CW00793390

Restructuring and Workouts

Strategies for Maximising Value,
Third Edition

Consulting Editor **Graham Lane**

Consulting editor
Graham Lane, Willkie Farr & Gallagher LLP

Managing director
Sian O'Neill

The publishers would like to thank Ben Larkin for his role as consulting editor of previous editions of this book.

Restructuring and Workouts: Strategies for Maximising Value, Third Edition **is published by**

Globe Law and Business Ltd
3 Mylor Close
Horsell
Woking
Surrey GU21 4DD
United Kingdom
Tel: +44 20 3745 4770
www.globelawandbusiness.com

Printed and bound by CPI Group (UK) Ltd, Croydon CR0 4YY

Restructuring and Workouts: Strategies for Maximising Value, Third Edition

ISBN 9781787421882
EPUB ISBN 9781787421899
Adobe PDF ISBN 9781787421905
Mobi ISBN 9781787421912

Table of contents

Foreword

Graham Lane
Willkie Farr & Gallagher LLP

I am delighted to have the honour to serve as consulting editor for this new edition of *Restructuring and Workouts: Strategies for Maximising Value.*

This third edition has been fully updated from the second edition which was published in 2013. To put it mildly, the intervening period has seen a significant amount of geopolitical change and unrest. How has this impacted the restructuring environment and what do we have to look forward to in 2019 and beyond? These chapters aspire to assist in answering these (and many other) questions.

I am very privileged to have been able to work alongside leading legal, financial and operational practitioners who have found the time in their busy schedules to share their skills and experience and impart knowledge in a way that will be stimulating to the reader. We have brought together a first-class group of restructuring professionals to contribute thought leadership on interesting and relevant topics.

This edition features a number of entirely new chapters as well as fully updated chapters from prior editions. First, we are grateful to PJT Partners and the World Bank Group for providing updated overview chapters. Secondly, we have chapters on key themes and issues from leading restructuring and financial advisory experts at AlixPartners, BDO, Deloitte, Greenhill and Lincoln Pensions. Notably, there are bespoke chapters on valuation, pre-packs, pension issues in restructurings, distressed M&A and cross-border insolvency situations. Thirdly, we are fortunate to have been able to introduce sector specific chapters. Leading names from Evercore and Alvarez & Marsal, with significant pertinent expertise, summarise trends and issues in sectors which have seen, and will likely continue to see, significant restructuring activity – namely shipping and offshore, and retail. Fourthly, we have country-specific chapters covering the key jurisdictions of France, Spain and the United States. The US remains a pre-eminent destination for restructurings and workouts, and the chapter summarises many of the facets of the well-established Chapter 11 process. France and Spain, on the other hand, have seen many changes in their restructuring laws and regulations in recent years. These chapters provide a user-friendly roadmap to these countries which offer an increasingly attractive restructuring market. Finally, we are very grateful to hear from Russell Downs at PwC who guides us through some of the intricacies and lessons learned from the Lehman Brothers bankruptcy, the one case that has done more than any other to shape and influence theory and practice in the restructuring world over the last 10 years.

This work provides the reader with guidance in navigating an increasingly complex and intertwined international legal and business environment. It may be read cover to cover or used as a specific reference point when the need or opportunity arises.

I am extremely grateful to the authors who have contributed their time and intellects. I am also grateful to the authors and the consulting editor of prior editions of this work. This book will hopefully prove itself to be an essential resource in your practice as we look forward to the next wave of restructuring activity in 2019 and beyond.

The restructuring and workout environment in Europe

Martin Gudgeon
Shirish Joshi
PJT Partners

1. Introduction

The current restructuring and workout environment in Europe is characterised by diversity and complexity, and has witnessed several transformative trends. Steps continue to be taken to make workouts easier and to limit value destruction from financial distress, particularly in the form of revisions to local insolvency laws to make them more reorganisation-friendly within each jurisdiction, and attempts to coordinate and harmonise laws and processes across various jurisdictions. Several characteristics of corporate and financing structures and innovation in financing markets mean that financial restructurings in Europe continue to be complex.

These characteristics include:

- increased complexity in debt instruments, security packages and corporate capital structures;
- a secondary market in loans and other credit instruments that continues to grow;
- credit markets willing to refinance stressed credits with limited levers that creditors can rely on in a downside scenario;
- continued uncertainty and challenged prospects on a macro-economic level in several industries, particularly in terms of timing of recovery on an industry-wide level; and
- an increasing number and variety of credit investors.

In general, the course and outcome of any restructuring process will principally depend on:

- the prevalent insolvency regime, not just in the debtor's jurisdiction of incorporation or where its financial liabilities exist, but also in every jurisdiction where the debtor has material business operations;
- the size and complexity of a debtor's capital structure;
- the number of stakeholders in the company;
- the composition of the company's creditor/lender base;
- the degree of effectiveness of the contractual rights that creditors have against the company, as negotiated in the credit documentation; and

- the availability of alternative financing sources and general health of capital markets and, in particular, the banking system in the relevant jurisdiction.

The European markets have seen a transformation in each of these factors that will have a long-lasting impact on the restructuring environment going forward.

2. Legal environment

Relative to the United States, where Chapter 11 of the Bankruptcy Code is more debtor-friendly, European jurisdictions tend to be creditor-focused, with the exception of certain jurisdictions such as France and Italy. Often, control is ceded to creditors or the courts, either directly or through an appointee. Over the past several years many jurisdictions have made tangible efforts to move away from regimes that almost seemed to encourage liquidation in any bankruptcy and towards regimes that encourage business rehabilitation (where justified), which may be viewed as an attempt to emulate the Chapter 11 framework that has prevailed in the United States. The intent has been to make restructurings and workouts easier to execute by facilitating elements such as super-priority new money financings, binding/cram-down mechanisms and debt-for-equity swaps via legal, rather than solely contractual, means.

Germany was one of the first European countries to implement a new insolvency regime, the *Insolvenzordung*, in January 1999. Italy has had the Prodi Bis since 1999 and the Marzano Decree, which was highlighted during the Parmalat restructuring, since December 2003. The United Kingdom reformed its insolvency law with the Enterprise Act that came into effect in September 2004. Incremental revisions to local insolvency and restructuring laws continue to take place, including the German Bondholder Act of 2009 (*Schuldverschreibungsgesetz*) and modifications to the Italian regime in 2010 and the German regime in 2012. France has implemented the *procedure de sauvegarde*. French restructuring and insolvency law remains debtor-friendly; however, certain amendments (which came into force in 2012 and 2014) and the CGG transaction precedent (where, relative to previous French-based company restructurings, pre-restructuring shareholders were provided a much smaller percentage of the post-transaction equity and more limited new money participation rights, and the vast majority of the post-restructured company was owned by creditors) may suggest a change, slightly rebalancing the bargaining power in favour of creditors. While many of these new regimes have been used on an *ad hoc* basis, few of them have been tested to the extent where they are sufficiently well understood to cater to the wide range of specific situations and outcomes that are typically seen in restructurings. The European Union in 2015 implemented a new regulation which made amendments to the existing 2002

EU Insolvency Regulation and which was aimed at making the pan-European restructuring and insolvency environment more coordinated and transparent (the 'Recast Regulation').

In contrast to the implied extraterritoriality of the US Chapter 11 process, individual jurisdictional analysis is an important part of European restructurings. For instance, a company may be headquartered in one jurisdiction, with the parent company incorporated in another; conduct business operations, own key assets and owe financial debt in a further half-dozen jurisdictions; and have its primary credit documentation governed by English law. While the overall relationship between the company and its creditors and among creditors themselves will be governed by English law, the efficacy and economic rationality of any enforcement of security or court procedure will be a function of each individual jurisdiction in which the company operates. For instance, certain jurisdictions allow a lender to take security and derive benefit from guarantees granted by other members of the corporate group, but the quantum of any such guarantee is limited to the amount of direct corporate benefit derived by that particular entity as a result of the provision of credit by the lenders.

Further, the test of insolvency or prospective insolvency differs from jurisdiction to jurisdiction, ranging from solely a mechanical balance sheet test to a cash flow test, either in isolation or in conjunction with a balance sheet test. Further, the cost and speed of enforcement action in certain European jurisdictions are quite high, making the threat of enforcement less effective in forcing a borrower or other creditors to negotiate a consensual transaction.

The approach and mindset of the relevant courts and the various participants, particularly banks and other creditors, in a workout process have changed to a large extent to make the European workout process through insolvency more efficient, from both a time and value perspective, but it still remains less efficient than in the United States. Advances continue to be made in terms of recognising restructuring and insolvency procedures across EU jurisdictions through the Recast Regulation, and steps are being taken to harmonise and coordinate local insolvency processes across the EU which, once implemented, should go a long way to addressing this issue. However, the lack of a fully fledged pan-European insolvency protocol remains an impediment to achieving a European multi-jurisdictional restructuring within a formal coordinated legal framework.

This inflexibility and uncertainty has resulted in the majority of European restructurings being accomplished on an out-of-court basis. These consensual restructurings add several layers of complexity to the restructuring process. In general, they require the unanimous consent of all stakeholders to be successfully implemented. The absence of court-imposed binding decisions or an alternative means to cram down dissenting creditors means that individual stakeholders may have disproportionate levels of influence in the negotiating process. The holdout value extracted by out-of-the-money creditors and existing shareholders, who in theory hold investments of no value and should have no voice in the restructuring process, can be significant in practice.

A compromise between the flexibility offered by out-of-court commercial restructuring negotiations and the legal power of insolvency law has resulted in many transactions being negotiated, structured and agreed on an out-of-court basis, but formally implemented through a formal court process. This is particularly evident when there are a very large number of constituent creditors (eg, widely held public bonds) or there is a particular risk of a small number of holdouts. For instance, in France, an Accelerated Financial Safeguard (AFS) procedure is available to implement a pre-pack plan with only a two-thirds majority by value of those voting (in both committees – bank and bond). The AFS procedure has rarely been implemented but is often used as a threat to incentivise holdouts to agree to a consensual deal. Similarly, an English law scheme of arrangement is a corporate process, not an insolvency process, and allows for the entire class of similarly situated creditors to be bound by a particular commercial proposal so long as a simple majority in number and 75% by value of creditors in that class support it.

The differences in insolvency laws across Europe have led to an increase in jurisdiction shopping, where companies in distress relocate either their jurisdiction of incorporation or their 'centre of main interests' (COMI) to more favourable jurisdictions solely to implement restructurings via a legal process that may not be available in their home jurisdictions. For example, the English law scheme of arrangement procedure has been used by a number of non-UK companies. Many have transferred their COMI to the UK, relying on EU regulations, or alternatively have established sufficient connection to the English courts, based on the governing law of the underlying credit documentation, to access the scheme of arrangement procedure.

3. Financial innovation

The European credit markets have seen an unprecedented level of financial innovation over the past several years. Credit markets have been characterised by the increasing complexity of capital structures and new classes of lenders and investors.

3.1 Complexity of corporate, capital and financial structures

Historically, European companies were funded by loans from traditional commercial banks. These loans were generally senior in nature and in some cases secured by all of the borrower's assets (especially in leveraged transactions). Large, well-established corporations had access to the public bond markets. Leveraged buyout activity in Europe has led to innovative financing structures and instruments such as second lien and mezzanine debt structures and payment-in-kind loans. Second lien and mezzanine instruments may be structured as either loans or tradable notes, similar to bonds. These are junior instruments that are usually held not by traditional banks, but by alternative investors such as hedge funds, dedicated mezzanine funds, collateralised loan obligation (CLO) and collateralised debt obligation (CDO) funds and other 'special situations' investors.

The number of layers in a company's financial structure makes workouts particularly problematic, as it increases the number of stakeholders that need to consent to a restructuring. For instance, as the term suggests, 'second lien' loans are debt instruments that share the same security package as a first lien loan, but are second in priority of payment from any value realised through the disposal of collateral. Conflicts often arise between the senior and junior lien holders with respect to the collateral, especially in the event that the immediate disposal of the collateral is value maximising for the first lien claim, but not for all the claims on the security package. In such an instance, the first lien lenders would be incentivised to dispose of the collateral, to the extent that the value generated at least covers their claim, as quickly as possible. However, junior lien holders would be incentivised to maximise the value of the entire security package, and that might imply adopting a wait-and-see approach or a more extensive disposal process that may take more time and resources. This difference in approach would bring the two lien holders in conflict with one another. Furthermore, certain transactions have featured instruments that have third and fourth liens on the same security package, which makes inter-creditor negotiations significantly more complex.

In addition to traditional corporate restructurings, Europe has seen a number of financial restructurings of non-corporate vehicles, such as securitisations, and the growth of highly structured transactions as a financing tool, such as mortgage-backed securities (both residential and commercial) and opco-propco financing structures. Many of these structures are long term in nature and have correspondingly long-term hedging instruments such as interest rate, inflation and currency swaps. Coupled with the current low interest rate environment, the associated hedging swaps have become a substantial part of the total liabilities of the borrower, which was hitherto not the case. These vehicles are complex, not well understood amongst the wider investment community, set up very differently from traditional corporate entities, and saddled with original governing documentation that did not contemplate a refinancing or restructuring involving existing stakeholders and investors. Accordingly, existing corporate-type restructuring constructs have had to be modified or new techniques created to deal with such situations.

There are two additional trends impacting the European restructuring scene. First, bond markets have become a much greater source of corporate capital.

Bonds have fewer covenants, involve considerably more constituent creditors relative to bank loans, have public–private information issues, and are subject to trading much more than bank loans. Secondly, in response to the withdrawal of several traditional banking institutions, alternative credit funds have filled the void. Financing from credit funds is more expensive but also more flexible (eg, covenant-lite) and bespoke. Such borrower- or situation-specific solutions are becoming more evident.

3.2 Loan trading and alternative investors

Traditionally, corporate loans were syndicated to a limited number of commercial banks that generally held the debt on their balance sheets until final maturity (the 'originate and hold' model). The borrower had a close relationship with the lead banks and the lead banks, by virtue of their largest holdings, were heavily incentivised to monitor the borrower closely. Over the past several years, banks have begun to syndicate the loans they originate much more widely, even to the extent that the originating bank may not keep any of the loan on its books.

Under the traditional model, in the event of financial distress the banks would have been made aware at an early juncture and the borrower would have had to negotiate with a limited number of banks, which made it easier to execute the workout process and to maintain a relatively high level of confidentiality. During the negotiation process, the banks would act in close coordination with each other and would agree to provide the debtor with the liquidity and financial support necessary as it completed an agreed restructuring programme, which usually involved a disciplined sale of individual assets or entire divisions by the debtor or, in certain cases, the sale of the debtor in its entirety. Banks did not want to be active shareholders in the business. During this time the debtor could operate free from the stresses and distractions imposed by any formal insolvency procedure.

This consensual approach to the workout process has been more or less rendered obsolete by the rise of loan trading and the number of non-bank institutions in the credit markets. Traditional lending banks have shown an increasing appetite to sell their exposure in the secondary markets immediately upon the onset of financial distress rather than endure a protracted workout process. The pro-cyclical nature of the Basel capital adequacy requirements, where banks have to commit increasing levels of reserve capital against stressed or non-performing loans, has accelerated loan sales.

Several banks have sold off large portfolios of loans, particularly in the real estate and shipping/offshore space as part of a strategic repositioning. The willingness of banks to offload their exposure has resulted in a number of alternative investors taking an active role in the bank debt markets. Loan trading has made restructuring processes more complex as the number of debt holders has increased, and alternative investors can have a more aggressive negotiating stance than traditional banks. The larger number of lenders means that confidentiality is much harder to maintain. As rumours of financial distress circulate in the wider arena, the debtor faces increasing pressure from suppliers, credit insurers, customers and employees, which often delays, and even frustrates, the operational recovery of the business.

Alternative investors, such as special situations funds, are generally more experienced in distressed situations, not being burdened by the same regulatory and capital adequacy constraints as traditional banks, and being more willing to become equity holders in the restructured business and more amenable to injecting new capital into the company as part of the restructuring process. However, dedicated special situations investors may not have the same patience, incentives or return expectations as traditional banks, making negotiations more complicated. Further, bank debt markets are inherently opaque and loan trading adds an additional layer of complexity, in that it makes lender identification much more convoluted. Most existing credit documentation does not allow non-bank parties to become lenders. Consequently, hedge funds and alternative investors invest in loans through sub-participation agreements, where a commercial bank fronts the investment on behalf of the hedge fund while the underlying hedge fund controls the votes, and benefits from the economics of the exposure. Loan trading also has the potential to increase inter-lender conflicts during restructuring negotiations as the incentives of par lenders are not the same as those of secondary market participants. For instance, a given restructuring proposal may be acceptable to a lender that purchased the debt at substantially below par value, but unacceptable to a primary lender that advanced the original loan at par.

4. Negotiating leverage in an uncertain environment

The timing, form and nature of corporate financial restructurings are often a function of the relative negotiating leverage amongst a borrower's key stakeholders, particularly the company, creditors and shareholders.

While credit markets became more disciplined for several years post the financial crisis, the abundance of liquidity, low borrowing costs, and the European Central Bank's and several national governments' initiatives to enhance market liquidity, including techniques such as quantitative easing, have resulted in a weakening of creditor rights in borrowing agreements. Overall leverage levels continue to increase (though not as high as the peak before the 2007 financial crisis), while creditor rights continue to weaken.

Any financial restructuring transaction is based on an operating business plan that is agreed by all relevant stakeholders and forms the basis of developing a sustainable capital structure. Continued industry-level challenges in several sectors means that what was considered a reasonable and achievable business plan at the time of the initial restructuring transaction may cease to be viable. In a number of situations, the operating environment continues to be sufficiently volatile that no credible medium- to long-term operational business plan can be prepared. This lack of certainty means that the rational decision would be to preserve the option pending the greater level of certainty that would more fully justify a comprehensive restructuring. Accordingly, a number of restructurings in certain industries have taken much longer than anticipated, involved short-term sub-optimal solutions, and needed to be revisited multiple times over the course of several years.

This operating market uncertainty has resulted in a number of 'amend and extend' transactions, where the terms of the existing credit documentation are amended to extend the final maturity of the debt. While early amend and extend transactions were short term in nature and seen as a "bridge to a better day" with the expectation that refinancing would eventually be achieved through a new money bank or capital markets transaction, the continued downturn in certain industries has resulted in more long-term amend and extend transactions. The market has seen a few of the initial amend and extends being extended for a second or even a third time.

Ample financing market liquidity and lower borrowing costs has meant that even stressed companies have been able to refinance upcoming maturities. In theory, one would expect a greater number of stressed companies and restructurings as a result of the closure of credit markets. However, one of the characteristics of the credit cycle has been the prevalence of loan packages with delayed amortising or non-amortising financial structures. Delayed amortising structures have given borrowers greater flexibility to avoid engaging with creditors as no material principal payments are due for the first several years of a loan package. Further, a number of financing packages have had significant availability under revolving credit lines and other alternative sources of funding, such as capital expenditure, restructuring and acquisition facilities. The requirements under these alternative facilities are often weak, which allows the borrower to draw down on these lines when distress-related liquidity needs arise.

In Europe, the prevalence of financial restructurings has also been limited by the nature of financial borrowing. A significant number of companies, particularly in Germany, Italy and Spain, have borrowed from state-owned or state-backed banks and financial institutions, mainly local savings banks. These banks are motivated by more than just profitability, their remit encompassing additional considerations such as broad economic development and local or even regional employment creation. Additionally, many of these state-backed institutions may not be bound by the same mark-to-market and capital adequacy requirements to which traditional, publicly traded lending institutions are subject, and tend to take a longer-term approach to lending.

Such institutions are, to a degree, immune to the shareholder pressures faced by publicly traded financial institutions.

5. Conclusion

In summary, restructurings in Europe are characterised by several layers of complexity arising from a multitude of jurisdictions, types of debt, varied investor classes and general macro-economic uncertainty. Several recent developments have increased the complexity of the workout process, while others have made the restructuring process more efficient and less value destructive. The remaining level of complexity leads to greater uncertainty and execution risk requiring higher levels of specialist financial and legal analysis.

The World Bank Group: insolvency, restructuring and economic development

Olena Koltko
Ronen Nehmad
Mahesh Uttamchandani
World Bank Group[1]

1. Introduction

Micro, small and medium-sized enterprises (MSMEs) account for more than a third of the world's total labour force and around 50% of private sector value globally.[2] For this reason, much attention has been given to encouraging the formation and growth of MSMEs. Treatment of MSMEs in financial distress, however, has only recently generated interest among policymakers. Insolvency processes in many countries are too expensive, too complicated and too lengthy to fit the needs of MSMEs. In addition, financial distress of a small company is often closely related to the financial well-being of its owners, to the extent that one can be difficult to tackle without the other. Thus, MSME insolvency has presented unique challenges. How to meet those challenges is one of the questions inextricably tied to the World Bank Group's agenda for promoting financial inclusion, which focuses on providing individuals and businesses with access to useful and affordable financial products and services that meet their needs.[3]

2. Why insolvency matters

Having an effective legal, regulatory and institutional insolvency framework is critical to a well-functioning economy and society. Developed insolvency regimes improve financial inclusion and increase access to credit in the private sector, as predictability and thus lender confidence in loan recovery upon default is enhanced. Similarly, because insolvency laws directly affect both the loan terms set by lenders and their willingness to extend credit, sound insolvency systems result in an overall lower cost of credit, which in turn

1 This chapter has been updated from the original written by Andres F Martinez, Antonia Menezes and Mahesh Uttamchandani.

2 See Oya Pinar Ardic, Nataliya Mylenko and Valentina Saltane, "Small and Medium Enterprises : A Cross-Country Analysis with a New Data Set", Policy Research Working Paper WPS 5538, World Bank, 2011.

3 World Bank, July 2018. Financial Inclusion Overview, www.worldbank.org/en/topic/financialinclusion/overview.

encourages growth. Insolvency regimes allow for a more efficient and productive allocation of resources, as viable but financially distressed firms restructure their debt and thus preserve jobs in the economy, keep supply chains intact and retain value. Additionally, effective insolvency regimes have been shown to encourage the risk-taking necessary for entrepreneurship and innovation. Several studies have found a link between a country's personal insolvency laws and entrepreneurship. For example, a recent survey of over 20,000 families in the US showed that there are more entrepreneurs in states with higher asset exemptions.[4]

Insolvency regimes are an important factor in lending as they allow for the allocation of risk among participants in a market economy. An effective insolvency framework promotes confidence and stability in the wider credit system by allocating risks in a way that is predictable, equitable and transparent.[5] It also allows for an efficient process to clean up non-performing loans from banks' balance sheets, leading to a more robust and healthy financial sector.[6]

Insolvency laws play such an important role because they promote predictability for both creditors and borrowers by establishing the rules for the worst-case scenario. They allow borrowers to determine the maximum risk associated with a failed undertaking, and they allow creditors to calculate the maximum risk associated with an unpaid loan. Collection of debts through bankruptcy proceedings is undoubtedly an unattractive option for creditors, who have to compete for a share of the debtor's estate against each other. So, having transparent, enforceable rules on how this type of enforcement takes place and clear guidelines on the role each party plays in the process are critical for lenders.[7]

Competing in global markets requires that domestic businesses have maximum access to the fuel that drives modern commerce: credit and investment. Credit depends on willing lenders, requiring laws that facilitate lending on flexible terms and ensure reasonable and timely enforcement of remedies in the event of default. In mature markets, credit comes in all forms: secured, unsecured, trade, leasing, purchase money security, securitisations, inventory and receivables financing, factoring and other forms – each of which carries different risks and affords different legal rights to stakeholders.

---

4 Wei Fan and Michelle White, "Personal Bankruptcy and the Level of Entrepreneurial Activity", XLVI *Journal of Law and Economics* 543, 2003.

5 Fernando Montes-Negret, "Best Practice Insolvency and Creditor Rights Systems: Key for Financial Stability", NPL Initiative, April 2016. See: http://npl.vienna-initiative.com/wp-content/uploads/sites/2/2016/08/Montes-Negret-on-ICRs.pdf.

6 Wolfgang Bergthaler, Kenneth Kang, Yan Liu and Dermot Monaghan, *Tackling Small and Medium Sized Enterprise Problem Loans in Europe*, International Monetary Fund, Washington, DC, 2015.

7 Klaus Koch, Olena Koltko and María Antonia Quesada, "Resolving Insolvency: Measuring the strength of insolvency laws", Doing Business 2015 Report.

3. Recent trends in insolvency reform

3.1 Focus on MSME insolvency

Until recently, most of the discussion of insolvency regimes took place in the context of big corporate debtors, as cases involving big retailers like Toys "R" Us in the United States, industry giants like Electrosteel Steels in India, and major construction firms like Carillion in Europe captured the public's attention. However, policymakers are increasingly recognising the importance of MSMEs for national economic stability. Their sheer number is impressive. A joint IFC and McKinsey study in 2010 estimated the total number of formal and informal MSMEs globally at 420–510 million, with the majority – between 365 and 445 million – located in developing economies.[8] Inevitably, many of these firms fail, and traditional insolvency frameworks are not always well suited to process such failures efficiently. As the recent World Bank Group report on the treatment of MSME insolvencies highlights, smaller companies face very specific challenges:[9]

- complex insolvency systems, which deter MSMEs from resorting to formal procedures to tackle financial distress;
- creditor passivity, where creditors have few incentives to deal with MSME debtors through legal processes;
- lack of information about MSME debtors, making it harder to assess business viability and discouraging creditor trust in the MSME debtor;
- post-insolvency financing, where many insolvency systems do not permit or incentivise financing after formal insolvency proceedings are filed, even though such financing is typically vital to MSME survival;
- insufficient assets to fund a formal insolvency procedure, given that MSMEs often lack the resources to cover the costs and fees for a formal insolvency procedure;
- co-mingling of personal debts, as MSMEs are often financed by a mixture of corporate debt and personal debt taken on by the entrepreneur (potentially with personal guarantees); and
- natural persons operating as enterprises, as many MSMEs might be informal entities that have not been incorporated, such as sole proprietorships.

For these reasons, a key trend in the past few years has been the

---

8 Peer Stein, Tony Goland and Robert Shiff, "Two Trillion and Counting: Assessing the Credit Gap for Micro, Small and Medium-size Enterprises in the Developing World", Working Paper 71315, World Bank, Washington, DC, 2010.

9 Working Group on the Treatment of MSME Insolvency, World Bank Group Insolvency and Creditor/Debtor Regimes Task Force, "Report on the Treatment of MSME Insolvency", 2017. Available at: http://documents.worldbank.org/curated/en/973331494264489956/pdf/114823-REVISED-PUBLIC-MSME-Insolvency-report-low-res-final.pdf.

development of solutions targeted at restructuring and liquidation of insolvent MSMEs. A few jurisdictions, such as Japan and Korea, have created tailor-made MSME insolvency procedures; others have chosen to eliminate certain procedural requirements when dealing with MSMEs as compared with large corporate debtors, or otherwise to make the process faster.[10] In Argentina, for example, small debtors benefit from fewer filing and procedural formalities.[11] In Greece, small companies can benefit from expedited processing of claim verification.[12] A recent study of 153 economies showed that about 20% of countries worldwide have some form of simplified insolvency procedure available to MSMEs to restructure or to liquidate.[13]

Another mechanism closely tied to treatment of MSMEs is personal bankruptcy regimes. The financial claims of small companies are often co-mingled with personal funds and personal guarantees from the owners. Having an efficient way to deal with both personal and corporate debts, therefore, is of paramount importance. In addition to economic concerns, personal insolvency incorporates an important human element. Default is often the consequence of factors outside the debtor's control. In January 2018, for example, Romania's new personal bankruptcy law came into force. The law establishes three types of proceedings for personal debtors:[14]

- liquidation;
- debt rescheduling; and
- a simplified insolvency procedure for debtors who have no assets, have small outstanding obligations, or are retired or disabled.

One of the important elements of the personal bankruptcy law is that it provides for a discharge of debts at the end of the process, so that the individual debtor is not forever bound by his or her obligations.

The interest in MSMEs insolvency is only likely to increase in the future as policies aimed at facilitating and encouraging MSME formation produce results. As more MSMEs run into financial difficulties, more and more countries are likely to tackle the challenge of making sure that the viable ones survive and those that are not viable are quickly liquidated and removed from the market, with the owners able to make a fresh start.

3.2 Wave of insolvency reforms in the Middle East and North Africa

Historically, bankruptcy reforms were quite rare in the Middle East and North

10 *Ibid.*

11 Ley de Concurso 24522, Articles 288–289.

12 Greek Insolvency Code, Article 162.

13 "Improving Access to Finance for SMEs: Opportunities Through Credit Reporting, Secured Lending and Insolvency Practices", Doing Business, 2018. Available at: www.doingbusiness.org/~/media/WBG/DoingBusiness/Documents/Special-Reports/improving-access-to-finance-for-SMEs.pdf.

14 Law No. 151/2015 of 18 June 2015.

Africa (MENA).[15] A 2009 study by Hawkamah, The World Bank, OECD and INSOL International showed that insolvency systems across the MENA region were largely inconsistent with best practice.[16] Some countries had no standalone law, and others adopted archaic punitive approaches towards honest debtors who failed in their businesses or were affected by market downturns.

In the past few years, authorities in many MENA countries have been stressing (in different forums such as the Forum for Insolvency Reform in MENA (FIRM) comprising World Bank Group, Hawkamah, the OECD and INSOL International) the urgent need to adapt their current insolvency regimes to improve their investment climate. Committees have been formed in countries like Lebanon, Egypt and Jordan. And these efforts are paying off. On 20 September 2016, the United Arab Emirates adopted the Federal Law on Bankruptcy, which came into effect in December 2016. A positive feature of the new legislation is a reorganisation procedure as an alternative to liquidation, which was the only available bankruptcy mechanism under the old regime. Now viable but financially distressed companies in the UAE will have an opportunity to continue operating after restructuring their debts and/or operations. Egypt adopted a new Bankruptcy Law in March 2018 with a similar focus on restructuring and setting up specialised bankruptcy courts, as well as creating a list of bankruptcy experts to assist in the reorganisation process. Several countries in the region, such as Bahrain and Qatar, are expecting to finalise their own new insolvency frameworks in the near future.

3.3 Globalisation of insolvency proceedings

In today's globalised and interconnected economy, it is rare to find enterprises that operate exclusively in a single jurisdiction. As a result, having effective cross-border insolvency frameworks that deal with financially distressed debtors (usually companies) with assets and creditors in multiple jurisdictions has become crucial. To facilitate cooperation between different countries when the same debtor is involved, UNCITRAL Model Law on Cross-Border Insolvency was issued by the UNCITRAL Secretariat in May 1997.[17] The Model Law focuses on the procedural aspects of cross-border insolvency proceedings, such as establishing mechanisms for judges and insolvency practitioners in different jurisdictions to coordinate their activities. Although the Model Law is two decades old, it is becoming increasingly relevant. Forty-four states and a total of 46 jurisdictions have adopted legislation based on the Model Law, including Cameroon (2015), Canada (2005), Dominican Republic (2015), Israel (2018) and Singapore (2017).[18]

---

15 The Doing Business report, which tracks business regulations in 190 economies, recorded only three insolvency reforms in the region between 2008 and 2014. See: www.doingbusiness.org.

16 Available at: www.oecd.org/dataoecd/51/30/44375185.pdf.

17 See: www.uncitral.org/pdf/english/texts/insolven/1997-Model-Law-Insol-2013-Guide-Enactment-e.pdf.

18 See: www.uncitral.org/uncitral/en/uncitral_texts/insolvency/1997Model_status.html.

3.4 Regional harmonisation of insolvency laws

As access to markets is increased, numerous states are exploring economic and trade cooperation across borders in order to enhance competition and investment. Regional integration is considered an effective tool here.[19] Although such integration can take many forms, a common trend in Africa is to harmonise regional commercial law, including insolvency law, to improve uniformity, transparency and coordination across states. L'Organisation pour l'Harmonisation en Afrique du Droit des Affaires (OHADA) is a regional international organisation, first established by treaty in 1993, which focuses on harmonising the business laws of its 17 member states.[20] It has a number of uniform laws that apply throughout member states, including an insolvency law.[21]

The effect can be powerful for countries that are geographically close and have similar legal regimes, and other regions are considering following suit – for example, in the Caribbean. A number of jurisdictions in the region have already adopted similar insolvency models, and several institutions, such as the Eastern Caribbean Central Bank and the Commonwealth Secretariat, are exploring ways of promoting further regional cooperation.

Different models are available. For example, whereas OHADA's regime provides for direct applicability of insolvency law across member states, other countries are considering non-binding model laws or principles. Ultimately, the effectiveness of either model will depend upon its implementation and the efforts of the respective states to share knowledge, experiences and training.

4. Five lessons from developing and transition countries

In countries where lenders generally experience poor loan recoveries, a weak insolvency regulatory framework is often the culprit. Underdeveloped institutional capacity for targeting commercial dispute resolution and insolvency proceedings also contributes. Successful debt resolution and insolvency systems need to address financial distress through formal and out-of-court tools including mediation, arbitration and informal workout guidelines.

In many economies, enforcement tools are rigid, with outdated insolvency frameworks. The courts in many cases lack the capacity to deal with recovery claims and business distress in a timely manner. This negatively impacts on entrepreneurship, access to credit, bank loan recovery and jobs.

The World Bank Group works with governments in emerging markets and

---

19 Maurice Schiff and L Alan Winters, *Regional Integration and Development*, The World Bank Group, Washington, DC, 2003.

20 Benin, Burkina Faso, Cameroon, Central African Republic, Chad, Comoros, Cote d'Ivoire, Democratic Republic of Congo, Equatorial Guinea, Gabon, Guinea, Guinea-Bissau, Niger, Mali, Republic of Congo, Togo and Senegal. See: www.ohadalegis.com/anglais/presohadagb.htm.

21 The laws come under the following general heads: commercial law, secured transactions, commercial companies and economic group partnerships, debt collection procedures and measures of execution, insolvency, arbitration, company accounting, carriage of goods by road and cooperative credit by banks.

transition countries to improve the quality of insolvency regimes. Through a variety of technical assistance programmes, it has assisted numerous countries in achieving these improvements. While each country's challenges and opportunities are different, broad lessons can be drawn from years of reform experience.

4.1 The insolvency system is a key part of firm 'ecology'

Efficient entry and exit of firms is critical to the healthy functioning of a market economy. As new firms enter an economy, older and less efficient ones will be pushed out, with their productive assets 'recycled' into more efficient firms. This facilitates market dynamism and allows overall productivity in an economy to be maximised. The link between efficient exit and the redeployment of assets is well established. But what about other parts of the firm lifecycle? Practitioners have long acknowledged the impact of sound insolvency regimes on the availability and cost of credit, but this link has not been well documented in academic literature. Recently, however, two papers have focused on the economic environment pre- and post-insolvency reform and control, looking for factors that might influence credit. Both papers have found that improving the overall insolvency regime can have a measurable and positive impact on the availability and cost of credit.[22]

4.2 Ineffectual implementation of laws

Weak implementation and enforcement mechanisms in some countries hinder the achievement of a sound insolvency regime. Experience shows that a country with stronger and more effective institutional and regulatory frameworks will generally have more effective and efficient insolvency and creditors' rights systems, even where the relevant laws have not been modernised. The most common institutional problems are the result of

- inadequate training of judges and administrators;
- inefficient case administration practices and procedures;
- lack of transparency and inconsistency in decision-making; and
- ineffective regulation to redress problems of corruption and the risk that interested parties may unduly influence the courts, administrators, trustees or other stakeholders.

Problems in regulation often point to weakness in, or absence of, procedures and institutions to license, qualify and supervise practitioners and professionals such as insolvency administrators, enforcement and collection agents and other specialists.

22 B Funchal, "The effects of the 2005 Bankruptcy Reform in Brazil", *Economic Letters* 101, 2008, 84–86; N Serrano-Velarde, G Rodano and E Tarantino, "The Causal Effect of Bankruptcy Law on the Cost of Finance", Oxford University, October 2011. Available at: http://denning.law.ox.ac.uk/news/events_files/SERRANOVEL ARDE_15_Nov_2011.pdf.

4.3 The effects of the tax regime on business competition and corporate rescue

Out-of-court workouts are frequently hampered by tax laws that penalise parties for engaging in a debt rationalisation process. For example, creditors may want to write off (or rationalise) debt or convert their debt into an equity interest in the debtor company. However, tax laws frequently impose heavy tax burdens on such transactions, forcing creditors to adopt alternative measures that are tax safe, but which lead to unnecessary litigation and execution, or liquidation. Alternatively, parties may be forced to carry artificially inflated asset values on their books to avoid the incurrence of taxes or the burden of provisioning for losses. Such laws create disincentives to restructuring.

In other instances, the tax regime unfairly saddles the buyer of an insolvent debtor's assets with tax liabilities previously due and owing by the debtor. Thus, in addition to paying a fair market value for the assets, a buyer may be forced to assume a tax liability of an uncertain amount.

These kinds of rule are generally designed to protect the state in the event of an insolvency, but unfairly shift the risk of loss to other market participants in a manner that stifles competition and the efficient recycling of assets and businesses. While no empirical studies exist, common sense would suggest that the impact of adverse tax policies far outweighs any gains to the state in trying to recover taxes from a very small minority of insolvent enterprises.

4.4 Weak social protection mechanisms

The treatment of employee rights and social protection of labour is particularly weak in many emerging markets and is often the greatest obstacle to successful corporate restructuring. It is extremely difficult to establish a healthy balance sheet without reducing costs and this often means laying off employees. This can be difficult to accomplish and can result in excessive hardship in the absence of effective rules to enforce a fair process and to provide protection for redundant workers. Rampant layoffs are not always the best solution, as was seen in Indonesia during the early stages of its financial crisis.

In many developing countries, such as India, although social protections for employees are weak, the *de facto* leverage of labour is often high. One approach to protecting workers is to establish a protection fund or a guarantee payment fund for employees laid off during corporate restructuring. These techniques have been used in many countries, in particular throughout the European Union, with positive results.

4.5 Delay inhibits choice and success

Although possibly an obvious point, it bears restating that delays negatively impact on both recovery levels and the choice of outcome (ie, going concern sale versus piecemeal liquidation). The reasons for this are numerous: the longer a business is in distress, the more likely valuable human capital will flee, the brand will suffer damage the negotiating position with suppliers will weaken. All of this leads to a cumulative level of market devaluation of the distressed entity. At some point, this devaluation makes a going concern sale impossible and piecemeal liquidation becomes the only option. Recovery values in piecemeal liquidation are, on a macro level, lower than those in going concern sales, and the longer the liquidation period drags on, the older the assets become, which typically leads to a decline in value.

A survey of practitioners in over 190 countries (see figure below) shows that while going concern sales yield higher recoveries than liquidations, both yield lower recoveries over time, and eventually liquidations become the only option. This leads to the conclusion that while processes must be speeded up, it must be done in a way that does not result in a greater preference for liquidation. Higher recoveries mean bigger distributions, particularly to unsecured creditors (eg, employees and trade creditors), and going concern sales result in fewer job losses.

Figure 1: The effects of delay on recovery rate

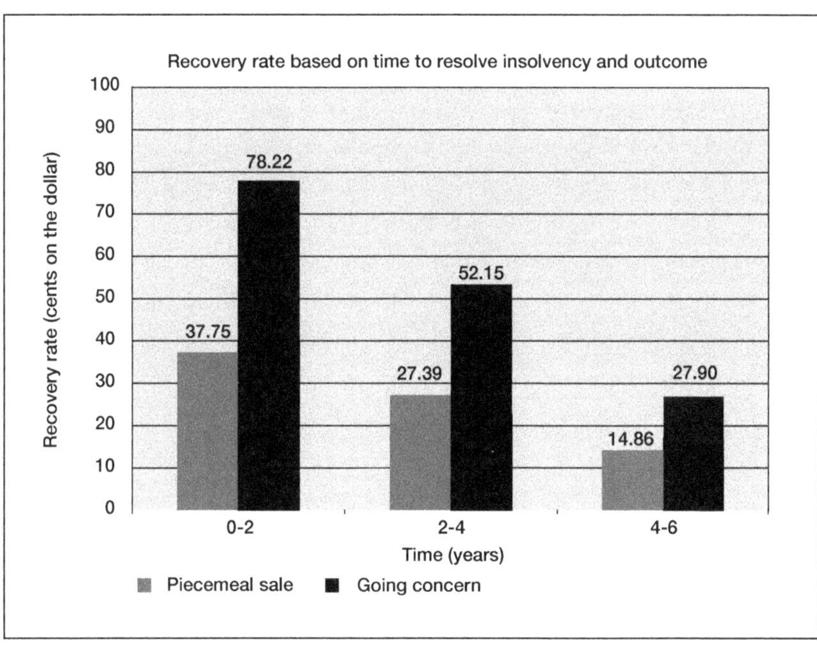

Source: Doing Business, see www.doingbusiness.org

5. Conclusion

Insolvency regimes are an integral part of the credit infrastructure. They help aspiring entrepreneurs determine the failure risks and allow banks to better price the risk of extending credit to businesses, thus increasing access to credit and lowering credit cost. This is especially important for start-ups and MSMEs, which play a central role in the global economy. It is not surprising that the topic of MSME insolvency is generating more and more interest among policymakers, who are designing mechanisms specifically targeting MSMEs, as well as regulating personal bankruptcy proceedings. At the same time, cross-border insolvency cases have become more common, prompting more countries to consider how their courts and practitioners coordinate with those in other jurisdictions, and whether regional models for insolvency regimes might foster greater international cooperation.

The importance of insolvency reform has been acknowledged even in regions previously reluctant to address the issue, such as the Middle East and North Africa. And while insolvency reforms must necessarily be tailored to the local legal and business environment, there are common themes across jurisdictions. These include addressing insolvency as an important and integral part of the business cycle; ensuring proper implementation of the reforms, especially at the institutional level; facilitating business restructuring by addressing tax consequences of debt write-off; extending social protections to those affected by business failure, where appropriate; and putting emphasis on timeliness to ensure higher recovery to creditors.

The publishers would like to thank Andres F Martinez and Antonia Menezes for their assistance in the preparation of the previous version of this chapter.

Valuation of distressed businesses

Kevin Coates
Craig Rachel
Graeme Smith
AlixPartners

---

1. Introduction

The valuation of distressed businesses is a key element of many restructuring and workout situations. It is a decision-making tool that can help to shape the exit strategy and guide planning in terms of seeking to sell the business or assets, or follow a restructuring process. Within a restructuring process, valuation is a central theme in negotiations to determine ownership levels and the required finance provision of the various stakeholder groups, which often have differing views and perspectives.

Where possible, distressed valuation follows the same principles and techniques as those used to value a healthy business, but the process needs to be more rigorous and reflect the realities of a distressed situation. With a structured approach, a sensible result can be achieved.

2. Valuation techniques

When considering the appropriate valuation approach, one needs to decide whether the business is a going concern or whether best value will be generated from a break-up sale of the assets. A going-concern valuation implies that the business will generate profit in the future, assuming:

- sound management;
- suitable future investment; and
- an appropriate funding structure.

Three basic valuation techniques are commonly applied to valuing a business:

- discounted cash flow (DCF);
- comparable multiples; and
- asset-based value.

Each technique has challenges that are amplified in a distressed situation. DCF, the purest valuation technique, depends on management's ability to produce reliable cash-flow forecasts. This is often extremely challenging in a distressed situation. The comparable multiples valuation methodology is applicable only if the business is generating a sensible level of pre-financing-cost profit (earnings before interest and tax (EBIT)) and earnings before interest, tax, depreciation and amortisation (EBITDA)), and if asset-based values are likely to vary considerably between a going-concern value and a break-up value.

As many of these techniques as possible should be used in order to build a valuation range for the business in question. A summary of each is set out in the table below.

Table 1: Summary of valuation techniques

	DCF	Comparable multiples	Asset-based value
Basis	Values free cash-flow potential by discounting these back to a present value using a relevant cost of capital.	Applies the market valuation multiples of similar companies, which either are quoted or have recently been acquired, to the subject company's relevant financial metric.	The asset value in current use for a going concern, which often equates to book value or the current realisable market value of the assets in a liquidation scenario.
Rationale	The value of a company is the potential future cash flows discounted to reflect the opportunity cost of the total capital investment.	The assumption is that the market applies fair valuations to companies. The value of the subject company can be considered comparable to companies in the same sector with similar economics.	For a going-concern valuation in an asset-intensive business, single year profitability may not be an appropriate guide to value. In a liquidation, realisable asset value gives the best guide to value as there is no going-concern premium.

continued on the next page

	DCF	**Comparable multiples**	**Asset-based value**
Requirements	• Medium- to long-term reliable cash-flow forecasts • Reasonable assessment of the relevant cost of capital	• Positive EBIT or EBITDA • Suitable comparable companies and transactions with similar economics to the subject company	Market values for the assets
Applicable companies	All companies with future cash-flow visibility	All companies with comparable data points	Asset-intensive businesses
Impact of distress	• Cash-flow forecasts need to be rigorously challenged to assess deliverability. • Discount rate needs to reflect increased risk. • Potential for failure should be factored in.	• Comparable data points must be thoroughly examined to assess level of comparability. • Discount should be applied to reflect distress and risk.	• Even in a going-concern sale, realisable value will be an important metric as it represents the buyer's downside position. • Quality and level of continued investment in assets will impact on value. • It is important to assess whether third-party claims exist on each asset.

These techniques can all be used to generate either equity or enterprise valuations (ie, the combined value of both equity and net debt). When valuing a distressed business, it is more appropriate to consider the enterprise valuation, as it is unlikely that the current capital structure will remain in place, and if the business is distressed then the equity is often of nil value. For this reason, all of the valuation approaches considered here are for enterprise value.

3. Valuation process

The process for valuing a distressed business can be broken down into four steps:

1. Understand and evaluate the business and the impact of the current and potential level of distress.
2. Review and adjust historical and forecast financial data.
3. Perform valuation analysis.
4. Consider other items that can impact on value.

This four-step process should enable all relevant aspects of the business and its current situation to be factored into the valuation. Distressed valuation is often required within an accelerated timetable, so the use of this structure can help to ensure that key points are not missed.

3.1 Understanding the business and the impact of distress

It is important to understand the quality and competitive positioning of the business in question. This reflects the importance of relativity in valuation. A business that holds a dominant position in its markets with high barriers to entry would typically carry a valuation premium over a weaker competitor that faces a high risk of substitution.

It is unusual to find a distressed business that holds such a dominant position and a review of its competitive position would be expected to highlight a number of risk areas that pose threats to future growth and prosperity.

Another key area when performing the initial review of the business is to assess the management team in terms of stability and quality. Distressed situations are often characterised by a great deal of management change and by management teams that have been unable to deliver on strategic goals. When a business is in distress, the ability of the management team to turn the business around and deliver on the business plan is critical. Without this, the achievability of a business plan can be highly questionable.

(a) Balance sheet v operational distress

Companies become distressed for many reasons and understanding the underlying causes is essential in order to arrive at a sensible valuation.

In some cases the company is a well-run and viable business, but is overleveraged. The most common cause of overleveraging is major acquisitions, whether from the business's own leveraged buyout or from the acquisition of other businesses. In many sectors, private equity-backed transactions have built up high levels of leverage with little headroom for underperformance.

Despite a sound underlying business, the leverage structure, repayment profile or refinancing requirements can leave companies unable to service debts as they fall due, making them technically insolvent. This scenario will be referred to as 'balance-sheet distress'.

Failure to tackle balance-sheet distress at an early stage through reset covenants, rescheduled debt repayments or some debt restructuring to reduce the current interest burden often leads to more significant operational issues because of lack of funds for investment in the development of the business.

Valuation of a business in early stage balance-sheet distress should not differ greatly from that of a healthy company, as alterations to the capital structure should eliminate the cause of distress rather than requiring operational changes.

At the other end of the spectrum, businesses may face a marked decline in revenue or an unsupportable cost base due to changes in their markets. Without significant operational restructuring, these businesses may not be viable as going concerns in the short or medium term. This scenario will be referred to as 'operational distress'. A good example is the UK high street retail market. This market grew its property footprint to meet continually rising consumer demand. It has since been hit not only by declining consumer spending and an increase in labour and property costs, but also by the switch to online purchasing. This has left many companies with leasehold estates containing a significant number of loss-making sites. Companies in this market that are unable to take advantage of the switch to online, and to exit loss-making sites, face major operational distress that often results in restructuring events.

Businesses in operational distress typically require significant investment to deliver their turnaround plans, and they present different valuation challenges to a healthy business. The valuation approach should be modified accordingly, reflecting the additional cost and risk associated with the turnaround.

In the real world, of course, a distressed business will lie somewhere between the two extremes. It is a matter of judgement how detrimental an impact distress has had, and the level of discount that should apply as a result.

(b) Distress and value

Before considering how to value a distressed business, it is worth understanding why distress has an impact on value.

Figure 1 demonstrates the relationship that can typically be found between the level of distress faced by a business and its potential valuation.

Figure 1: Relationship between level of distress and valuation

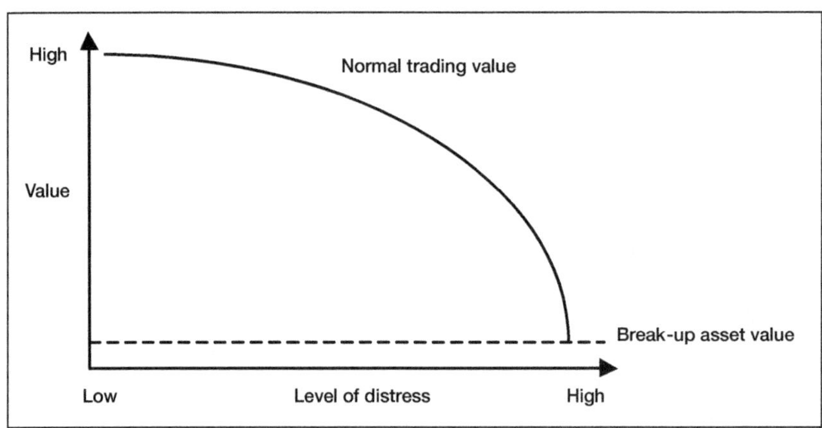

As the level of distress increases, the value of a business can be expected to fall rapidly as the risk of failure becomes a realistic possibility. The enterprise value can be expressed using the following equation:

Real enterprise value = enterprise value – present value (PV) of costs of financial distress

The equation recognises that there are real costs associated with financial distress and the risk of business failure. The risk of business failure grows rapidly with increasing distress, and the costs of financial distress can significantly reduce the real enterprise value.

The costs of financial distress are numerous and exist both when the business is at risk of insolvency and during a formal process.

Table 2: Examples of costs of financial distress

Operational and financial	Strategic and management
• detrimental credit terms • reduced access to lines of credit for overseas supply • higher incremental financing costs • fire-sale asset values • investment required for business recovery • professional fees	• restraints on capital investment • project decision-making focused on short-term rather than long-term value • distraction from running the business • conflicts of interest between stakeholders

3.2 Review and adjust historical and forecast financial data

(a) *Lies, damn lies and business plans*

The one certainty of a company's business plan is that actual trading will always be different from the financial forecasts. This means that before the valuation analysis has started, a source of error has already been introduced.

When considering a distressed business, it is likely that the financial forecasts will have been prepared some time ago – potentially, before the business had fully appreciated its true circumstances. It may even be that the person who prepared the forecasts is no longer with the company. It is therefore essential that the current management re-forecast based on current macro market issues and the company's own position. Any underperforming business with significant leverage is likely to have had an independent business review – a review of the deliverability of the financial forecast that highlights appropriate sensitivities and vulnerabilities to the management's forecasts.

It is also possible that the results from the last financial year may no longer be an appropriate basis for a valuation, as they may not represent the new realities facing the business.

Financial forecasts and historical results, therefore, need to be analysed more thoroughly than may usually be necessary for a healthy business. The analysis needs to drill down into the underlying assumptions and to challenge them, in order to check that they still hold given the current conditions facing the business. This is especially important in the absence of an independent business review.

(b) *Future net maintainable earnings*

It is vital, as part of any distressed valuation, to consider what adjustments need to be made to ensure that both the comparable multiples and DCF analysis use the appropriate financial data. These adjustments are all made with the objective of determining the company's future net maintainable earnings, which reflect the earning capacity of the business when the impact of distress has been eliminated through either a refinancing or a formal insolvency process.

When considering adjustments, only items that are ongoing in nature should be included. Any items that are considered situational, caused only by the current level of distress, should be excluded. Typical ongoing adjustments include:

- step reductions in sales – for example, due to changing market conditions or contract losses (eg, service companies supplying the public sector and bricks and mortar retailers following the move towards online retailing);
- increased costs due to input cost inflation (eg, labour costs due to

national minimum wage and pension auto-enrolment, property, rent and rates, utility prices and metal commodity prices such as copper and platinum); and
- increased capital, maintenance or research and development (R&D) expenditure where these costs have been cut to preserve cash.

These ongoing adjustments also need to be taken into account in relation to the historical results. When reviewing the historical results, additional consideration needs to be given to assessing whether there are any one-off or non-recurring costs that can be eradicated once the company emerges from distress and which should therefore be excluded. Examples include:
- less favourable credit terms and discounts from suppliers;
- professional fees associated with restructuring or other corporate activity;
- above-market salaries and other distributions made to related parties in anticipation of distress; and
- profits or losses from asset sales.

Once these adjustments have been quantified and an assessment of the future net maintainable earnings made, the financials are in a position to be analysed for valuation purposes. Care should always be taken to ensure that any adjustments are supportable under scrutiny by third parties.

(c) Continued investment?

A tool used by management in distressed situations to conserve cash is to cut back on investment in the business. This may be through a reduction in capital, repairs and maintenance or R&D expenditure. No matter what categories of cost are cut, there will almost certainly be a detrimental impact on the business if they have been in place for any significant period of time.

Business plans typically underestimate the impact of lack of investment on the future profitability of the business. New investment takes time to implement and even longer to impact on profitability, and should be carefully considered as a sensitivity for the valuation.

To assess the impact on value, it is necessary to understand the extent to which the business is underinvested. This can be achieved by comparing the current investment levels in the management accounts with those of prior periods and by benchmarking the investment levels with comparable companies.

Any catch-up investment should be included in the cash flows used for the DCF analysis, and its discounted value deducted from the comparable multiples valuations.

This approach takes into account the physical shortfall in investment and the cash impact of rectifying it. What it does not consider is the long-term damage that lack of investment causes to the business and its brands.

(d) *Is goodwill now badwill?*

Building and maintaining goodwill and brand value is crucial to the success of many businesses. This is normally an expensive and long-term process that can be undone in a much shorter time period by mismanagement and underinvestment.

Even in non-brand-led businesses, successful performance is often directly linked to strong relationships with customers, suppliers and even finance providers. This goodwill generates customer loyalty, enables favourable terms to be negotiated and allows flexibility to cope with business fluctuations.

In times of distress, however, new priorities appear for management. Conserving cash, either through aggressive working capital management or cutting investment, has the potential to damage the goodwill and brand value built by the business.

Typically, the damage caused by a limited period of distress is short-lived and can quickly be repaired. However, where measures to address distress are in place for any substantial period of time, the damage can be more serious. Stock shortages are a classic consequence of distress. Short-term shortages can lead to long-term reputation issues associated with a lack of reliability, which can have a lasting impact on the business.

The extent of any damage caused to the goodwill and brand value of a business is important in assessing the deliverability of its financial forecasts. Market-leading growth rates and profitability indicate that management believes that the company's goodwill has not suffered material impairment. If this is not the case, then either the growth and profitability rates need to be reduced or additional investment needs to be factored into the plan.

A practical point not to be overlooked in a distressed situation is the legal ownership of any intellectual property that is necessary for the business. When times are good, informal arrangements in place over important intellectual property may well be sufficient for the ongoing operation of the business. When the situation becomes distressed and the future of the business is uncertain, these informal relationships can break down.

If informal relationships do exist and a formal insolvency process is undertaken, the holder of any business-critical intellectual property will often try to extract as much value as possible from the situation. It is better for a business to deal with such issues in advance, when trading is still good and the spirit of a long-term partnership still exists with the owner of the intellectual property.

In summary, the following should be considered when reviewing financial forecasts:

- When were they prepared, and by whom?

- Do they reflect current market conditions?
- Have any necessary future net maintainable earnings adjustments been made?
- Do they show any step changes to sales or costs?
- Are there any current distress costs that require to be excluded?
- Are proposed adjustments supportable?
- Has allowance been made for reversal of underinvestment?

3.3 Perform valuation analysis

The main techniques that are used to value a normal business – comparable multiples and DCF analysis – can be difficult to apply in a distressed situation.

The main reason for this is that these techniques start with the assumption that the business in question will continue into perpetuity. This is a bold assertion for any company, but for one already in distress it is a step too far, as the business has already demonstrated its capacity to be at risk of failure. When using these techniques, this risk of failure needs to be factored into the analysis.

(a) Comparable multiples analysis

Comparable multiples analysis looks at the valuation multiples that apply to comparable companies quoted on the public markets and comparable (or precedent) transactions that have taken place. This analysis is based on the assumption that similar valuation multiples apply for businesses with similar economics. It can be applied only to businesses that are profitable at least at the EBITDA level.

The quoted companies that are considered to be comparable will likely be in much stronger financial shape than the distressed business being valued, and as such their enterprise value as a multiple of EBIT or EBITDA will be higher. The degree of comparability and the number of comparable companies can vary greatly, and the appropriate discount will be a matter of judgement based on the individual circumstances. However, value is likely to be at the bottom of the multiple range suggested by the comparable company analysis or even at a further discount, given the risk associated with the specific distressed business.

When valuing a healthy business, it is common practice to consider the level of control premium that should be applied to the comparable company data. This premium for control is applied to take account of the fact that the share price of a quoted company reflects the valuation of a minority shareholding. To acquire the company, a party will generally need to pay a premium over the current share price in order to acquire control. In a restructuring, the restructured company often has a wide shareholder base, which would mean that a control premium would not be applicable, and in general it is unlikely that a premium for control will be appropriate in a distressed valuation as it is likely to be offset by the risk factors in the business.

The publicly available data for comparable transactions can often be misleading when used for valuation purposes, as there is generally a lack of information about the future prospects of the target company for all but the larger public company transactions. The dynamics and drivers for each transaction will vary widely. Most deals are driven by current and future prospects rather than historical profitability and therefore the implied historical multiple can be a particularly unreliable comparator. Additionally, with a corporate acquisition, the valuation may have assumed that significant synergies would be available when the businesses are merged which would not be applicable to a standalone business valuation.

Comparable transaction data therefore needs to be analysed fully to try to eliminate these distorting factors. As with the comparable company analysis, the comparative health and growth prospects of the subject company should be considered when assessing the most appropriate multiple, and the most comparable deals weighted accordingly.

Precedent transactions may provide the most appropriate guide to valuation multiples in a situation where companies have previously been acquired out of distress, as the value paid will have reflected the distressed situation and is likely to have focused more heavily on recovery prospects at the time. Again, it is important to try to analyse the publicly available information to ensure that the most applicable underlying financial data is considered.

With either comparable company or transaction analysis, care needs to be taken to apply the resultant multiple to the most appropriate underlying financials. The multiples should be applied to the future net maintainable earnings of the business.

An example of the importance of this would be the valuation of a drug company with its main drug coming off-patent. At the point where manufacturers can launch generic versions of the drug, the profitability of the patented product is likely to drop significantly. If this change happens towards the end of an accounting period, the full-year impact will not be evident in the year-end results. Applying a historical multiple to unadjusted results would overvalue the business by being based on unsustainable profit levels.

Normalised working capital: When a business becomes distressed, one of the first operational areas to suffer is working capital. As cash becomes short, management tends to seek ways to preserve it through stretching creditors and chasing debtors more aggressively. However, as a situation becomes more distressed and this becomes apparent to suppliers, they may seek to protect their positions by moving to more adverse credit terms and, in extreme cases, cash on delivery.

These factors mean that in a distressed situation, working capital levels are unlikely to be representative of normal conditions. Following an acquisition and a return to normal trading conditions, these working capital balances will return to normal levels.

If the business is to be acquired out of administration, then all non-essential creditors will remain with the administrators and the purchaser will benefit from a buildup of these creditor balances post-acquisition, which will improve the cash flow of the business in the short term.

These working capital effects need to be taken into account in a valuation. When considering a DCF analysis, the effects will be accounted for by the inflow or outflow of cash in the post-acquisition period. Comparable company and transaction analysis assumes that the business is being acquired with a normal level of working capital. For these methodologies the short-term cash impact of working capital returning to normal levels should be an adjustment to the valuation. This adjustment would be the discounted value of these short-term cash flows.

In assessing the normal level of working capital, it may be necessary to consider business performance in previous financial periods, before the effects of trading in distress became apparent.

Figure 2: Impact of working capital stretch on consideration

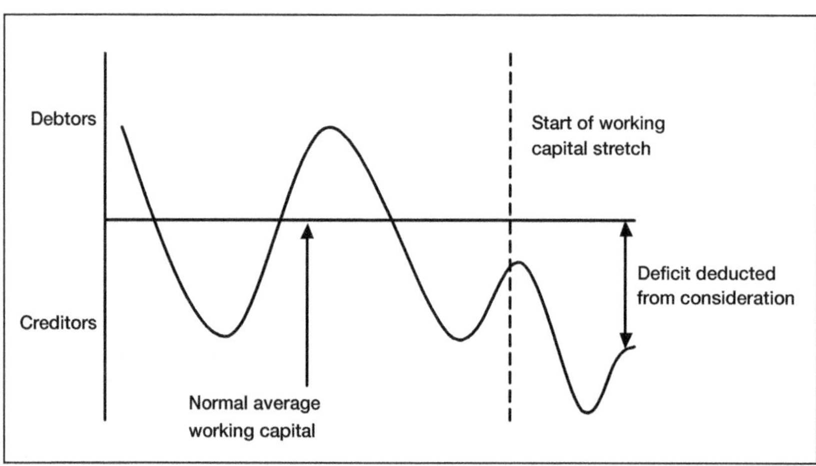

(b) ***Discounted cash flow***

DCF analysis is a flexible valuation methodology that can be tailored to the outlook of the subject company. Whereas comparable multiples attempt to apply the economics of similar businesses, a DCF approach analyses the cash flows of the business in question. This enables the impact of specific issues facing the company to be factored into the cash-flow forecasts and consequently the valuation.

As this analysis is based on medium-term financial forecasts, a sensible estimate of value relies on the reasonableness of the forecasts. For this reason, it becomes vital that the financial forecasts have been subjected to the rigorous review discussed above, and adjusted to reflect future net maintainable earnings of the business.

DCF analysis provides an estimate of value by considering the net present value (NPV) of the future cash flows implied by the financial forecasts of a business. They include a terminal value to take account of cash flows into perpetuity beyond the forecast period at the point where the cash flows have reached a stable growth state. When considering enterprise value, the analysis is performed before taking into account any financing costs.

These cash flows are discounted at a rate that reflects the required rate of return of the company's equity and debt providers, weighted according to the proportion of funding provided. This discount rate is known as the weighted average cost of capital (WACC) and is defined as follows:

$$WACC = rd\,(1 - tc)\,D / (D + E) + re\,E / (D + E)$$

Where:

rd = cost of debt

tc = marginal tax rate

re = return on equity

D = level of debt

E = level of equity

These rates of return compensate the finance providers for the level of risk that they are accepting by making an investment in the company. The returns required for equity providers are much higher than those for the debt providers; this to reflect the security that debt providers enjoy, primarily from holding specific security on a company's assets or structural priority in the event of insolvency.

In the case of a distressed business, this perceived risk level will be higher than that of a healthy business, and equity and debt finance providers will likely require higher rates of return to compensate for the increased risk. This in turn will require that a higher discount rate be applied to future cash flows.

A higher discount rate will partially reflect the impact of distress in a DCF, but will not be sufficient on its own. This is because a real risk facing a distressed business is that it will eventually fail and there will be no further cash flows beyond those of an insolvency process. By using a higher discount rate, the present value of the future cash flows is reduced, but value is still attributed to cash flows into perpetuity.

The area where ignoring this risk has the most material impact on valuation is in terminal value. Terminal value often accounts for the majority of the DCF valuation and represents the value of the company beyond the financial forecast period. Terminal value is typically calculated in one of two ways:

- using a perpetuity formula: the terminal-year cash flow is divided by the delta of WACC and the terminal growth rate. This assumes that the business continues to trade into perpetuity; or
- using the exit multiple methodology: this assumes that the business is sold in the terminal year and an appropriate valuation multiple is applied to the relevant financial metric in the terminal year to estimate a sale value; and that the new owner derives value from the business into perpetuity.

Terminal value should be estimated using both methodologies in order to sense-check the results. This is important because the terminal growth value relies on an estimate for the growth of the cash flows of the business into perpetuity – and this rate is difficult to predict.

A guideline for a healthy business is that the terminal growth rate should be roughly equal to the long-term forecast gross domestic product (GDP) growth rate for its country of operation. For a distressed business, the long-term prospects are likely to be more uncertain and a terminal growth rate between zero and GDP is typical.

Both methodologies make the assumption that the cash flows continue into perpetuity. For a healthy business this is a reasonable assumption, but for a business in operational distress it is far less certain given the associated risks.

To take account of these risks, an estimate of the break-up asset value of the business in the terminal year should be used as a third terminal value data point in a distressed situation. The break-up asset value provides an estimate of the return that could be realised in an insolvent sale and would represent a floor value for the terminal year. In order to determine a reasonable range for the terminal value, it is necessary to assess the likelihood of the business recovering fully by the terminal year and the likelihood that its business model has longevity.

If there is a high probability of the business recovering fully with good long-term prospects, then a terminal value based on the growth and exit multiple methodologies would be appropriate. If it is highly uncertain whether the business will be secure in the long term, then a terminal value based on break-up asset value would be more appropriate.

(c) Pricing probability of failure

The traditional method for performing a DCF does not take adequate account of the risk of corporate failure. One methodology that can be used to rectify this is to apply the basic principles of adjusting bond prices for the risk of default (this methodology does not claim to reflect all the complexities of bond pricing, only the basic principles).

In basic bond pricing, if a one-year bond with a face value of £1,000 carried an interest rate of 5%, it would be expected to pay out £1,050 at the end of one year. If this bond had no risk of default and the risk-free rate were 5%, then the bond would be priced as follows:

$$\text{PV of bond} = \frac{£1{,}000 + 50}{1.05} = £1{,}000$$

However, if these bonds carried a 10% risk of default this risk would need to be factored into their price. In this example there would be a 10% chance that the bondholder received nothing and a 90% chance that the bondholder would receive full payment. The probability-weighted expected return would therefore be (90% × £1,050) + (10% × 0) = £945.

$$\text{Probability-weighted PV of the bond} = \frac{£945}{1.05} = £900$$

This would make the implied yield of the bond £1,050/£900 = 17%.

This methodology can be applied to DCF analysis by replacing the risk-free rate with the calculated WACC (discount rate) and the break-up value of the business with the pay-out in the event of default (replacing the zero return to bondholders assumed in the previous example).

Shown below is a simple worked example using a three-year cash flow with free cash-flow and break-up value growing at a constant rate. The terminal value is calculated using an exit multiple and the probability of failure in any one year is assumed to be constant (in reality, the risk of failure may change from year to year).

This methodology considers the following possible outcomes that can occur in each year: the company

- survives to generate free cash flow; or
- becomes insolvent so the break-up value is realised.

The present value of each of these potential outcomes is calculated and then multiplied by the probability that each outcome will occur. By adding these results together, a probability-weighted NPV can be calculated.

Table 3: DCF analysis including failure potential

Assumptions	
Annual growth rate of free cash flow and break-up value	2.0%
Discount rate	2.0%
Annual probability of failure	15.0%
Terminal year exit multiple (of free cash flow)	10.0×
Break-up value year 1	£20m

	Period			**Terminal value**
£m	**1**	**2**	**3**	
Free cash flow	10	10.2	10.4	106.1
Discount factor	0.89	0.80	0.71	0.71
Present value	8.9	8.1	7.4	75.5
Break-up value	20	20.4	20.8	21.2
Discount factor	0.89	0.80	0.71	0.71
Present value	17.9	16.3	14.8	15.1

	Present value by period (£m)				
Scenario	**1**	**2**	**3**	**TY***	**NPV (£m)**
No failure	8.9	8.1	7.4	75.5	100.0
Failure in exit year	8.9	8.1	7.4	15.1	39.6
Failure in year 3	8.9	8.1	14.8		31.9
Failure in year 2	8.9	16.3			25.2
Failure in year 1	17.9				17.9

Scenario	Probability by period				Probability (%)
	1	2	3	TY	
No failure	85%	85%	85%	85%	52
Failure in exit year	85%	85%	85%	15%	9
Failure in year 3	85%	85%	15%		11
Failure in year 2	85%	15%			13
Failure in year 1	15%				15
					100

Scenario	NPV (£m)	Probability	Probability-weighted NPV (£m)
No failure	100.0	52%	52.2
Failure in exit year	39.6	9%	3.6
Failure in year 3	31.9	11%	3.5
Failure in year 2	25.2	13%	3.2
Failure in year 1	17.9	15%	2.7
	Total	100%	65.2

*TY = terminal year

This example shows that the DCF valuation with no risk of failure would be £100 million. When this is adjusted to take account of the estimate probability of failure, the NPV falls to £65 million. This implies a 35% discount to compensate the buyer for the additional risk of acquiring this distressed business.

This methodology enables the potential for failure to be factored into the DCF analysis and also forces the user to consider in more depth that potential for failure and the break-up value for the business that may be recovered in this scenario.

(d) *Risk and return*

One area that is often overlooked when considering the valuation of distressed businesses is the requirements of the buyer. There are now more and more investment vehicles and funds specialising in investing in distressed assets. These funds often have a mandate from their limited partners to pursue specific types of investment and specific levels of risk. Funds allocated by limited partners to these investment vehicles will typically demand a higher level of return to compensate for the increased level of risk assumed when making distressed investments.

This requirement for increased rates of return has a direct impact on the price that the buyer is able to pay for the asset. When performing a returns analysis on a distressed asset, the typical private equity rule of thumb of a target increased rate of return of 20% to 25% needs to be revised upwards towards 35% or more.

(e) *Asset value*

When considering a seriously distressed business, there are often severe time constraints on the restructuring or sale. This makes preparation of reliable financial forecasts unrealistic, either because future prospects cannot be predicted with any degree of certainty or because the existing forecasts do not reflect reality. In this circumstance a reliable DCF-based valuation is impossible.

In addition, the business may be loss-making or generating only a relatively small profit. This undermines the use of the comparable multiples-based valuation methods, leaving an asset-based valuation as the most appropriate, and sometimes only, valuation basis.

Asset-based valuations are therefore core to many distressed valuations. As outlined at the start of this chapter, there are two asset valuations: the going-concern value and the realisable value.

If a business is being sold as a going concern – that is, if the operations of the business will be kept together and the business will continue to trade – then the appropriate asset value will represent the value in use of the assets being considered. A good proxy for this value will often be the depreciated book value of the assets in the accounts. A review should be made of the depreciation policy adopted by the company to check that the depreciation rate reflects the useful economic life of the assets, and that the value of the assets is representative.

Asset valuations are particularly useful for capital-intensive businesses where investment in equipment and tooling is made to support long-term cash-flow generation, typically against supply contracts. Examples of this would be the automotive supply industry, where heavy capital investment against multiple-year supply contracts provides the majority of value when a business becomes distressed.

In asset-light businesses, however, the future value of the business is tied into intangible assets such as supply contracts, brand names and human capital. In these businesses, value is better assessed through the consideration of future cash-flow potential using DCF or comparable multiples analysis.

In a going-concern situation, the net asset value of a business should be considered with the liabilities of the business taken into account.

(f) *Realising asset value in insolvency*

If the subject business does not represent a going concern, then the assets should be valued on a realisable value basis, often referred to as a 'break-up basis'. This represents the value that can be realised from selling individual assets or collections of assets, with the business ceasing to trade.

This method of valuing a business is typically the base valuation considered when estimating recoveries from an insolvent situation. It is important to consider the realisation costs associated with asset sales (eg, intermediaries' fees and distribution costs).

The realisable value of assets is very much dependent on the specific assets in question, particularly their condition, portability, flexibility of use and the presence of a secondary market. In addition, when realising asset value in an insolvent situation, the risk of successful retention of title claims by third parties needs to be considered. If third parties are well placed to enforce retention of title, the assets to which this applies should be considered of nil realisable value.

In addition to these general issues, Table 4, on the next page, outlines some of the key factors to be taken into consideration when assessing realisable value for the major asset classes.

When acquiring a distressed business, break-up value is used as the contingency value to determine the level of financial risk being assumed at a given purchase price. The delta between break-up value and consideration is the initial value at risk for the buyer in the acquisition.

When assessing the level of net realisation from an insolvency, it is important to seek specific tax advice to understand how the timing of certain actions, such as the sale of freehold property, can impact on the priority of payment of any resultant tax charges.

3.4 Other items that can impact on value

(a) *Partial business sale – solvent*

Careful analysis should be performed to understand whether value can be maximised by selling parts of a business rather than the whole.

In a solvent situation, this may be driven by the potential to divest part of the business which offers no synergies with the rest of the group, but which would be attractive to third parties. Selling this business may realise more value than the ongoing value of that business to the group.

Table 4: Key considerations for assessing realisable value for different asset classes

Asset class	Key factors impacting value
Fixed assets	
Freehold property	Alternative use potential, planning permissions, environmental liabilities, tenants
Leasehold property	(In addition to the freehold points above), remaining lease term, assignment provisions, Landlord and Tenant Act 1954 protection, ability to assign, rent review provisions, pre-emption rights
Leasehold improvements	Limited value on a break-up basis
Plant and machinery	Age, ownership of associated tooling, risk of property damage on removal, decommissioning to installation costs
Fixtures and fittings	Limited value on a break-up basis
Intellectual property	Documented legal ownership, ability to assign, associated litigation
Current assets	
Stock	Ownership (third-party stock held on site), recoverability (stock held by third parties), age, obsolescence
Debtors	Age, ability to collect, foreign exchange exposure, legal documentation, offsetting creditor balances

In this situation the whole business should be valued on a sum-of-the-parts basis. A sum-of-the-parts valuation considers each part of the business separately and applies different valuation metrics to reflect the different economics of each business.

It is important when performing a sum-of-the-parts valuation to make sure that the costs of any business support functions carried out by the business being sold are reflected in the remaining business's financials, and that any cross-selling benefits should be excluded.

(b) *Partial business sale – insolvent*

When a business has reached a more advanced level of distress, maximum value may be achieved by leaving behind loss-making or value-impairing elements of the business through the use of an insolvency procedure.

This situation can occur for a number of reasons, but common examples include the presence of onerous leases or contracts, loss-making locations or potentially high exposure to past legal liabilities. One example would be the restructuring of a retail business with a number of loss-making sites. The profitable sites could be sold as a group in a trade and assets sale out of insolvency, with the loss-making units remaining with the administrator.

If value for a business is to be realised through an insolvent sale, careful analysis needs to be undertaken to determine which assets and liabilities will transfer as part of the sale.

In a theoretical insolvent transaction, only the assets necessary to continue the operations of the business would transfer and the valuation would be based on these alone, with all liabilities excluded. In reality, a number of historical creditor balances and liabilities need to be taken into account.

Some of the most common liabilities that need to be taken into account are the employee costs associated with the Transfer of Undertakings (Protection of Employment) Regulations 2006, as amended by the Collective Redundancies and Transfer of Undertakings (Protection of Employment) (Amendment) Regulations 2014 (TUPE). This provides protection to employees when all or substantially all of the business is sold. This will impact on value because the buyer will often stipulate as a condition of the deal that an amount be held back from consideration to cover the potential TUPE liability. The eventual TUPE cost that is suffered varies from case to case, but the range should be assessed up front so that the potential impact on value can be understood.

Other liabilities to be considered are set out in the table below.

Table 5: Main creditor balances/liabilities to be considered in insolvent sales

Creditor or liability	Considerations
Trade creditors	• Existing suppliers may be necessary to continue trade, meaning that their credit balances need to be settled or assumed by the buyer. • Certain creditors may hold important information or assets which require 'ransom' payments to be made to the creditor.
Leasehold properties	• If there are common landlords of both profitable and loss-making sites, it may not be possible to secure assignments of only the profitable sites. Loss-making units may need to be included as part of the transaction.
Loss-making contracts	• Loss-making contracts may need to be retained if they serve an important ongoing customer.

The analysis of which liabilities need to be taken into account in the valuation is situation-specific and typically requires a line-by-line review.

(c) ***Pensions***

A defined benefit pension scheme may be the largest single creditor on a company's balance sheet. The treatment of the scheme will have a significant impact on the enterprise valuation of a business.

Where a defined benefit pension scheme is transferring to the buyer as part of the transaction, it is important to treat past liabilities and the funding for future service benefits separately. Past liabilities should be considered as an additional debt and factored into the enterprise valuation. The funding for future service liabilities should be included in the forecast profits and cash flows considered in the DCF and comparable multiples analysis.

Past liabilities are held on the company's balance sheet and carried at a value calculated under the provisions of Financial Reporting Standard 102 (UK only) or International Accounting Standard 19. This is normally used as the starting point for the quantification of the debt value to be included as part of the enterprise valuation.

When executing a transaction, however, the terms of the servicing of the historical deficit and future service benefits are agreed with the pension trustees as part of the deal. The terms agreed can then be analysed on a DCF basis to assess the impact on value and an actuarial valuation should then be carried out to estimate the historical liability.

If a business is being acquired out of insolvency, then the defined benefit pension scheme may remain with the seller. If certain conditions are met, the scheme will fall within the pension protection fund, which will then provide 90% of the expected employee benefits to the majority of scheme members. In this scenario, the buyer will need to factor only the future pension costs of a replacement scheme into the financial forecasts. No allowance needs to be made for the historical liability.

Defined benefit pension schemes are highly complex products and specialist advice should be obtained when considering their valuation impact.

(d) Debt financing

An important driver for value in a distressed transaction is the availability of debt financing. In this area of the market, the most common source of debt finance is asset-based lending. Asset-based lending provides debt finance secured on specific assets. The most common assets secured are stock and debtors, due to their relatively high level of liquidity, and also freehold property due to its security and marketability. In very specific circumstances, asset-based borrowing can be raised using other assets as security, such as plant and machinery.

The level of debt financing available affects valuation due to its impact on potential equity returns. The greater the proportion of acquisition value sourced from debt rather than equity, the higher the eventual returns will be for the equity provider. This is due to the reduced amount of equity required and the lower returns paid to debt providers as interest compared with the capital growth that accrues to equity holders.

4. Conclusion

The bottom line is that although the valuation of a distressed business follows the same fundamentals as that of a healthy business, it is essential to select the most appropriate methodologies for the particular circumstances, and apply the various methodologies to the right data.

The critical factors that typically need to be taken into account when valuing a distressed business are as follows:

- Distressed businesses are higher risk than healthy businesses.
- The probability of failure is real.
- Investors require higher returns to compensate for the increased risk and this drives down their entry value.
- The level of distress and associated damage to the business impacts on value.

- The underlying financial data needs to be adjusted to reflect future net maintainable earnings, given the new reality facing the business.

With these factors in mind and using the tools outlined above, you should be well placed to value a distressed business.

The publishers would like to thank Paul Hemming and Alastair Beveridge for their assistance in the preparation of the previous version of this chapter.

Pre-packs at an operational level

Mark Shaw
BDO LLP

1. Introduction

The term 'pre-pack' has become near-ubiquitous in modern insolvency and restructuring practice, notwithstanding that it applies to only a very small proportion of insolvencies. A pre-pack insolvency process is one in which an insolvency practitioner, immediately following his or her appointment, sells all or some of a company's assets, having reached an agreement to do so in the run-up to appointment. The term can cover a range of transactions, from the sale of assets of very small companies to their directors to highly sophisticated transactions worth billions of pounds.

Public concern has been expressed over pre-packs, stemming principally from:

- a generally perceived lack of transparency;
- the marketing process adopted before the sale;
- the valuation of the business sold; and
- considerations as to whether the business will be viable post-sale.

Pre-packs have remained an area of focus for government, regulators and the wider business community over recent years.

This chapter concentrates on operational or trading companies in the context of mid-market and upwards transactions. It does not deal specifically with the issues that arise in private equity-backed structures, involving only holding companies and more limited numbers of financial stakeholders. However, the same issues and considerations are likely to apply to virtually all pre-packs, to one degree or another.

Pre-pack sales of operational or trading companies tend to have a greater impact on the underlying business in a group than, for example, those that take place only at the holding company level.

Some years ago, it was relatively common for appointments of administrative receivers or administrators in even quite large and complex insolvencies to be made with little warning or planning. The appointed insolvency practitioner would then need to decide whether the business should be traded-on with a view to it being marketed and, hopefully, sold as a going concern. This meant that any business sale would be executed some time after appointment.

However, stakeholders – and especially lenders – are now usually adept at identifying potential problem exposures early on, which has meant that there is normally a period of time between the identification of a problem and the likelihood of an insolvency process. This in turn means that the business can often be marketed for sale prior to, rather than after, an insolvency process has commenced. While a detailed discussion of distressed M&A and accelerated M&A processes ("AM&A processes") is beyond the scope of this chapter, such processes are nonetheless relevant, as they represent the usual means of marketing a business for sale in advance of a pre-pack. The development of AM&A processes has gone hand-in-hand with the development of pre-pack sales.

AM&A processes market a business for sale using a variant of more traditional M&A techniques. The timeframe is usually much shorter than for a traditional M&A process and information/due diligence is comparatively limited, but the focus remains the sale of a bundle of underlying cash flows to a purchaser in as seamless a manner as possible, as opposed to the historically more common sale of a bundle of assets. The aim of this approach is to preserve and maximise value.

Once the AM&A process has been run and the price maximised through such competitive tension as it has been possible to create in the circumstances, the sale is commonly executed using a pre-pack.

Another factor which is likely to have contributed to the use of pre-packs is the risk of litigation for loss-making trading against insolvency practitioners following appointment. The use of the pre-pack mitigates much of this risk – although, as discussed below, it does create other risks instead.

Therefore, a pre-pack is usually a near-seamless sale of a business from within a company to a new owner, which has been arranged and documented prior to the commencement of an insolvency process. In a pre-pack, the first transaction which the appointed insolvency practitioner enters into is a pre-arranged and pre-negotiated sale agreement.

Pre-packs also tend to reduce costs, as the work must be carried out within a limited timeframe. In some circumstances, very much less work needs to be carried out to arrange a pre-pack sale compared to that required to trade on post-insolvency.

This chapter is a high-level discussion of some of the practical issues that affect pre-pack sales at an operational level. It is not intended to be a complete guide or checklist for all issues to which an insolvency practitioner should have regard. Each situation will be different and insolvency practitioners will need to use their own judgement and seek appropriate advice as needed.

2. The decision to pre-pack

In broad terms, any appointed insolvency practitioner owes a duty to take reasonable steps to obtain a proper value for a company's assets as the circumstances permit, and then to distribute the resulting realisations among creditors in the right manner. 'Reasonable steps' will be judged by the standard of what an ordinary, skilled insolvency practitioner would have done.

There are additional specific overlays to this broad proposition which arise in relation to an insolvency practitioner acting as an administrator, which are commented on further below (see section 4.2).

In a pre-pack sale, there is always a risk that the insolvency practitioner could be criticised by courts or regulators, or be sued for not achieving such proper value. The prudent insolvency practitioner will therefore wish to consider carefully any decision to execute a pre-pack sale, given the potential for such criticism or litigation.

Some factors that may be taken into account in deciding whether to execute a pre-pack sale are discussed below. This list is not intended to be exhaustive.

However, the essence of the decision to pre-pack is the answer to the following question: Is it likely that a pre-pack sale will, overall, be better than any realistically achievable next best option? In some cases, the answer to this will be clear. In others, the insolvency practitioner will need to undertake careful analysis and risk management processes in exercising his or her judgement.

The following illustrative factors are all likely to be supportive, if not determinative, of a decision to pre-pack.

2.1 The position of senior debt

If a bank is owed a significant sum of money that is secured on all assets of the company, this can make a decision to pre-pack more straightforward in certain circumstances.

An example could be a highly-geared business that has under-performed significantly at an operational level and now needs additional funds, which the current lenders are unwilling to provide and which cannot be obtained from an alternative lender.

Let us assume that, over time, £70 million of debt has built up in the business. Its assets on a break-up are worth less than £10 million. The enterprise (ie, cash-free, debt-free) value of the business is currently, say, £35 million – as determined by market testing, independent valuation or both.

Therefore, the business would need to be worth £35 million more before the insolvency practitioner would be at risk of a justifiable claim of undervalue, on the assumption that the holder of the £70 million of debt agreed with the strategy. For simplicity, it is assumed that all of the company's assets fall to fixed charge realisations.

Put another way, the lender can decide for itself whether a given level of loss is acceptable to it and the outcome does not affect other stakeholders in practical terms. The closer the value gets to the next level of debt down – say, unsecured creditors – the greater the risk becomes.

An important factor surrounding senior debt is the ability to deliver the assets to a buyer. If a senior lender has security over the assets, a deed of release will likely be needed to deliver the assets unencumbered to a buyer in the requisite timescales. Therefore, in most circumstances, the lender needs to be in agreement with the strategy to be able to do this. Similar issues can arise in relation to lower-ranking creditors, such as bondholders, where a change of control consent is required in the indenture. This can give rise to complex contractual positions, making proper legal advice essential.

2.2 Loss of customers in insolvency

Some businesses will have customers that dissipate quickly once the prospect of formal insolvency is scented. This is not necessarily the same as the situation in which contracts for sale of a debtor's goods or services are determined on insolvency; it is more a commercial issue about being able to rely on a debtor for continued supply.

A pre-pack sale is still a sale following a formal insolvency process, hence contracts which determine automatically on insolvency will still do so.

An example of such commercial customer risk could come from a supply of engineered goods where warranties are essential. In such cases, customers are likely to move to alternative suppliers rather than risk the potential loss of warranty or after-sales care. Trading by an insolvency practitioner after the commencement of insolvency would therefore be more difficult.

In a pre-pack sale, the message to customers could be: "X Ltd has bought the business, your past warranties will be honoured and X Ltd has ample resources to fund the business in the future." Revenues would thus be preserved, and therefore value. If this were contrasted with an insolvency process, with post-appointment trading and a subsequent sale, the value of the business would likely be lower due to loss of revenues. Debtor and stock realisations would likely be consequently suppressed as well.

2.3 Loss of key people

This can happen where there are highly mobile people whose retention is key to preserving business value. An example would be a professional services firm. Again, the issue would arise not so much from determination of employment contracts as from rivals calling directly to poach key staff and to exploit the debtor's distressed position. It is axiomatic that the staff who are best, and hence most valuable to the business, will be most desired by rivals.

2.4 Regulated businesses

Some businesses are regulated such that a formal insolvency process would destroy value in them, through withdrawal of that regulated status. A pre-pack may avoid this as the formal insolvency process happens only at the instant of sale – usually to another regulated business with the consent of the relevant regulator.

Financial services and legal businesses are good examples of such situations.

2.5 Post-insolvency trading would be loss-making or require significant funding

This is commonly the case, as suppliers can hold a debtor to ransom for ongoing supplies – not just in terms of, say, *pro forma* supplies for new deliveries, but also for past debts and/or retention of title claims.

An example is useful to illustrate the issues. An insolvency practitioner has identified that four weeks would be needed meaningfully to market the business for sale post-appointment. In that time, the debtor would make an accounting loss of approximately £5 million, on the assumption that no customers would be lost. Further, the insolvency practitioner has formed the view that he or she would need to borrow £3 million to achieve that £5 million loss. On the assumption of no customer losses, the £3 million of borrowings would likely be repaid at the end of the four-week trading period. It is far from certain that the value of the underlying assets/business would be increased from such trading.

Meanwhile, current lenders have stated that they see that the debtor is over-borrowed already and therefore would lend money to the insolvency practitioner only if he or she were to accept personal liability for the loans. There is no logical argument for an insolvency practitioner having to borrow money personally in such circumstances, when the underlying stakeholders themselves do not see the economic sense in it.

In these circumstances, overall, it could well be better to consider the use of a pre-pack sale. This example also begins to highlight some of the potential conflicts and risks which pre-packs create. If the business is to lose money and require funding, surely some of that would happen under the directors' trading during, say, an AM&A process? Who, then, provides funding or bears the effects of these losses? This issue is important, especially in the context of the perception of pre-packs by stakeholders and the public in general, and is considered in further detail in section 5.2 below.

2.6 A good business, but with historical liabilities

A good example of this would be a manufacturer that is operationally profitable, but has legacy environmental or health and safety liabilities which render the business unsustainable for the future.

In certain circumstances, a pre-pack can be used to clean up a business, passing it to new owners but without the liabilities which would otherwise render it unviable. This can carry significant reputational risk and hence careful consideration of alternative options is needed, especially around value. For example, a compromise/cram-down process (eg, a company voluntary arrangement (CVA) or scheme of arrangement) may be worthy of consideration. The cascading priority of administration objectives requires that these alternatives be considered before a pre-pack sale of assets is used.

Legacy defined benefit pension schemes are another common example of such situations.

2.7 Other issues

It could be said that an AM&A process followed by a pre-pack is intended to facilitate a seamless sale of a business, with minimal taint from insolvency.

While it is true that the taint from insolvency would be less than in, say, an insolvency appointment followed by a marketing period and a sale, not all of the problems would disappear.

For example, property leases cannot just be 'sold' to a buyer. They need to be assigned by tri-partite agreement between landlord, tenant (ie, seller) and buyer. Therefore, in a pre-pack, the solution is usually to grant a licence to occupy in the sale agreement to the buyer. This will normally be in breach of the lease and can give rise to applications for forfeiture. This will need to be considered and the risks mitigated in advance. It is also one of the reasons why businesses which are heavily reliant on property leases (eg, retailers) now tend to be restructured using a CVA.

Trade creditors, to the extent that they are not paid or otherwise taken over by the buyer, may well refuse to supply the buyer without their debts being settled. The position is similar for retention of title claims.

Generally, a review of contracts should be undertaken to ascertain whether they determine automatically in an insolvency process, or whether they may be determined by the counterparty on an insolvency process. If key contracts vanish, this can go to value.

Generally, insofar as possible, with an AM&A process for a trading business, it makes sense to identify and be able to deal up-front with potential problems that could go to value which the insolvency process might cause, so that potential buyers can be comfortable with the consequent effect on value. Suggestions for post-sale communications processes are also important to this. This may appear counterintuitive, but time constraints create a need for a more open and up-front approach to prevent issues otherwise derailing a sale at an inopportune moment.

3. Documenting the decision

Having set out the position where criticism could be levelled at an insolvency practitioner for failing to achieve proper value before executing a pre-pack sale, it follows that having a detailed written justification of why that decision was made would be sound risk management.

This justification should be an answer to the potential questions that, for example, an unsecured creditor which is left out of the money on such a sale could ask of the insolvency practitioner. In recent years government, and hence regulators, have additionally focused not just on what was done by the insolvency practitioner, but on how the pre-pack is likely to be perceived by stakeholders, the business community and the public more generally.

It is vital, in making and documenting the decision to execute a pre-pack sale, that the insolvency practitioner think objectively about the sorts of criticism they would level at another insolvency practitioner if they were engaged by, say, an unsecured creditor to assess the appropriateness of a pre-pack sale – a poacher-turned-gamekeeper thought process. The insolvency practitioner should, as above, also have regard to how he or she transparently communicates this to persons with an interest in the pre-pack.

Robust internal procedures are vital. In making the decision and preparing the consequent file note to evidence this decision, it should always be borne in mind that there is the potential for regulator review around disclosure and value and/or litigation around value; the note being prepared could be adduced in evidence in disciplinary or legal proceedings. It is far better to consider and document such issues at the time, in order to deal with likely questions in advance of any review/litigation.

The file note documenting the decision must be carefully structured and fully worked. It should include an assessment of the matters set out in the table below at a high level. The file note should form the basis of the required disclosure to creditors under Statement of Insolvency Practice 16 (ie, the SIP16 letter), as set out in more detail in section 7.2 below. In practice, the latter is likely to be a distilled version of this file note. Statements of insolvency practice are issued to insolvency practitioners by the regulators who authorise them to act as such.

Table 1: File note evidencing the pre-pack sale decision

Evidence of insolvency	• What evidence do you have that the debtor is, or will shortly be, insolvent? • How did you come to that conclusion? • From which source(s) did you draw information?

continued on next page

Why the business cannot trade post-insolvency	• Explain why such trading would not be appropriate (eg, lack of funding, supply difficulties, people difficulties, nature of business). • Explain why even perhaps limited trading should not be conducted post-insolvency. • Comment on post-appointment trading profitability and funding needs (and likely sources).
Why the offer in the pre-pack is better than the next best alternative	• Prepare an outcome statement for all classes of creditor for the pre-pack, contrasting with the reasonably achievable next best alternative(s). • Explain why a break-up would not be more appropriate. • Explain why it would not be possible or as effective to market the business post-insolvency. • Consider the impact of costs in each alternative. • Set out what valuation methodology for the assets was adopted and explain why. • Set out what marketing process was adopted and explain why.
Who will lose money?	• Which creditors/shareholders will be adversely affected by the pre-pack sale and what is their likely reaction? • How will you be able to defend your decision against such reactions?
Other matters	• Consider the three statutory administration objectives, in the required order. • Confirm that each of the requirements of SIP16 has been complied with, including as to valuation and marketing. • Consider any other matters that a person who does not fully understand the pre-pack sale decision at hand would need in order to understand the issues and the conclusions reached. • What would an investigative journalist make of the transaction? How would you hypothetically answer his or her criticisms?

continued on next page

	• Take account of choice of insolvency process issues (discussed further below at section 4). • Consider the use of a scorecard to aid decision-making.
Conclusion	• Include a summary and clear conclusion as to why this pre-pack sale is justifiable and the best course of action in the circumstances. • Attach the proposed SIP16 letter to creditors.

The file note should be signed off by its originator, the insolvency practitioners who are to be appointed and any internal risk controllers. All documents relevant to the file note should be cross-referenced in a clear, structured manner, and appended if appropriate. The disciplined process of doing this will usually mean that most, if not all, relevant issues are considered before final sign-off is given.

There will naturally be a cost/benefit analysis as to the amount of detail and justification that is provided in the file note – a matter for the insolvency practitioner's judgement in each case.

4. Choice of insolvency process

Readers will note that, so far, this chapter has referred to the terms 'insolvency practitioner' and 'insolvency process' in generic terms.

In reality, more than one process could well be available. These are discussed below, together with some relevant issues which would need to be considered. However, the majority of pre-packs these days will likely be executed using administration. Not all of the issues relating to these processes are discussed – just some key ones which may be relevant to pre-pack sales.

4.1 Administrative receivership

An administrative receivership appointment is made by a lender who holds appropriate security. In effect, administrative receivership is a dying process, as it can be initiated only by holders of certain security which, bar some exceptions, it has not been possible to create since September 2003.

The lender can make demand and appoint on just a few hours' notice. There is no need for the involvement of the courts in any way. It is entirely a private remedy.

Of relevance to pre-packs is that the administrative receiver's duties are relatively limited: in commercial terms, they are to realise the assets that are the subject of the relevant security in order to repay (insofar as circumstances permit) the appointer without undue disadvantage to preferential creditors and, by implication, unsecured creditors and the debtor. In situations where there is a clear shortfall to a secured lender, an administrative receiver has a great deal of latitude.

An administrative receiver has few tax issues to deal with, as the majority fall to be dealt with by the company in a subsequent liquidation. Other than in situations where the secured lender would be repaid in full, an administrative receiver can largely ignore tax issues, especially those relating to chargeable gains.

Administrative receivership does not, however, provide a moratorium against legal proceedings in the same way as administration. Practically, where administrative receivership is available, the trade-off between tax and moratorium issues will be a key consideration in the choice between administrative receivership and administration. Certain other matters, for example antecedent transactions, may also be relevant.

Technically, the disclosure obligations of SIP16 do not apply to administrative receiverships, but it would arguably be good practice to apply them in such situations.

4.2 Administration

These days, the majority of pre-pack sales are executed in administrations. The process can be initiated by the directors of a company directly, by application to the court or by the holder of a qualifying floating charge (usually a lender with rights analogous to those which would have historically allowed them to appoint an administrative receiver). For most pre-pack sales, it is likely that the director route or qualifying floating charge route will be used, as these require no court decision, only filing.

Except for certain types of company, the appointed administrator has a 'waterfall' of objectives to meet. These objectives are, in commercial terms:

1. to rescue the company as a going concern; failing which
2. to achieve a better result for creditors than in a winding-up; failing which
3. to realise property in order to make a distribution to one or more secured or preferential creditors.

The administrator may cascade down the waterfall only in the event that an objective cannot be met. There are two important additional overlays to these objectives. The first is that the administrator must generally perform his or her duties in the interests of the company's creditors as a whole. The second is that, if the objective is that stated in 3. above, the administrator must instead not unnecessarily harm the interests of creditors as a whole.

It is likely that insolvency law intended that the administrator would consider these duties only once in office. However, in a pre-pack, the prospective administrator must consider them before accepting the appointment. Therefore, to the extent that the first or, where relevant, the second objective cannot be achieved, the administrator will need to be able to show he or she has considered in appropriate detail why that is the case. As set out in the table above, this should be documented in the file note justifying the pre-pack sale.

There has been increasing litigation against administrators over the last few years based on allegations of:

- insufficient effort made to rescue a company as a going concern, before taking the decision to realise its assets;
- failing to achieve proper value for assets; and/or
- not acting in the interest of creditors as a whole or unnecessarily harming their interests.

The majority of these cases have focused on administrations that did not involve pre-packs. However, the principles and risks apply equally to pre-packs. The significant rise in the availability of litigation funding is likely to mean that, as things stand, these kinds of cases will continue to be brought.

An administrator is an officer of the court and under its ultimate control, and administration is a collective procedure (as evidenced by the objectives and overlays above). However, the decision of whether and how to exercise the power to execute a pre-pack sale is one for the administrator, not the court. Despite the court-supervised nature of administration, in practice the administrator gets on with the job, using his or her commercial judgement, unless and until a creditor or other stakeholder applies to the court to argue otherwise. Any attempt by the administrator to get the court to sanction the exercise of his or her commercial judgement is unlikely to be successful.

The administrator's status as an officer of the court, in broad terms, obliges him or her to be fair and balanced to all interested parties in any decisions beyond strict legal rights; this can add extra considerations in certain pre-pack sales.

Recognition in other European Union member states may be helpful in the aftermath of a pre-pack. Administration automatically allows this as one of the specified collective insolvency procedures. Following the UK's decision to leave the European Union, the future of such recognition is (at least at the time of writing) uncertain.

Tax planning in contemplation of a pre-pack is touched upon below at section 6, as this is much more relevant in the context of an administration.

Another issue of relevance to administrations relates to the costs of advisers in the run-up to the pre-pack. If these are not settled before the administration is started, they must meet certain criteria to be paid as expenses of the administration.

4.3 Other types of receivership

Receivers may also be appointed under certain fixed/legal charges. They are not discussed further in this chapter as they have practical limitations for pre-pack sales at the operational level, not providing the ability to sell assets which are subject to floating charges – just those subject to certain fixed charges or mortgages.

4.4 Liquidations

Liquidation is not discussed in detail as, in practice, it is rarely seen in the context of pre-pack sales, especially at the operational level. This is because of the time delays that legislation and practical matters impose on a liquidator in exercising his discretion to sell.

However, there are certain situations and types of corporate body for which administration is not possible; here, liquidation or provisional liquidation may provide the solution, although such situations will be rare.

4.5 CVAs and schemes of arrangement

These tend to establish arrangements to compromise claims, as opposed to providing a framework for the sale of assets from a debtor in satisfaction of claims. They therefore tend to be an alternative to pre-packs, as opposed to a means of achieving them. There could well be specific circumstances in which this is not the case, but the scope of this chapter is on more usual practice.

An example of such specific circumstances would be (as mentioned above) the use of CVAs to restructure retail and similar businesses over the last few years. As such, in practice, the consideration of CVAs and schemes of arrangement is more likely to be an alternative to a pre-pack than a means of executing one. They are particularly important in considering the first administration objective above: both CVAs and schemes of arrangement can be a means of rescuing a company as a going concern.

5. Risk

Certain risk issues warrant further discussion.

5.1 Advisers/insolvency practitioners

For the sake of simplicity, it is assumed for these purposes that the adviser is the insolvency practitioner in waiting.

The most significant likely risk for an insolvency practitioner is the allegation of not achieving proper value in the circumstances. This can be mitigated to some extent by ensuring that the guidelines outlined above on making and documenting the decision to execute a pre-pack sale are followed. There is also a very real regulatory risk of not complying with the provisions of SIP16.

It is usually important to obtain professional valuations for physical assets (eg, real estate, plant and machinery) on a break-up basis, an existing use basis and – especially for real estate – an alternative use basis. The latter could include development potential, for example.

The insolvency practitioner will need to provide estimates of the values of monetary assets, such as debtors, stock and work in progress. The judgement and experience of the insolvency practitioner and the nature of the relevant business will be important here.

Goodwill and intellectual property are much harder to value, especially in distressed situations. It is particularly in respect of these types of asset that market exposure is useful in reducing risk.

For this reason, it is always best that some form of market exposure be used wherever possible. This is likely to be through an AM&A process. The insolvency practitioner will need to ensure that any such process is run properly, especially if (as is likely) their own firm runs the process.

In certain circumstances, it can be appropriate to obtain a range of likely valuations from a third-party valuer on whole business value, whether that be in conjunction with exposure to the market or in place of it. Current practice – and judicial view – dictates that market exposure is the normal starting point and is a better measure of value than a valuer's opinion. Sometimes, such market exposure may be only to financial buyers and not to trade buyers. Although this is not the best means of market exposure, it may be a pragmatic compromise where the business is at risk from a sales process being made public by competitors for their own commercial advantage, hence damaging the very value you wish to realise.

There can be circumstances in which an insolvency practitioner engaged to run an AM&A process advises the directors of the relevant company that they should expose the business for sale more widely than the directors wish to. The insolvency practitioner may then be faced with a decision to execute a pre-pack sale in circumstances where his or her advice has not been followed. This situation is not of the insolvency practitioner's making, but nevertheless may require careful consideration and disclosure. The issue of potential conflicts between pre-insolvency advice and the duties of an administrator has arisen in a recent well-publicised court case.

There is reputational risk for the insolvency practitioner. For example, if a case is likely to attract press attention due to the fact that, although a pre-pack may be commercially desirable, a high-profile group of creditors or shareholders will lose money, steps must be taken to manage this. This will involve a combination of robust internal risk management processes and ensuring that appropriate communications are in place for the firm when the pre-pack is made public, such that the insolvency practitioner's position is explained before concerns are raised in the press. Considering likely public reaction can often be a good way of assessing the risks of a pre-pack sale in itself, especially given the current focus on perception and transparency.

Conflicts can arise (eg, between the insolvency practitioner advising the directors in respect of their duties and a lender, which may be perceived to desire a continuation of trade) in achieving a pre-pack sale following an AM&A process. The insolvency practitioner will need to be sure that he or she is not left in a position of unmanageable conflict.

If the pre-pack sale is in effect to the directors, there is nothing to stop the insolvency practitioner from requesting warranties from them personally to minimise the risk. This would be on the basis that the directors would effectively be on both sides of the transaction, with the insolvency practitioner in the middle, standing to benefit only from his or her fees, not the value in the business now or in the future.

It is helpful to have internal risk management policies that require an independent senior partner or risk committee to approve a pre-pack sale to make sure that there is proper consultation on, and objective consideration of, the decision. This helps to protect not only the firm, but also the individuals within it.

The insolvency practitioner acting as such cannot limit his liability contractually against claims from creditors or other stakeholders.

5.2 Directors

In a pre-pack sale, the directors will not be executing the sale and so are unlikely to be at risk of breach of duty claims that they did not achieve a proper price on the sale. All the same, they do need to take steps to realise a proper value and hence returns to creditors, and to ensure that the decisions that they take are defensible after the event. This usually means that directors should take expert advice from someone who is clear of unmanageable conflicts.

Commonly, a lender will want trading to continue during an AM&A process where further funds are not being provided. If the business is loss-making, this gives rise to the question of who should bear that loss. If the directors allow the position of, for example, trade creditors to worsen by such continued trading when the benefits of so doing may accrue to a senior lender, this could be a *prima facie* case of wrongful trading. This exposes the directors to the risk of personal liability for restitution, as well as disqualification from acting as a director in the future.

The language of the wrongful trading provisions can be summarised in commercial terms as follows: once a formal insolvency process is inevitable, directors should not do anything or suffer anything to be done, including allowing a company to trade on, that reduces the return to creditors.

This is not the same as the legal wording, but it conveys the commercial reality in straightforward terms.

In a pre-pack sale, directors are in the unusual position of generally knowing that insolvency will happen and roughly at what point in the future. Therefore, they cannot use the defence that a formal insolvency process was not inevitable. In the case of a pre-pack sale, the directors need to ensure that creditors are held in broadly the same position at the time of the pre-pack sale as they were when the pre-pack sale (ie, formal insolvency process) became inevitable. This is not just in terms of the amount of debt owed to a class of creditors; it should be applied to the return they would likely receive in an insolvency process – and to the creditors as between themselves in order to minimise the risk of other director claims. This requires careful consideration and advice from appropriate advisers.

Creditors' positions can be preserved by managing their respective exposures or using creditor payment trusts. In the latter case, funds are declared to be held on trust for creditors whose claims arose after a certain date, with the aim of protecting their positions. Apart from the need for free funds to place on trust in this manner, legal challenges to the validity of such trusts have increased in recent years. They require careful consideration and setting up in order to be effective and are less commonly used as a result these days.

Directors will wish to avoid such risk of claims against them, and careful, reasoned, well-advised and well-documented decisions are thus essential.

A further complication for directors can arise if they are contemplating a pre-pack sale to themselves or similar connected party – for example, a management buy-out from a pre-pack. In such circumstances, they will wish to ensure that the marketing or valuation process is robust to prevent accusations of breach of duty. Such conflicts of interest need to be managed, based on professional advice. Pre-pack sales to connected parties have been a particular area of government and regulator focus in recent years.

5.3 Valuations

Any professional providing a valuation for use in support of a pre-pack sale will seek to minimise their risk. Unlike the insolvency practitioner, such advisers can (and usually do) seek to limit their liability.

For example, an insolvency practitioner could seek to rely on the opinion of a third-party valuer on the value of a business (as opposed to its assets) when executing a pre-pack sale. If the sale were attacked, the claim would likely be against the insolvency practitioner for breach of duty. He or she might then seek to join in the valuer who provided the valuation, although the extent of that adviser's liability would be limited. A similar position could be seen with asset (as opposed to business) valuers.

The insolvency practitioner will wish to ensure that any instructions to such valuers are clear, including recording that the advice will be relied upon for the execution of a pre-pack sale.

The insolvency practitioner will also want to understand fully all provisions that relate to limitation of liability in such engagement terms, such as proportional liability clauses.

That said, the insolvency practitioner will only be liable for negligence if he or she falls below the standard of an ordinary skilled practitioner. If he or she reasonably relies on an apparently competent valuer whose advice turns out to be wrong, it does not necessarily follow that the insolvency practitioner is negligent or liable.

5.4 Stakeholders

This section concentrates on lenders, as they are most likely to be involved in a pre-pack transaction in this context. Other stakeholders can also have exposure to risk in pre-packs.

Lenders will be alive to reputational risks, especially in situations where a management buy-out (ie, connected party sale) is likely and trade creditors or shareholders could lose money. The same is true where there is a loss of employment or a defined benefit pension scheme. Steps to mitigate would include well-planned communications and public relations. This has become a bigger issue in recent years.

Lenders will also wish to make sure that they do not engage in behaviour which could be argued to favour a claim that they somehow took part in the management of a debtor company. In extreme circumstances, this could give rise to claims against a lender for loss to creditors, or disqualification.

5.5 Pensions

The Pensions Act 2004 includes various 'moral hazard' provisions concerning certain persons connected to debtors where there is a deficit on a defined benefit pension scheme.

These moral hazard rules can allow the Pensions Regulator to pierce the corporate veil in significant ways. Given the amounts of money that are usually at stake in pension schemes, as well as the public attention they generate, pensions can be a significant issue.

Although a detailed discussion of pension issues is beyond the scope of this chapter, if there is a defined benefit pension scheme in any company for which a pre-pack sale is contemplated, specialist advice should be sought as to whether there should be a clearance application or other protective steps.

6. Tax planning

A detailed discussion of tax issues is also beyond the scope of a relatively short chapter such as this. However, it would not be complete without some mention of the potential significance of tax planning in pre-pack sales. The issues that can arise in relation to tax in pre-packs include:

- whether gains on the sale of goodwill or other relevant assets can be sheltered by losses when administration triggers a new accounting period;
- that tax on gains which are triggered post-administration is usually an expense of the administration, as opposed to an unsecured claim;
- other considerations relating to group relief shelters where only part of the group goes into insolvency; and
- the tax advantages that administrative receivership, where the charge allows it, has over administration. For example, it does not trigger a new accounting period or impact on group relationships and the resulting liability is not an expense of the administrative receivership.

The above, particularly in relation to administrations, may well make it more tax-efficient for sales to take place immediately before the commencement of the formal insolvency process (eg, administration). However, this would not, strictly speaking, be a pre-pack, but rather a sale prior to an insolvency appointment.

There are often practical and legal difficulties in achieving such sales. For example, directors may be concerned about their own positions in executing a sale prior to insolvency and a well-advised buyer may also have concerns about the risk of being pursued by an insolvency practitioner for additional value on the basis that the price was not high enough (ie, a transaction at an undervalue claim). These issues do not arise in a sale executed by an insolvency practitioner.

Also, if the directors sell the business before the insolvency process, it is arguable that administration may not be an appropriate procedure, due to difficulties in achieving the relevant statutory objective of an administration.

The author is unaware of any insolvency practitioner being sued for negligence relating to tax planning on a pre-pack, but it would be prudent to assume that such a claim might be made.

7. Legal and other documents

These need to be negotiated in advance so that they are ready to be signed at the instant of appointment.

A practical point is that the insolvency practitioner will want to ensure that the buyer will go through with the agreed purchase once the company is in insolvency. If not, the buyer could seek to reduce the price and the insolvency practitioner might have no other strategy to preserve value in a business which, by that point, will be in an insolvency process.

Conversely, the proposed buyer may want to ensure that the time and cost that it has invested in the process up to that point will not be lost if the insolvency practitioner decides to market the business post-appointment.

The logical answer is to have pre-negotiated and signed documents that are held on solicitors' undertakings, pending the appointment being made – a kind of lock-up agreement.

The key documents are likely to include the following.

7.1 Sale and purchase agreement

A sale and purchase agreement should include any ancillary documents, such as property licences and IP assignments. It will likely take the same form as a normal insolvency practitioner sale agreement.

Although insolvency practitioners do not give warranties, directors sometimes do so in pre-pack sales and these will need to be negotiated and agreed before appointment.

It is important that confidentiality clauses in sale and purchase agreements do not prevent the insolvency practitioner from issuing the reports/disclosures that are required under best practice, and particularly SIP16, and in general statutory reports to creditors.

Where the sale is to a mortgagee (see below at section 9 for more issues relating to this) or to directors, it is important that they have separate legal advice to manage conflicts of interest.

7.2 SIP16 and SIP16 letters

Certain SIPs deal with the steps and disclosures necessary where sales are made to directors and in pre-packs generally. These disclosure requirements are not listed in full here; suffice to say that insolvency practitioners need to ensure that they comply with their provisions where needed. The insolvency practitioner will need to consider compliance in spirit as well as in letter.

SIP16, however, does warrant further mention. Compliance with SIP16 deals specifically with pre-pack sales and has become an important issue for insolvency practitioners. A copy of all SIP16 letters needs to be sent to the insolvency practitioner's regulator. Compliance is closely monitored by such regulators and breaches are investigated as a matter of course.

SIP16 was introduced in 2009, and has since been revised twice: in 2013 and 2015. The latter revision followed a lengthy report to the government in response to concerns about public confidence in the pre-pack process.

The latest revision to SIP16 contains specific steps to deal with concerns about transparency, marketing, valuation and viability of successor businesses. In broad terms:

- On transparency, there is now an increased emphasis, as mentioned above, on how the transaction will be viewed by a wide range of interested parties.
- On valuation, details of the valuer's independence and professional qualifications are to be provided, as well as an explanation of the valuation methodology adopted.

- On the marketing process, there is a list of "marketing essentials" which are to be complied with, or an explanation of why not.
- On viability, there has been created a 'pre-pack pool'. The pool can provide an independent opinion:
  - that the pre-pack is not unreasonable;
  - that it is not unreasonable but there are minor limitations in evidence to support it; or
  - that the case for the pre-pack is not made.

The pre-pack pool was intended to provide an independent view to interested parties that the pre-pack was appropriate. However, in practice, its utility has been limited because there is no requirement on connected buyers to engage with it: the insolvency practitioner only has to make connected buyers aware of its existence. The same is true for 'viability statements' for the buyer. Put simply, there is no real incentive for connected buyers to engage with the pre-pack pool or in viability statements.

Regulation and legislation surrounding pre-packs remain under review, particularly those to connected parties.

7.3 Deeds of release

These are usually needed to sell assets which are the subject of a lender's security. The buyer will want to see deeds of release to be sure that it is buying the assets free of such security interests. From a practical perspective, this means that the insolvency practitioner will have to organise this in advance. This is usually achieved by their lawyers holding the documents to the lender's order pending completion.

7.4 Appointment documents

These will need to be ready to effect an appointment at the desired time, remembering that this could be outside normal business hours. This means that the relevant logistical arrangements will need to be made to effect the appointment when needed. There may be limitations on who can effect an administration appointment outside normal business hours.

Buyers' lawyers may wish to look at appointment documentation to ensure that the insolvency practitioner has been validly appointed and hence can execute the sale. There have been several cases where the validity of an administrator's appointment has been challenged.

Before an administration appointment becomes effective, what is known as a 'notice of intention to appoint an administrator' is usually served by the directors on the holder of a qualifying floating charge. This allows the latter a five-day period in which to impose a different administrator to the one chosen by the directors. Crucially, the notice of intention creates a 10-day moratorium on all legal actions and similar against the debtor company, even before it goes into administration.

A practice had developed in which, sometimes, several such notices had been issued in sequence; this practice has been the subject of recent court challenge. The current judicial view is that such notices can only be issued:

- when there is a qualifying floating charge holder; and
- when there is a settled intention to place the company into administration.

It follows that it could in some circumstances be an abuse of process to issue such notices, for example to achieve a moratorium to complete a sale of the business outside of administration.

8. Substantial property transactions with directors

Until recently, a conflict existed between the significant powers given to an insolvency practitioner under insolvency law to dispose of a company's assets and other provisions of company law which related to directors' duties.

The Companies Act 1985 (as amended) stated that shareholder approval was needed where a substantial amount of a company's property was sold to directors of a company or another company controlled by them. This makes sense from a fiduciary duty perspective in relation to solvent companies, to prevent directors dealing with themselves to the detriment of shareholders. However, it was somewhat strange that an insolvency practitioner appointed under statute with a power to sell an insolvent company's assets, when the shareholders had no economic interest, should be restricted in the same manner.

That was nonetheless the effect of a legal case decided some years ago. Since then, the Companies Act 2006 has replaced the earlier law in this respect so that this is no longer an issue in administrations.

However, it remains something to be dealt with in administrative receiverships. Therefore, in the context of administrative receivership pre-pack sales where the buyer and seller have some common directors, it will need to be dealt with at or before sale by obtaining shareholder approval or by ensuring that none of the directors in the seller has a financial interest in the buyer at the point of sale.

9. Sales to mortgagees

There is a legal restriction on sales to a mortgagee or self-dealing in administrative receiverships. This is, in essence, that a mortgagee – and, by extension, its receiver – cannot sell to the mortgagee.

The usual solution here is for a new special purpose vehicle to be created, which may even be a subsidiary of the mortgagee. It is unclear whether this applies to an administrator in analogous circumstances, but it would make sense to use a similar structure.

The economics of an insolvency practitioner selling to a mortgagee are similar to a debt-for-equity swap in favour of a mortgagee.

10. 'Post-packs'

This is one of a number of terms used to describe a situation in which a pre-pack sale is executed, but with some form of buy-back option for a limited period. The buy-back is usually at the original price, but with some allowance for costs.

A few years ago, there was much market commentary on such arrangements, but very few practical uses are known. SIP16 requires disclosure of such arrangements to creditors.

An example of a potential use would be a business where even an AM&A process would be fatal to value – for example, due to customer loss, a run on working capital which could not be funded or regulatory issues. Therefore, a sale is executed with market exposure to take place afterwards.

The economics of such arrangements are similar to asset hive-downs. This is where the business is hived down in clean form to a new company and that company is sold.

Such arrangements can arguably have useful applications, but they are most likely to be limited to situations in which they are no more than a belt and braces on value risk. An example could be where a business is sold to its lenders and there is no reasonable belief that anyone else would pay more for it than the lender has done.

Put another way, it is designed to be a defence to the possible assertion from a potential buyer of, "Had I known it was for sale, I would have paid more for it than you did." This is an easy assertion to make when you know that you will not have to go through with it. However, post-pack provisions can neutralise this.

Use in any other situations would usually be limited due to the risks of the deal being undone. It is much easier for an existing lender or similar to make a calculated risk assessment than a trade buyer. This is not always the case and each situation inevitably has its own facts and would need to be considered carefully.

UK defined benefit pension schemes and restructuring situations

Luke Hartley
Alex Hutton-Mills
Lincoln Pensions

1. Introduction

BHS. Carillion. House of Fraser. Kodak. Lehman Brothers. Nortel. Tata Steel.

The list of public restructuring situations where a UK defined benefit (DB) pension scheme has been a critical stakeholder has grown every year since the current pensions regime was established through the Pensions Act 2004.

Changes in UK legislation since 2004 have strengthened DB scheme protection significantly and further legislation is now expected to be introduced, including criminal sanctions for those found guilty of 'wilful or reckless' behaviour.

In tandem with a general under-appreciation of the impact of DB schemes on restructurings, an increase in DB scheme deficits (and therefore claims in restructuring) has occurred, driven by the 2008 financial crisis and subsequent, sustained low interest rates.

With Brexit and tectonic shifts in global trade arrangements on the horizon, as well as major structural changes affecting certain industries (eg, retail and print journalism), many companies will undergo some form of restructuring over the next five years. This is likely to have implications for a number of significant pension schemes.

Additional restructuring challenges facing those companies with DB pension schemes include dealing with a wider range of stakeholders, complex claim structures, and the risk of retrospective litigation. Failure to engage early and to adequately address DB pension issues in a restructuring can lead to additional costs, delays and ultimately failure.

This chapter is relevant in UK-only and/or cross-border restructurings where an overseas group has a UK DB scheme (eg, Kodak, Lehman Brothers and Nortel).

2. Key stakeholders

There are a number of key pension-related stakeholders, including:

- DB scheme trustees;

- the Pensions Regulator (TPR);
- the Pension Protection Fund (PPF);
- employees;
- DB scheme members; and
- the UK Government.

2.1 Pension scheme trustees

The trustees, who can often include senior executives of the sponsoring company, are custodians of the scheme's assets on behalf of the scheme members.

Broadly, their role involves paying the correct benefits to members, investing scheme assets appropriately, and acting in the best interests of scheme members. Extensive duties are imposed on trustees by both trust law and current legislation.

Professional trusteeship (broadly analogous to corporate non-executive directorship) has increased in recent years. A professional trustee may be appointed to balance, or provide particular expertise to, the trustee board – for example, a number of professional trustees now have expertise in restructuring situations.

Given the time-critical nature of such restructurings, there is frequently a concern that trustees will not be able to act quickly or decisively enough when a decision needs to be made. This is a valid concern, not least because trustees are drawn from a variety of backgrounds and often have full-time jobs to perform alongside their duties.

It will therefore be important to ensure that any decisions required from the trustees are well understood; that they are active participants in discussions; and that they are supported by advisors and, potentially, an appropriately qualified professional trustee on the board.

2.2 The Pensions Regulator (TPR)

TPR is the regulatory and supervisory body for work-based pension schemes, including occupational pension schemes. Its statutory aims are set out in the Pensions Act 2004 (as amended), the most relevant for this chapter being:

- protecting members' benefits;
- reducing the risk of schemes needing recourse to the PPF; and
- minimising any adverse impact on the sustainable growth of an employer.[1]

TPR has also been given wide-ranging powers affecting employers (ie, corporates supporting pension schemes) and trustees, including its 'moral hazard' powers, which are designed to reduce the risk of pension liabilities being

1 In practice this objective is focused more on ongoing situations than restructurings.

transferred to the PPF and to permit TPR to pierce the corporate veil and use its moral hazard powers (see section 4) against "associated or connected" entities.[2]

TPR also produces guidance and codes of practice setting out what it expects of employers and trustees in certain situations. For example, guidance has been issued relating to scheme abandonment, clearance of corporate transactions, and conflicts of interest.[3]

2.3 The Pension Protection Fund (PPF)

The PPF is a statutory fund, managed by the board of the PPF and established under the Pensions Act 2004. It was created to pay compensation to members of eligible DB pension schemes in the event of employer insolvency – in effect, a form of statutory insurance. It is important to note that this compensation caps certain benefits and is therefore typically lower than the promised pension.

It is funded through levies charged on all UK DB schemes, with the quantum determined by factors such as scheme funding level and estimated risk of sponsor insolvency.[4]

Where an employer suffers a "qualifying insolvency event",[5] the PPF assumes the responsibility from trustees for managing the scheme's claim(s) in restructurings. The PPF also leads negotiations where the scheme claim is to be 'compromised' outside formal insolvency, for example via a regulated apportionment arrangement (RAA).

2.4 Employees

Many employees, particularly in unionised industries, may be members of the pension scheme. Corporates should be aware that pension considerations may become intermingled with employee discussions, particularly in solvent restructurings.

2.5 Scheme members

While trustees are expected to act on behalf of scheme members, it is not always the case that every member feels appropriately represented. Small but vocal groups of members can provide further challenges to a restructuring, and it is possible that members could challenge the decisions of trustees in court.

---

2 The Insolvency Act 1986 provides the definitions for 'connected' and 'associated' persons broadly to include directors, shadow directors and all companies in a corporate group (including shareholders holding at least one-third of the voting rights). However, FSDs cannot currently be issued against individual directors or shadow directors.

3 For more information on TPR, and for copies of the various codes of practice and guidance, see www.thepensionsregulator.gov.uk.

4 For more information on the PPF, see the PPF's website at www.pensionprotectionfund.org.uk.

5 The list of categories includes most of the usual types of insolvency, including administration, voluntary arrangements, administrative receivership and most types of liquidation. However, voluntary liquidations, where the directors of the employer have signed a declaration of solvency, and schemes of arrangement, are excluded. In addition, it must be the first insolvency event to have occurred to the employer on or after 6 April 2005.

2.6 UK Government

Recent restructurings such as Carillion, Tata Steel, Toys "R" Us and BHS have been highly politicised as a consequence of pension issues. While most restructurings will not involve a key government outsourcer or a divisive public figure, parties should be aware of the risk of a post-ante parliamentary investigation, particularly given the current parliamentary focus on DB pensions outcomes.

3. Importance of scheme structure

In order to consider the potential impact of the pension scheme in a restructuring, corporates and their advisers should understand both the size of any potential claim and the entities against which such a claim may exist.

3.1 Size of the obligation

A DB scheme comprises two elements – a pool of assets and an obligation to pay members' benefits in future. The extent of this obligation depends on a number of factors including length of employment service, expected retirement date, life expectancy, employee salary and inflation.

To establish the present value of the liabilities, a discount rate is used. There is a plethora of liability measures, each using a different discount rate. Essentially, they are linked to the assumed investment strategy associated with each relevant liability measure. A present value of the aggregated liabilities is calculated, which is then compared to the asset pool to establish the scheme's 'deficit'.

Every three years, pension schemes complete a valuation to estimate the present value of the liabilities ('ongoing liabilities'). If this results in a deficit (known as the 'ongoing deficit'), a 'recovery plan' (or amortisation schedule) is agreed, such that the group pays monthly contributions to cover the shortfall over a period of time.

The ongoing liabilities therefore determine the size of the deficit that must be corrected by cash payments to the scheme.

However, in the context of restructuring, there are several other liability calculations that you should be aware of:

- 'accounting' liabilities;[6]
- 'self-sufficiency' liabilities;[7]

---

6 Accounting liabilities are those disclosed in the statutory accounts. They are calculated using a flat discount rate based around returns on AA corporate bonds, as permitted under current, applicable accounting standards. While this may sound low-risk, it is generally a less prudent assumption than adopted by the majority of schemes. In other words, accounting liabilities (and associated deficit) are typically lower than ongoing liabilities (and associated deficit).

7 Self-sufficiency liabilities are estimated using a low-risk investment strategy – typically a margin of up to 50 basis points over UK gilt yields, giving a correspondingly low discount rate. As a consequence, they are typically higher than ongoing liabilities (and significantly higher than accounting liabilities), often returning a large deficit. The self-sufficiency estimate shows the level of assets required for the scheme to run on with minimal risk of future contributions being required from the sponsor, and is therefore often a key target for schemes to achieve in a restructuring.

- 'buyout' liabilities;[8] and
- PPF liabilities.[9]

3.2 Legal obligation(s)

A DB scheme's 'employer' is the entity under the scheme's constitution[10] with the obligation to meet any shortfall in the assets. It is the entity against which the buyout deficit will crystallise if it enters insolvency, for example. In order to understand subordination and other issues (through guarantees, asset security etc from the broader group in favour of the scheme) it is critical to understand which entities are the scheme's employers and the potential impact of broader group capital and security structures.

Many pension schemes have a single employer. For these schemes, the equation is relatively simple as the focus needs to be on this entity.

Some schemes, however, have multiple employers. These are known as 'multi-employer schemes' and each employer will have a share of the overall deficit attributable to it, which could change over time, or through a restructuring, as particular employers become insolvent or debts are transferred.

In a restructuring context, it is possible that any restructuring could affect none, some or all of these entities directly.

4. TPR's powers

TPR has several statutory powers,[11] including the ability to wind up schemes, set contribution schedules or appoint trustees. The most relevant for restructuring purposes are its 'moral hazard' powers – the power to issue contribution notices (CNs) and financial support directions (FSDs).

Broadly speaking, these powers enable TPR to create an obligation on entities and persons to support the pension scheme, either through a specific monetary contribution (CN) or a more general obligation (FSD). They are intended to pierce the corporate veil and allow pension schemes to attribute liabilities to connected or associated parties that may not have previously considered the pension scheme as a liability.

Since inception in 2005, TPR has brought its moral hazard powers to bear in several high-profile insolvencies including Sea Containers, Nortel, Lehman Brothers, BHS and Boxclever.

---

8 Buyout liabilities are based on the expected cost to buy annuities for all scheme members with an insurance company and are typically the largest estimate. Also known as the 'Section 75 debt', the buyout deficit is the claim that the scheme would have on insolvency. Together with the PPF liabilities (see below) it is the most important deficit to be aware of in the context of restructuring.

9 PPF liabilities represent the level of liabilities insured by the PPF. Because the PPF caps certain liabilities, this estimate is typically lower than either self-sufficiency or buyout liabilities. It is important in restructuring because the PPF deficit represents the shortfall that would be suffered by the PPF in the event of insolvency – if there is no shortfall, there may be no need for the PPF to become involved.

10 Trust deed and rules.

11 Derived from Pensions Act 1995, Pensions Act 2004 and Pensions Act 2008.

4.1 Contribution notices

CNs can be issued against any individual or company "connected or associated" with an employer that has been involved in an act or failure to act, where either:

- the main purpose of the act/failure is to avoid pension liabilities; or
- a scheme has suffered a 'material detriment' to the likelihood of scheme benefits being received as a consequence of the act/failure.

In each case, the issuance of a CN is predicated on such action being "reasonable". Factors contributing to reasonableness are both varied and circumstance-dependent, but essentially seek to answer why another individual or entity should be required to contribute. An example might be because they have received a financial benefit at the expense of the scheme creditor.

A CN requires the target to pay a specified sum into the scheme and proceedings can be commenced up to six years after the relevant act or failure.

4.2 Financial support directions

FSDs can be issued against any company associated or connected with an employer within the last two years, where that employer is insufficiently resourced[12] or a service company,[13] and (similarly to a CN) where it is determined to be "reasonable" to do so.

An FSD requires the target to put in place arrangements (which do not need to be an immediate provision of cash) to provide financial support to the scheme. An FSD is not based around a specific act or failure, nor does it require fault on any part. Rather, it is designed to extend the scope of legal support for a pension scheme to connected entities where it is determined reasonable to do so.

Unlike a CN, which is focused on a specific act or failure within the last six years, there is no time limit on the acts that contribute towards reasonableness for an FSD.[14] These could, for example, include distributions to connected parties seven or more years ago.

4.3 Risk mitigation

Many of the successful uses of TPR's powers to date have been in situations where some measure of value was transferred from the sponsoring employers

12 An employer is insufficiently resourced if the value of its resources is less than 50% of the estimated Section 75 (or buyout) liability of the scheme, and the value of the resources of a connected or associated person when added to the employer's resources would be 50% or more of the estimated Section 75 liability.

13 A company is a service company if its revenues are mainly derived from providing services to other companies within the same corporate group.

14 As confirmed in the Upper Tribunal Tax and Chancery decision of Mrs Justice Rose, Judge Herrington and Member Abrams on 18 May 2018 in *ITV Plc and others v The Pensions Regulator with Box Clever Trustees Ltd as an Interested Party*.

(and therefore the pension schemes) to the wider group, prior to their insolvency.

Restructuring professionals, investors and corporate groups can therefore seek to understand (and potentially mitigate) a group's potential exposure to TPR's powers through close consideration of the following factors:

- *Value movements.* To what extent could financial value be deemed to have moved from the employers to the group prior to insolvency or as part of a solvent restructuring, for example, through under-value asset transfers, intercompany trading or dividends?
- *Reasons for and timing of insolvency process.* The rationale behind an employer entering insolvency may have a bearing on whether a use of TPR's powers is reasonable, for example, where the main driver of insolvency was to limit exposure to a pension scheme.
- *Due process and marketing in insolvency.* Where fair value is obtained and fairly distributed, there is likely to be little additional justification for TPR involvement, even where the business and assets of an employer are returned to a group via a pre-pack administration.

If corporates and/or individuals wish a greater level of assurance, they have two principal options: invoking the 'statutory defence' or applying for 'clearance'.

(a) Statutory defence

The statutory defence can be invoked where the act or failure has caused "material detriment" to the likelihood of scheme benefits being met.[15] It is not available where a CN is being issued on the basis that the main purpose of the act or failure is to avoid pension liabilities.

If a party can successfully avail itself of the statutory defence, TPR is unlikely to be successful in any CN-related proceedings against that party. In order to do so, the party must demonstrate that all three elements of the statutory defence are met:

- Prior to the act or failure, the corporate considered whether the act/failure might constitute material detriment.
- If it concluded that there was a risk of material detriment, it took all reasonable steps to minimise potential detrimental effects.
- Having regard to all relevant circumstances prevailing at the time, it was reasonable to conclude that there was no material detriment.

Although professional advice should be sought in establishing the statutory defence, it is clear how this could proceed in practice; namely, by ensuring that

15 Section 38 of the Pensions Act 2008.

the risk of material detriment is recognised and appropriately assessed, and where identified, mitigation is agreed. This would typically require engagement with the trustees, to either agree mitigation or more generally, as part of demonstrating reasonableness.

(b) Clearance

Clearance is a voluntary process under which parties can apply to TPR for advance assurance that TPR will not use its moral hazard powers in the context of specific corporate events or series of events.

Clearance can be sought for what TPR calls 'Type A' events, which are categorised as either employer-related or scheme-related. Essentially, any event that is materially detrimental (see above) is likely to be a Type A event.

Employer-related events: These are events that affect the employer and/or its group. For an employer-related event to be a Type A event, the scheme must also have a 'relevant deficit'.[16]

TPR guidance provides a non-exhaustive list of events that constitute employer-related events. The following are likely to be most relevant in a workout:

- a change in the level of security to creditors;
- the return of capital;
- a change in group structure (including a change of control which may be the result of a debt-for-equity swap by creditors); or
- asset sales (eg, with sale proceeds going to creditors as a means of reducing indebtedness).

No thresholds are provided in the guidance. Instead, for an event to be determined as a Type A event (assuming there is also a relevant deficit), parties need to consider whether the event is materially detrimental to the scheme.

Scheme-related events: These are events directly affecting the scheme. Examples include compromising a debt owed to the scheme or re-apportioning the deficit between employers.

Unlike with employer-related events, a scheme-related event can be a Type A event regardless of whether there is a relevant deficit; rather, material detriment is considered on a case-by-case basis.

If parties voluntarily seek clearance for either an employer- or scheme-related event, TPR will expect to hear from trustees, employers and other affected parties. Trustees will be expected to have considered whether

16 The relevant deficit will usually be the highest of the accounting deficit, PPF deficit and ongoing deficit, but in some circumstances, such as scheme abandonment or where there are going concern issues, it will be measured on a higher basis (eg, the buyout deficit).

appropriate mitigation has been agreed to offset any detriment to the employer covenant caused by a restructuring. This could range from direct cash or asset contributions to the scheme, to contingent assets that would provide funding on the occurrence of specified events.

Once granted, clearance provides assurance that no CN or FSD will be made against those parties named in the application, in relation to events specified in the clearance application.[17]

Despite the obvious benefits of clearance, since its introduction applications have declined year on year, from over 250 in 2005/6 to only nine in 2015/16.[18] Potential reasons for the decline include a greater level of understanding in the industry as to what may or may not constitute material detriment; the introduction of the statutory defence in the Pensions Act 2008; and the time and cost involved in negotiating with TPR to obtain clearance, noting that TPR will often seek to enhance mitigation before granting clearance.

Ultimately, parties should weigh up the risk and cost of potential TPR intervention with the implications on costs and timing of seeking clearance. Recent parliamentary pressure put on TPR to be more decisive, and its adoption of a new strategy to become "clearer, quicker and tougher" may see a reversal in the recent downward trend in clearance applications.[19]

5. Pension considerations in different types of restructuring

In this section, we consider some key pension considerations, including the potential impact of TPR and the PPF, in four different types of restructuring solutions:

- corporate reorganisations;
- solvent restructurings with no scheme compromise;
- solvent restructurings where the scheme is compromised; and
- insolvent restructurings.

The list is not exhaustive and there will be many circumstances that exhibit characteristics of each, such as the use of Chapter 11 to compromise debt secured on UK assets or a solvent scheme of arrangement used to compromise only a single creditor class. However, the principles highlighted below can be applied across the variety of different methods/procedures that could be used to deliver a restructuring.

5.1 Corporate reorganisations

Trustees have a statutory obligation to consider the 'employer covenant' provided to a scheme, defined as "the extent of the employer's legal obligation

17 Please note that clearance will not bind TPR if the actual circumstances are materially different from those set out in the clearance application.

18 Based on TPR website (see note *supra*) and freedom of information requests.

19 TPR Corporate Plan 2018–21.

and financial ability to support the scheme now and in the future".[20] In other words, the credit risk of their employers relative to the size of, and risks associated with, the relevant DB scheme. The employer covenant is not to be confused with covenants in bank/bondholder documentation!

The strength of the employer covenant informs the approach taken by trustees and other stakeholders to investment risk and funding outcomes. Broadly speaking, a stronger covenant gives trustees greater flexibility regarding investment risk, given the employer's ability to remedy adverse investment performance. Consequently, the potential impact of reorganisation proposals on the covenant is a key factor and early planning (including consideration of mitigation options) is a must.

For example, if an employer disposed of business and assets as part of a reorganisation, leaving significantly reduced operations, the covenant impact could be significantly negative. Conversely, if business and assets were acquired, the covenant could improve.

Where there is perceived detriment, trustees are encouraged by TPR to seek mitigation, which could include a share of any proceeds received.

In a multi-employer scheme, the situation is further complicated. Not only are there more employers, but where employers cease to have any active members in the pension scheme, individual Section 75 debts (as noted earlier, the largest estimate) can crystallise at those employers, crystallising statutory debts of the allocated Section 75 liabilities of those employers.[21]

Understanding the scheme structure and the employer covenant should therefore be on the critical path to any reorganisation. Once understood, there are a number of tools available to facilitate such restructurings without having a negative impact on the pension scheme. These are set out in TPR's guidance on multi-employer scheme departures.[22]

The employer should also be cognisant of material detriment in the context of TPR's moral hazard powers, as discussed at section 4 above.

5.2 Solvent restructuring – no scheme compromise

Solvent restructurings/refinancings range from simple covenant resets or terming out maturity dates to more complicated balance sheet restructurings and debt compromises.

To the extent corporate reorganisations result from solvent restructurings, the same principles as set out above will apply.

In a solvent restructuring, trustees will want to understand the terms of any restructuring agreed with other stakeholders, given the potential employer covenant impact.

20 TPR Code of Practice 3: Funding Defined Benefits.

21 Section 75 of the Pensions Act 1995 (as amended) and the Occupational Pension Schemes (Employer Debt) Regulations 2005.

For example, while a debt-for-equity swap might reduce the overall debt burden on the group, unencumber previously secured assets and reduce the interest cost to employers, it might also create restrictive covenants or commit the group to future actions that could be detrimental to the employer covenant, requiring the provision of mitigation to the trustees.

The trustees will be focused not just on the immediate impact of the restructuring, but also on the ability of the corporate to support the scheme going forward, including the extent to which the employer can meet future payments to the scheme post-restructuring.

It is not unusual for these two aspects to be dealt with side by side, with any restructuring also seeking to commit the scheme to a future level of deficit reduction contributions.

(a) TPR's role in solvent restructurings

TPR often has a key role to play, both in working with the company and trustees to understand the impact on the pension scheme and in ratifying any subsequent funding arrangement.

In circumstances where the trustees have identified a risk of material detriment, they may seek support from TPR in negotiating mitigation, including asking TPR to consider using its powers. TPR will also negotiate directly with corporates in any application for clearance.

(b) PPF role in solvent restructurings

Generally speaking, the PPF would not be expected to have a direct role in reorganisations or solvent restructurings where there are no proposals to compromise the scheme's claim(s) or the level of benefits paid.

That said, there is one notable exception to this rule – company voluntary arrangements (CVAs), discussed below – and the PPF will also often have an indirect involvement through TPR, given the latter's statutory objectives. Consequently, the PPF may be involved in the background, particularly where there are concerns over increasing PPF exposure, often referred to as 'PPF drift'.[23]

If a CVA is used to effect a solvent restructuring, the PPF can have a direct role even if the scheme is not compromised. This is because the filing of a CVA proposal is a 'qualifying insolvency event' for the purposes of PPF entry and means that the PPF potentially assumes voting rights from the trustees.[24]

---

23 PPF drift refers to the fact that, because the PPF pays full benefits to pensioners but caps benefits paid to non-pensioners, the PPF's total exposure grows over time as members retire and avoid being capped. The rate of growth of this exposure is referred to as PPF drift. If pensions contributions are insufficient to cover this drift, the PPF's exposure worsens.

24 Whether the PPF assumes voting rights depends on the scheme structure – in a 'last man standing' scheme the trustees would retain control of voting rights if one or more employers was not affected by the CVA. This was the case with House of Fraser in 2018.

In June 2018, the PPF issued guidance in relation to CVAs,[25] setting out its expectations for both CVAs that sought to compromise the scheme (see section 5.3 below) and those that did not. Notably, even where the scheme is unaffected by the CVA and would expect to be a beneficiary from other claims (such as landlord claims) that are being compromised, the PPF has established a checklist of 11 items on which they would expect corporates to engage with them, namely:

- the restructuring plan and whether there is a viable business going forward;
- management's capabilities to deliver the plan;
- whether there is sufficient finance to deliver the proposals;
- the impact of the CVA on any bank creditor;
- the level of deficit reduction contributions;
- future dividend expectations and protections for the scheme;
- the quantum of PPF drift and any protections;
- the exposure of the scheme to the PPF levy during the CVA and any protections;
- proposed pension scheme de-risking;
- protection for the pension scheme on finance and equity exit; and
- preservation of contributions to the scheme.

The list is comprehensive and will require significantly more engagement than might be expected with a nominally unaffected creditor. However, given that the scheme is often the largest single unsecured creditor, agreement can be critical to achieving the necessary 75% of creditor approvals for any CVA. Consequently, some level of engagement with the PPF is likely to be necessary. Even where the PPF is not directly involved, we would expect trustees to be guided by the PPF's checklist to avoid criticism in the event of subsequent corporate failure.

5.3 Solvent restructuring – scheme compromise

In the above section we discussed solvent restructurings where there is no intent to compromise the scheme's debt. In many circumstances, however, the scheme itself is the problem, either exclusively or alongside other challenges.

Even for an otherwise healthy business, a large pension scheme can create significant viability concerns.

Under scheme-specific funding requirements, trustees are obliged to assess the covenant of the sponsoring employer and reflect this assessment in setting the "ongoing liabilities" or "technical provisions" – see section 3.1 above. However, the covenant is a relative measure of the entity's ability to fund the scheme. Even where the entity is financially healthy, a large and significantly underfunded scheme may not be supportable in much the same way that a

25 PPF Restructuring & Insolvency Team, Guidance Note 4: Company Voluntary Arrangements.

business can be overleveraged with debt. Accordingly, the covenant could be rated 'weak' – typically driving a higher ongoing deficit and putting strain on the employer's cash flows in agreeing an appropriate recovery plan.

Over time, such a strain can have a significant negative impact on the viability of a business. In particular, it may restrict the business's access to investment or credit lines due to concerns that additional funding will be absorbed into the pension scheme rather than providing a return to the business's investors.

If the business's performance becomes stressed, this becomes more acute, with cash flow pressure impacting the ability to raise credit or undertake necessary restructuring.

In such circumstances it may be appropriate to consider a solvent restructuring to compromise the scheme rather than an insolvent restructuring that could destroy value in the business by, for example, terminating key contracts or operating licences.

One such method of compromising the pension scheme that will be familiar to readers is a CVA, where the scheme would be one of the affected creditors.

An alternative to a CVA is an RAA, which is a restructuring tool established by the Occupational Pension Schemes (Employer Debt Regulations) 2005 for the very purpose of compromising a scheme debt. Under an RAA, the scheme's claim can be moved from one employer to another and, in a restructuring context, is typically moved to a shell employer outside the group which subsequently enters insolvency to trigger the entry of the pension scheme into the PPF.

The key advantage of an RAA is that it is not public and therefore avoids the potential stigma and notification requirements of a CVA. The key disadvantages are that there are certain qualifying criteria for the PPF to agree a compromise that are easier to demonstrate in a CVA, and TPR's approval is also required.

(a) TPR and PPF roles in scheme compromises

Whilst trustees have the power to agree a compromise arrangement for the employer statutory debt, any such compromise is almost certain to involve both TPR and the PPF[26] and they will generally both have to provide their consent to any deal.

In order to participate in any scheme compromise arrangement, TPR and the PPF have agreed a set of principles to govern their participation:

- Insolvency must be otherwise inevitable ("within 12 months" is often added as a rider, due to RAA requirements).
- The scheme must receive cash or assets that are significantly more (in value) than it would otherwise receive on insolvency. The proposal also

26 Any such compromise that takes place without the agreement of the PPF or, in any event, is below the PPF's calculated level of protected liabilities, would otherwise render the scheme ineligible for PPF protection going forward.

needs to be "realistic" in the context of the Section 75 debt – this is generally interpreted to mean that the cash/assets must represent a material portion of the debt.

- What is offered must be "fair" compared to the treatment of other stakeholders (this usually requires an element of sharing the pain).
- The PPF will seek equity in the restructured company of at least 10% if the future shareholders are not currently involved with the company and at least 33% if the future shareholders are currently involved with the business (this is essentially an anti-embarrassment provision, particularly in relation to MBOs or debt-for-equity conversions, to protect the PPF against negative consequences arising from information asymmetry).
- A better outcome could not be achieved for the scheme through the use of TPR's powers (CNs or FSDs).
- Where an RAA is proposed, TPR clearance must be obtained.
- Where the deal involves a refinancing, bank fees must be considered reasonable.
- The corporate must pay the costs of both the PPF and trustees, including adviser fees.

The above principles are not necessarily set in stone and examples exist where the PPF and TPR have deviated from them. However, such deviations are very much a case of give with one hand and take with the other – any proposal that does not meet one criteria would need to compensate with another. One example is Uniq, where the compensation was wholly in equity, but with the equity component increased to 90% rather than the 33% under the guidelines.

More recently, in cases such as Kodak and Halcrow, part of the compensation was met through the transfer of members to a new, smaller, pension scheme, with the members' benefits being restructured as part of the overall process. This reduced the burden on the PPF and therefore the size of the necessary compensation.

It is also worth noting that the PPF and TPR are not wholly governed by short-term commercial considerations. In its CVA guidance,[27] for example, the PPF goes so far as to say that it is "always concerned to ensure that no precedents are set that would permit any schemes to be weakened where there is a possibility of PPF entry in the foreseeable future". In this regard TPR or the PPF can and have walked away from prospective deals, even *prima facie* commercially attractive ones, that do not meet the criteria above or are otherwise unfavourable.

Finally, directors considering a solvent restructuring should be cognisant of a potential conflict between their duties and the requirements of TPR and the

27 *Supra.*

PPF to engage in compromise discussions. In particular, whilst the cash flow and balance sheet tests set out in Section 123 of the Insolvency Act 1986 are governed by the balance of probabilities, TPR and the PPF require insolvency to be inevitable for agreement to be reached. This is a significantly higher hurdle, particularly in the case of the balance sheet test.

5.4 Insolvent restructuring

For the purposes of this chapter, insolvent restructuring means administration, administrative receivership or liquidation. As these processes will be familiar to most readers, this section focuses on the roles of the PPF and TPR.

(a) TPR role in insolvent restructuring

TPR has no formal role in insolvency, with responsibility for the scheme fully devolved to the PPF. However, insolvency often forms the catalyst for TPR to consider whether there is scope for it to use its moral hazard powers to benefit the scheme, essentially by extending the scheme's obligations to other entities.

(b) PPF role in insolvent restructuring

In the event of an insolvent restructuring of the scheme's sponsor, the scheme will enter a PPF "assessment period" and the PPF will assume voting rights in insolvency. The PPF will also appoint a trustee to the scheme from its pre-approved panel, to monitor the insolvency and commence the wind-up of the scheme.

The PPF assumes responsibility for a scheme only where:

- a "qualifying insolvency event" has occurred with respect to an eligible scheme;
- the scheme has not been rescued (eg, by the sale of the business to a new employer that takes over the scheme's funding obligations); and
- the scheme's assets (post-liquidation dividend) are below the PPF's calculated level of protected liabilities.

If the above conditions are not met, the PPF will cease to be involved once the relevant assessment procedures have been completed, handing control back to the trustees. If the conditions are met, however, the scheme will transfer to the PPF and the scheme members will receive compensation payments in lieu of their pensions.

Broadly, the level of compensation payable will depend on whether the members in question are over or under normal pension age on the date of the insolvency event. The rules for calculating compensation are complex and beyond the scope of this chapter but can be found on the PPF's website.[28]

---

28 See: www.pensionprotectionfund.org.uk.

As noted earlier, the PPF may also have a role to play in insolvent restructurings through its assumption of scheme voting rights. These voting rights may allow it to participate in the insolvency – through voting at creditor meetings, approving fees and potentially appointing its own insolvency practitioner, either as liquidator or alongside an administrator.

6. Outlook

Following the demise of BHS in 2016 and of Carillion in early 2018, and the subsequent UK parliamentary select committee hearings for each situation, UK DB schemes have been very much in the spotlight.

Amidst a plethora of criticism for its failure to act sooner on BHS and Carillion, TPR has set out its revised objective to be "clearer, quicker and tougher" – a marked change from their previous approach of "educate, enable and enforce". Early signs are that TPR is intervening more frequently in interactions between trustees and corporates and actively seeking to use its powers more widely.

In March 2018 the Department for Work and Pensions issued its white paper, Protecting Defined Benefit Pension Schemes. Although not perhaps quite as far-reaching as many commentators had predicted, the white paper made several key proposals, including the introduction of criminal sanctions against individuals in certain circumstances and new investigative powers for TPR.

Finally, new CVA guidance from the PPF issued in June 2018 indicates a desire to become more influential in ongoing funding decisions, in order to provide further protection for the PPF from loss.

Taken together, it is clear that the regulatory environment for UK pensions is becoming more active. Companies looking to restructure need to be cognisant of the threat of retrospective action and the desire of the PPF to become more involved in discussions.

Away from the specific world of pensions, Brexit and, more broadly, global trade disputes continue to loom large on the horizon. While the eventual impact is far from clear, many are predicting recessionary pressure on both the demand and supply side when Britain leaves the EU. There are also potentially significant adverse effects for global groups (and global trade more generally) from potential import tariff tit for tat moves.

These pressures, together with the increased public scrutiny of DB pensions highlighted above, mean that DB pension issues will remain firmly on the restructuring agenda for the next few years and will be a key aspect to resolve as part of restructuring situations.

The publishers would like to thank Michael Bushnell for his assistance in the preparation of the previous version of this chapter.

Cross-border insolvency: solutions to maximise stakeholder value

Matthew Mawhinney
David Soden
Deloitte

1. Introduction

As businesses have become increasingly global, with record levels of M&A activity fuelled by historically low interest rates and covenant-lite financing facilities from an increasingly diverse lending base, there has been a corresponding need for global restructuring solutions.

There have been various attempts to harmonise laws and regulations, be it the European Insolvency Regulation, the UNCITRAL Model Law or the mooted Restructuring Professional concept across Europe. However, these have been met with a healthy dose of professional scepticism and some resistance by those in the profession, as restructuring hubs position themselves to be the destination of choice for complex financial restructurings, notwithstanding some of the practical impediments to their implementation.

The advantages and disadvantages of Chapter 11, UK or Singaporean schemes of arrangement, Cayman provisional liquidations and countless others are well documented. This chapter is not designed to be a critique of individual processes but, working through some recent examples, highlights the importance of both working flexibly across borders and using a combination of insolvency processes to drive the optimal restructuring solution.

Equally important is understanding the pitfalls of failing to work collaboratively across borders, where practitioners seeking to maximise the benefit of an individual estate end up limiting value realisable to all. Furthermore, following recent high profile corporate insolvencies in the UK and the well-publicised use of CVAs to compromise retail landlords, there is mounting pressure on restructuring advisers to consider the public interest in their work. In this context it is important to highlight that the profession has also deployed innovative solutions to save businesses from collapse, right-sizing balance sheets and providing stable platforms for management teams to rebuild in the process.

2. Paragon Offshore

2.1 Background

The primary case study for this chapter is Paragon Offshore Plc ("Paragon"), selected for the wide range of complex issues faced by management and their advisers and the creative solution implemented to drive maximum stakeholder value. We have revisited the key issues faced and solutions identified for a wide range of competing stakeholders, to highlight key learning points.

To provide some context to Paragon, it was a global oil field services company, operating jack-up rigs and semi-submersibles in the Gulf of Mexico, Africa, the North Sea and across the Middle East. Its customers were large multinational oil and gas companies and government agencies across the globe. Laden with ca. $2.4 billion of debt comprising a $756 million RCF, $642 million term debt and $1,020 million of bonds, as well as $215 million of specific asset financing relating to its two most valuable rigs, the company struggled when oil prices hit $40 per barrel in 2016, as major customers reined in exploratory deep sea drilling in favour of cheaper shallow water and land-based shale production.

Management recognised the need for a balance sheet restructuring, as although the group had significant levels of cash it had an ageing fleet of rigs requiring significant capex and a business plan reliant on a dramatic uptick in the price of oil. Competition intensified as a number of private equity-backed businesses rapidly expanded, driving up supply in a sub-market that is notoriously fragile to supply- and demand-side shocks.

2.2 No one size fits all

The US Chapter 11 process has long been the standard for global restructuring processes, and with good reason. It is flexible, corporates remain in control and can compromise onerous liabilities and contracts, there is a well-trodden path for debtor in possession funding, relatively minimal insolvency stigma and apparent global stay of proceedings. All have offset the cost and time periods associated with delivering a transaction.

Paragon Offshore Plc, a UK public company listed in New York, and certain of its material subsidiaries filed for Chapter 11 in February 2016 and began the process of negotiating with its stakeholder group under the protection of the US Bankruptcy Court.

Having filed a plan of reorganisation in April 2016 and two subsequent plans in August 2016 and February 2017 (which were rejected by the presiding judge for, amongst other reasons, lacking commercial prudence – an inconceivable reason in many jurisdictions but demonstrating the commercial acumen of the US court process) it was becoming apparent that a reappraisal of the situation was required and that at least one of the stakeholder groups needed to take more of the pain and absorb further losses.

Third-party valuations were received from different advisers on different bases, and on any analysis it was clear that the group's shareholders were significantly out of the money and lenders were facing losses running into the hundreds of millions. Attempts to consensually agree a restructuring with the lenders, the group and its shareholders stalled, and detailed contingency planning commenced.

A significant component of the stakeholder debates centred around contingent tax liabilities in Brazil and Mexico and the terms of a settlement agreement with Noble Corporation Plc (the listed oil company from which Paragon was spun off in August 2014). The creditors were not satisfied with the group's proposal, their apprehension focusing on the ability of the relevant tax authorities to pursue the reorganised group (in which the lenders were proposing to be the equity holders), in particular their ability to pierce the corporate veil.

2.3 The search for a solution

Breaking the deadlock had to focus on driving value for the fulcrum creditors and offering them a concrete solution that delivered tangible results. Given that the value of the assets was restricted by the oversupply of similar vessels in a flat market, value had to be created by limiting the reorganised Paragon group's liabilities.

There were two material hurdles to overcome:

- A US bankruptcy judge is unable to fetter the rights of shareholders (some of whom had become increasingly vociferous in their objection to the plan) of non-US domiciled entities – a legal nuance, but a critical implementation hurdle that needed to be addressed.
- The Chapter 11 process is designed to save a group of filing debtors, not just the more valuable entities, so the concept of hiving off contingent or real liabilities within certain debtors is a relatively alien concept.

When seeking to establish a precedent transaction against which to base analysis and assumptions, there was limited case law. There are numerous examples of foreign domiciled entities seeking recognition in the US through Chapter 15 (Harkand or Ocean Rig for example, which will be revisited later in this chapter) or local processes for differing entities in the group (CHC Helicopters) but an entity already a debtor in a Chapter 11 case, filing for a concurrent insolvency process? This was unchartered territory.

As mentioned, the parent company was a UK plc so the traditional menu of UK restructuring options was, in theory, available to complement the Chapter 11 process, albeit this would be highly unusual. These options obviously included the now-commonplace pre-packaged sale whereby the key assets can be sold immediately following an administrator's appointment to ensure value is maintained, whilst the remaining group is not sold and is wound down or otherwise liquidated.

Legal advice from leading counsel and lawyers from both sides of the Atlantic was clear: Paragon Offshore Plc was an English-registered entity with its head office and regular board meetings in London. Despite arguably having its COMI outside the UK (significant management control was exercised in Houston) and already being a debtor in Chapter 11, the directors submitted an application to court for the appointment of administrators in accordance with paragraph 12(1)(b) of Schedule B1 to the Insolvency Act on 17 May 2017.

In the context of Paragon, the two crucial powers bestowed upon administrators under the Insolvency Act were as follows:

- the ability to sell the shares owned by the parent company, free and clear of any encumbrances and without recourse by the shareholders; and
- the ability to implement a corporate restructuring that split the group into two distinct parts:
  - New Paragon: the entities and operations that management wished to continue to drive forward; and
  - Old Paragon: the entities deemed surplus to requirements, which could be wound down and realised for value (where appropriate).

An additional complexity in this case was that certain of the company's shareholders were seeking, at the AGM and a proposed EGM, the removal of the directors in order to try to frustrate the restructuring process that they believed unfairly prejudiced them. The directors resolved to appoint administrators in advance of any meeting of shareholders in order to provide the stability required to deliver the transaction.

This alone caused significant uncertainty for the directors, who on the one hand were trying to save the business and negotiate with their significantly out-of-the-money creditors, while on the other trying to ensure that any agreement made with those creditors would be appropriately binding in the event of their removal. Shareholder activism, at a time where, by any analysis, the shareholders were out of the money, was threatening to destabilise a heavily negotiated restructuring plan.

2.4 Delivering the solution – was it a pre-packaged sale?

Given the scrutiny (and occasional objections) the Chapter 11 was receiving from stakeholders across the globe, the administrators were keen to ensure that all elements of the process were transparent and all critical issues considered. Although the transaction did not complete immediately after appointment of the administrators, as it could not be consummated until the Fifth Plan was ratified by the US courts, it was in substance pre-agreed with the company's lenders prior to the appointment. The administrators therefore considered it to be a pre-packaged sale for the purposes of complying with SIP 16.

A significant amount of debt was written off – $2.4 billion in total – in return for a split of the cash in the business at the date of the transaction, reinstated debt of under $100 million and a share of the equity. Whilst this result is not exceptional in the context of large leverage restructurings, the mechanics used to achieve it were, and the combination of different regimes was critical to ensure that the transaction could be completed. It then provided stability for the reorganised group, with significantly reduced debt, to focus on its original purpose and maximise value for all stakeholders.

2.5 Liquidating subsidiaries – the do's and don'ts

Whilst the overall transaction was a success, it represented a material departure from a typical Chapter 11 transaction, which focuses on a group-wide solution to, typically, a balance sheet problem. As noted above, a key element of this transaction was a clear split in the group, with only the entities and assets specifically identified as part of the approved business plan being sold to the lender-owned newco. This enabled the restructure of certain contingent liabilities in jurisdictions that management had sought to exit.

Managed exits of conglomerates with dedicated project teams is challenging enough. However, zero funding, incomplete information, litigation risk and disenfranchised employees add further layers of complexity. Some key pointers:

- *Understand the stakeholders.* A key part of the wind-down focused on which external stakeholders would be impacted. The development of an entity priority model that could efficiently marshal the intercompany claims and give a global view on likely distributions allowed the locally appointed liquidators (or equivalent) to come to a commercial position on dividend distributions without the need for circular payments and many iterations of distributions. This strong commercial approach cut through the potentially divisive legal complexities by jurisdiction.
- *Seek initial approval for the Chapter 11 plan.* The judge's buy-in is a fundamental first step before any of the preparatory work can commence. The argument needs to be commercially compelling as it flies in the face of the notion that a debtor group would emerge from Chapter 11 as one constituency. The case here was very clearly articulated and the pressure the creditors were applying added credibility to the arguments.
- *Seek collaboration and a global team.* Liquidations have completed or are ongoing in Cayman, Delaware, Mexico, Brazil, Norway, Gibraltar, Luxembourg and Switzerland with a variety of different firms acting under the supervision of the parent company administrators. Without a coordinated global team and collaborative approach the costs would be many times higher and creditor distributions lower, particularly in light of the intercompany positions.

As we shall see later in this chapter, where there are liquidators from multiple firms representing distinct creditor groups the results can be hugely inefficient.

2.6 Challenges to global stay

Certain of the group's borrowing entities remained outside of Chapter 11, separate financing arrangements with non-US lenders totalling some $200 million. The lenders were seen as potentially peripheral to the process and would "probably just fall in line" if the US creditors consented to the plan. This nearly caused the collapse of the Paragon transaction but again, both the UK and US courts and practitioners showed flexibility in the face of adversity. Having exited Chapter 11 and effected the main restructuring, the UK parent (whilst still in administration and acting through its administrators) re-petitioned for Chapter 11 to ensure that a valuable part of the group – for which creditor consent was not obtained during the initial phase – could be dealt with again within the US and UK courts.

Whilst the global stay on proceedings is often rightly vaunted as a key benefit of the Chapter 11 process, the reality is that a creditor or stakeholder without any US nexus can seek to challenge that global stay. In the Paragon case, neither an Asian bank nor an overseas tax authority considered themselves bound by the Chapter 11. Stakeholders with minimal exposure to the US may take issue with a US-centric Chapter 11 approach and careful consideration needs to be given to stakeholders who can frustrate the process. A failure to consider the options available to such stakeholders can have a potentially terminal impact on a restructuring.

3. CHC Group Ltd

3.1 Background

Chapter 11 was combined with another insolvency process in the context of the CHC Group Ltd restructuring. Headquartered in Canada, CHC was a global helicopter services business, specialising in transportation to offshore oil and gas platforms. The group comprised 87 entities registered in around 30 countries, serving a global client base. The group began to struggle, like Paragon, as oil and gas multinationals began to pull out of exploratory and deep sea drilling in 2015.

CHC, along with 42 affiliated group entities, petitioned for relief under Chapter 11 in May 2016. At the date of the petition, the group had outstanding debts of approximately $1.6 billion. The group proposed a debt-for-equity restructuring as part of the Chapter 11 proceedings that would allow the group to continue trading, and for partial satisfaction of its creditor claims.

As the group's ultimate parent company was domiciled in the Cayman

Islands (outside the jurisdiction of the US courts), it was deemed necessary to obtain an order from a Cayman court validating the transfer of assets proposed in the plan, subject to its being confirmed in the US court.

The question was whether the US Bankruptcy Court had jurisdiction over a Cayman-registered company and its creditors. The general working assumption is that in a consensual restructuring solution, a US Chapter 11 provides a global stay on proceedings and can effect the necessary amendments to financing facilities. However, as with Paragon, where there are dissenting creditors or shareholders, companies will seek the additional protection of local courts. In the case of CHC, the disenfranchised shareholders were seeking to challenge the Chapter 11, and a successful challenge in the Cayman court could have derailed the restructuring.

Furthermore, the UK pension scheme had a Section 75 deficit of £150 million, and a key component of the plan involved a significant reduction to the scheme deficit. Could the company rely on the Chapter 11 to force a reduction in the scheme deficit plan?

3.2 The solution

Here again, the restructuring professionals thought around the problem and combined the US Chapter 11 process with an overseas process, to overcome the shortfalls of Chapter 11 that had not been envisaged originally. Given the Cayman-domiciled parent company, provisional liquidators (PLs) were appointed under Cayman law in January 2017. Although its name suggests otherwise, a Cayman provisional liquidator is very much a restructuring tool as opposed to a precursor to an official liquidation, and in this case provided all the powers required to deliver a transaction.

The provisional liquidation was an ancillary proceeding to the Chapter 11 proceedings in the US, in which a restructuring plan had been proposed. The PLs' ultimate objective was to independently assess the plan and support, or otherwise, the company's application in the Cayman court for a validation order which would have the effect of approving the transfer of assets proposed by the plan under Cayman law, thus nullifying any challenge from the affected stakeholders.

As part of this analysis, the PLs had to consider the following questions:

- Was the plan in the best interests of the creditors of the company and the group?
- Was there any evidence that any creditors had been unfairly prejudiced?
- Was the process to notify the company's creditors of the Chapter 11 proceedings and the provisional liquidation appropriate?

After a period of financial and qualitative analysis on the proposed plan in order to answer the above questions (which was completed within the time frame of the overall Chapter 11 proceedings) a comprehensive report was prepared and submitted to the Cayman court, which granted a validation order protecting the company from the risk of a local challenge. With the blessing of the US Court and the validation order, the PLs were able to successfully renegotiate the pension scheme deficit reduction plan.

This flexibility in approach and willingness to consider alternative options rather than to merely follow a pre-ordained plan was again critical in delivering this cross-border restructuring.

4. Ocean Rig

4.1 Background

The Cayman courts were also utilised in the restructuring of Ocean Rig, a Greece-based operator of oil rigs. The group's holding company was domiciled in the US and listed on NASDAQ. Notwithstanding this, restructuring professionals proactively considered which restructuring tool was most relevant to the situation faced by the company, and avoided the constraints of what was currently available by making use of that tool.

The significant learning point from the Ocean Rig restructuring was the innovative use of COMI shifts. It was the first high profile COMI shift pre-insolvency and subsequent Cayman Island court restructure of foreign companies.

The COMI shift solution required:

- the incorporation of a Cayman Islands subsidiary directly below the original holding company;
- appointment of local Cayman directors who conducted board meetings and made the fundamental business decisions in Cayman in the lead-up to the restructuring;
- notification by the directors of all known creditors of the group, and a press release informing the public of the change in COMI in good time prior to the restructure; and
- all key restructuring negotiations with creditors to be held locally in the Cayman Islands.

4.2 The outcome

The group benefited from the provisions of Section 91(d)(ii) of the Cayman Islands Company Law giving the court jurisdiction over a foreign company which is carrying on business in the Cayman Islands. This enabled the group to implement its restructuring in Cayman and resulted in a compromise of $3.7 billion of New York law debt.

This was an excellent example of the defensive strategic capabilities of Cayman Islands restructurings, allowing the group the breathing space to negotiate with its creditors in a debtor-friendly environment.

5. How not to do it – Espirito Santo

Restructuring professionals do not always get it right, and insolvency does not always work across borders. We have covered examples of highly flexible regimes to date – the Cayman Islands, the US and the UK – each of which have been used to restructure foreign debt successfully, with pragmatic practitioners and a commercial approach taken by both the legal profession and the courts in each jurisdiction, irrespective of the initial centre of main interests of the company.

However, in all but the largest cases where management is prepared to proactively consider a restructure, too often we see local processes applied to global businesses which are neither designed nor appropriate for achieving practical solutions. A good example of this is the case of Espirito Santo from 2014. Whilst outside the scope of this chapter, it is a good example of why the pan-European regulators are seeking a coordinated approach to bank insolvency, as local insolvency regimes are ill-prepared for a global corporate restructure, let alone a global bank restructure. That it was a bank is not important for current purposes – indeed the bank was only part of operations that spanned Europe, Africa and South America and covered banking, real estate, infrastructure, agriculture, insurance and healthcare. Espirito Santo is of interest here because it involved concurrent insolvencies in Luxembourg, Switzerland, Panama, Dubai and Portugal, amongst others.

If the examples used so far demonstrate how restructuring professionals can use innovative solutions and work together cross-border to maximise value, these liquidations provide a reminder of what happens when conflicting priorities and a local approach collide.

The Espirito Santo Group had locally appointed liquidators in each of the aforementioned jurisdictions, over both banking and non-banking entities and, whilst there were different creditors in each jurisdiction, there were overarching creditors at the Luxembourg parent companies (Rio Forte Investments, SA and Espirito Santo International SA) which had issued ca. $6 billion in Luxembourg law debt.

The group proactively sought a restructuring plan with regulatory authorities and creditors through a Luxembourg *gestion contrôlée*. However, this plan did not involve comprehensive debt write-off nor third-party and court verification of a restructuring, which proved to be so important in each of the Paragon, CHC and Ocean Rig cases discussed above.

After the inevitable failure of the *gestion contrôlée* process, and despite the best efforts of the board and management teams of subsidiary companies, a group-wide insolvency was inevitable. Again, there was another opportunity to seek a protective solution – perhaps a Luxembourg process combined with a Chapter 11 – but this was not progressed and local liquidators were appointed.

Separate liquidators being appointed does not mean that an effective process cannot be run, provided each liquidator focuses on the realisation of assets in order to maximise recoveries for every creditor as a priority, rather than being concerned with claims between group companies that could not increase the overall asset pool. However, this did not happen in the Espirito Santo case. In particular:

- Liquidators commenced proceedings against other group companies which had no assets.
- Liquidators applied a very literal reading of national insolvency laws and asserted claims of billions of dollars against:
  - client assets (which of course are intended to be sacrosanct – whether monetary or physical); and
  - other group companies with no realisations.
- Secondary proceedings were begun in certain jurisdictions to protect local assets for local creditors.

Meanwhile, the key assets of value in Portugal, Latin America and Switzerland were seized by the relevant government authorities, the proceeds of sale being intended to be applied for the benefit of locally affected creditors (in this instance in particular, Portuguese depositors who had lost out due to the failure of the bank, and not the creditors of the Luxembourg companies which ostensibly owned the assets).

Whether a single group-wide process would have resulted in better realisations for creditors in this particular situation is impossible to say. However, realisations have suffered because of the lack of sophistication and the incompatibility of different restructuring regimes, with the losers being the creditors that each liquidator was there to protect.

It is worth mentioning that the European Insolvency Regulation and UNCITRAL Model Law are both effective guidelines for an international restructure, if followed. However, a key issue experienced in Espirito Santo was that neither Luxembourg nor Switzerland recognise the Model Law. The weakness of both was thus exposed – a number of large issuers are based in Luxembourg and international collaboration cannot be compelled under either.

6. Conclusion

Despite the relatively benign restructuring market of recent years, the examples listed in this chapter demonstrate the innovation taking place across the industry. Whilst the large corporate failures – from Enron to Carillion – will always grab the headlines, significant progress is being made in harmonising restructuring approaches, notwithstanding local differences. By working cross-border, in a collaborative manner, restructuring professionals can continue to drive real value for stakeholders at all points on the distress curve.

It is critical that all parties understand the tools in the box, and increasingly the use of a single restructuring process is insufficient to get to the result required. Unfamiliarity, time horizon and the cost of Chapter 11 in Europe have historically dissuaded issuers from pursuing Chapter 11, but an increasing quantum of debt from European issuers is subject to New York law – and often issued to US-resident investors – so its use is expected to continue to increase for traditionally non-US businesses. Furthermore, complex group structures and increasingly complex stakeholder groups, combined with local law issues, may compel a combination of restructuring procedures.

It is also notable that each of the successful cases considered here were driven by a pragmatic management team that understood the risks and issues in the lead-up to a restructuring. This should not be underestimated. Creditor-friendly regimes have their place and are important for the efficient flow of international capital, but as we have seen in the UK (and as will be more relevant as the next wave of covenant-lite financing structures begin to fail), a proactive management team – taking appropriate action at the appropriate time – will always be a critical ingredient to a successful restructure.

Creating value in distressed M&A transactions

Carlo Bosco
Greenhill

1. Introduction

There is a significant amount of literature on merger and acquisitions (M&A) in general, but very little has been written about M&A in a distressed context. This chapter focuses on distressed M&A for control, leaving aside the wider investment options for distressed assets.

It is not the intention to provide universal solutions. Every restructuring situation is different and requires both method (in order to have an orderly and effective process) and creativity (in order to find solutions to complex problems). The chapter is aimed at all practitioners of financial restructuring, from investors to financial and legal advisers, and from executives to turnaround specialists.

2. Identifying distressed assets

The standard definition of a distressed company is a company with debt trading with a spread of more than 1,000 bps above the risk-free rate. A simpler definition is a company that faces a liquidity crisis due to operational needs, a covenant breach, or upcoming maturities that cannot be refinanced. Both definitions are helpful, but leave out a number of potential targets including, for example, business units of a larger and healthier corporate that need to be restructured.

Restructuring professionals and distressed debt investors spend a lot of time identifying these targets to gain an edge over their competitors, leveraging a wide-ranging network of M&A and work-out bankers, accountants and legal advisers.

3. Parties involved in a distressed sale

In contrast to a normal M&A transaction, a distressed sale usually involves a wider number of parties and stakeholders. This is because the enterprise value of the firm does not necessarily break in the equity and therefore the transaction might require the consent of other parties, including creditors – financial and trade – regulators and administrators. The behaviour and psychology of stakeholders is also very different from that in a regular M&A transaction.

3.1 Shareholders

Shareholders are the ultimate decision makers in a regular M&A transaction. However, in a distressed sale they could be completely cut out of the decision-making process. At the same time, if they play their cards well they could extract value from a situation where, theoretically, there is no value left for them.

Shareholders face an interesting dilemma. If out of the money, they are tempted to kick the can down the road for as long as possible to see if things improve for the business, taking increasingly riskier bets to retain any remaining value; but the longer they wait, the lower the chance that they will be able to control the restructuring process and extract any value at all, all else being equal.

Shareholders often disregard the potential opportunity that a financial restructuring can present to reset the capital structure. Instead, they frequently risk throwing good money after bad, only to realise that they have not properly restructured the business. The same money might have been used to negotiate a proper recapitalisation and retain control from creditors, participating in the sale process or even pre-empting it.

3.2 Creditors

Creditors play a key role in a distressed situation. They have usually earned a seat at the table and can facilitate or frustrate the process, depending on their ultimate objectives. Creditors are not a homogenous group and often include different classes and types, with differing objectives depending on where the value breaks (or is perceived to break) in the capital structure.

(a) Secured creditors

Secured creditors usually have more control. They have rights to specific assets and can protect their claim, potentially preventing options that could enhance value for other stakeholders. Their priority is to make sure that their collateral does not deteriorate further in value, so maximising value will not be top on their agenda, especially if the expected value of the collateral covers their claim.

If the expected value does not cover their claim, they are likely to be more engaged; however, the behaviour of banks and other par lenders will typically be very different to that of hedge funds that entered the capital structure at a discount. Banks are generally less proactive and like to explore all possible options prior to making a decision. Funds tend to be more aggressive and can seek to take control of the assets through an enforcement or credit bid.

Other stakeholders will need to take secured creditors' rights into account, and make them whole if they want to implement alternative transactions.

(b) ***Junior creditors***

Junior creditors are in a more difficult spot, running the risk of being "bullied" by secured creditors and shareholders. To take control of the process and protect their interest they will first need to ensure that the secured creditors are made whole, either through repayment, refinancing or cram-up (in a Chapter 11 context, reinstating their debt at terms that are deemed not detrimental by a judge), depending on the jurisdiction and the specifics of the situation.

If they deal effectively with the senior creditors, they can become the *de facto* equity and drive the process.

(c) ***Trade creditors***

Trade creditors play a vital role for the company. Their ability to extend terms and continue to supply the target is critical, but at the same time exposes them to further losses if the restructuring does not yield the envisaged results. Proper engagement with trade creditors is important throughout the process.

3.3 Other stakeholders

A restructuring usually attracts the interest of the public at large, especially if jobs are at risk. Unions and political organisations can have an impact and facilitate a transaction, for example by providing improvements to collective contracts, incentives or tax reliefs. However, at the same time they can be a real roadblock if not carefully managed, as for example during the restructuring of an airline in 2017, when the unions voted down the restructuring and pushed the airline into an extraordinary administration process that is still ongoing.

Navigating this complexity requires a mix of corporate finance tools that straddle M&A and restructuring. On the one hand, a purist M&A approach could end up resulting in a non-deliverable solution or a botched process; on the other, a creditor-focused restructuring process could destroy significant value, focusing on covenants and cash preservation to the detriment of the best interests of the business.

To address this, it is critical for the financial advisers involved to educate all parties on what their real position is and what the available options are in order to create the right set of expectations for the implementation of a successful transaction. This education process will also need to outline, to the secured stakeholders, why the value maximising process would not put their position at risk versus the status quo.

For example, during the recent restructuring of an English plc, the status quo was not sustainable and the board of directors announced a strategic review to explore a number of options to finance a complex operational turnaround. Due to a looming covenant breach, the company's lenders were approached to negotiate and secure significant runway (sufficient to cover more than one full year of operations as per the business plan at the time), thereby allowing the company to explore options without an outstanding default. Creditors accepted the request after a detailed education process, which explained that they were not increasing their risk versus the status quo and that taking these steps would actually increase the chances of a full recovery in due course. The support of the lenders, which at the beginning was not forthcoming, enabled the company to run a comprehensive and extensive disposal process, resulting in the sale of the company to a competitor and unlocking value for the seller's shareholders.

It is worth noting that exploring all possible alternatives may not always be the best course of action and could even destroy value. Prolonged restructuring processes represent a significant distraction for management teams, often leading to severe loss of talent and resources, with transaction costs cutting out a very significant portion of the ultimate recovery.

In a recent transaction, both management and its advisers strongly believed that the business first needed to be stabilised and separated from non-core investments. They were advised against postponing any critical decisions, as any further delay would likely result in value destruction. Creditors could not agree on a path forward, due to the conflicting views of banks and hedge funds, prolonging the restructuring process until cash was depleted and a decision had to be made.

4. Company perspective

A company facing financial difficulties is an object of significant desire in the context of distressed M&A. It will be targeted by advisers and investors, who will want to play a role in the restructuring.

In the early stages of a restructuring, most management teams will struggle to recognise their real position. This is due to a number of factors, but boils down to the fact that entrepreneurs and managers are usually more optimistic than restructuring professionals. A financial adviser bringing the bad news can risk upsetting management and losing a mandate, even if eventually proven right.

The target and its management team will eventually come to terms with the issue at hand and will need to engage with their stakeholders to find a solution. Initially, the company will be in control of exploring options, but eventually, if nothing happens, creditors facing a distressed situation will force the company and its shareholders to confront the need to satisfy their obligations by either:

- refinancing the debt;
- raising more equity; or
- selling assets.

Time is of the essence in a restructuring. While the so-called 'runway' before a credit event (such as an upcoming maturity, liquidity need or a covenant breach) often varies, the recent growth of covenant-lite loans and loose fixed-income documentation have allowed stressed or distressed companies to artificially extend the runway before tougher options are explored. However, the absence of any covenants can be a devil in disguise as companies in distress only start reviewing their options ahead of severe events, such as a liquidity shortfall. In the absence of liquidity, the number of options available become fewer, putting value maximisation at risk.

If an asset sale is required, different stakeholders will have different objectives. For the benefit of all stakeholders, it is important to align all parties behind the solution that maximises value (or minimises losses). The company and the professionals involved will need to make sure that this objective is clear and avoid running into traps that would prevent value maximisation. A common example is a hedge fund buying a blocking position in the capital structure in order to drive the restructuring process to a result that would benefit its own investment, at the expense of the wider stakeholder universe.

So how does one enhance the value of a distressed asset for all stakeholders? It has been said that M&A does not happen in a restructuring, meaning that in order to a have a successful sale one needs to avoid a distressed sale in the first place. If an investor believes that the asset will become cheaper over time, they will naturally wait, hence the critical need to remove the perception of distress with a controllable solution.

This is not easy to achieve and often requires the support of creditors. It can happen in or out of court, depending on the jurisdiction. A few years ago, for example, during the sale of a mortgage insurance business in receivership, competitive tension was created with a mix of special situation funds with significant experience in insurance, and trade buyers. The message to all prospective buyers was clear: if nobody wanted to pay a full price, the receiver would be happy running the company for years. Ultimately, a very compelling offer was received from a trade buyer that took advantage of the powers of the receiver, and the sale was quickly executed.

As in this example, the key to implementing any successful sale is to build and maintain competitive tension, possibly removing the need for a sale. In a distressed context, this is more difficult for a number of reasons. The time to implement a transaction could be limited because the company desperately needs cash. The number of acquirers could also be limited, because available information is unclear or the process has an obvious outcome (for example a debt-for-equity swap driven by aggressive hedge funds in the fulcrum security) and nobody wants to invest the time and resources to come up with a better alternative.

5. The process

A management team and its advisers should quickly assess the causes of the current distress and what the business needs to recover and thrive. This exercise has to be grounded in reality and based on assumptions that can be credibly supported. Another important exercise is to see what management would do if they did not face the current financial constraints. These are complex exercises, but fundamental to support the process. They will allow the advisers to present the business to potential buyers and identify opportunities clearly. Even if potential buyers will have different plans for the asset, these exercises will accelerate their understanding of the business and motivate them to participate in the process.

Once management has identified what the business needs, it is also important to analyse the real position of each stakeholder. This is usually carried out in close collaboration with the company's legal counsel, given how relevant the input of the legal analysis under various scenarios will be. A stakeholder's real position might be very different from their perceived position. Aligning all stakeholders on the reality of their relative positions will reset expectations and facilitate the implementation of a successful transaction down the road.

These two analyses will lead to the development of a list of available options to restructure the business, which could include the option to sell the whole or parts of the going concern.

If a sale is contemplated, it would ideally have to be completed within a reasonable time frame (similar to a normal M&A process), thereby avoiding the perception of a burning platform. If the situation is time critical, it is important to negotiate the necessary runway with creditors. This flexibility is typically obtained if the company can show that the extended runway would lead to a better outcome for the stakeholder(s) that need to consent, potentially in exchange for concessions such as consent fees or margin bumps.

Once the assets to be disposed of are identified (which may constitute the company as a whole), the company and its advisers should prepare a clear and credible information pack, including a vendor due diligence report, and structure a process that demonstrates how the transaction can be implemented. The better the quality of the information provided, the more likely it is that parties will invest time and money in exploring the transaction.

A buyer universe also needs to be identified and will most likely include trade and financial buyers. The company should determine why the investment would be appealing for these parties and create the right environment for them to participate in a healthy and competitive process.

Attracting trade buyers can significantly increase value given the potential for synergies, but it is not always possible. If the business requires a significant turnaround, most corporates will shy away from getting involved to avoid contaminating their existing business.

Finally, a controllable contingency plan should also be put in place to support the sale process and avoid forcing the company's hand during the negotiation.

Figure 1: Launching the process

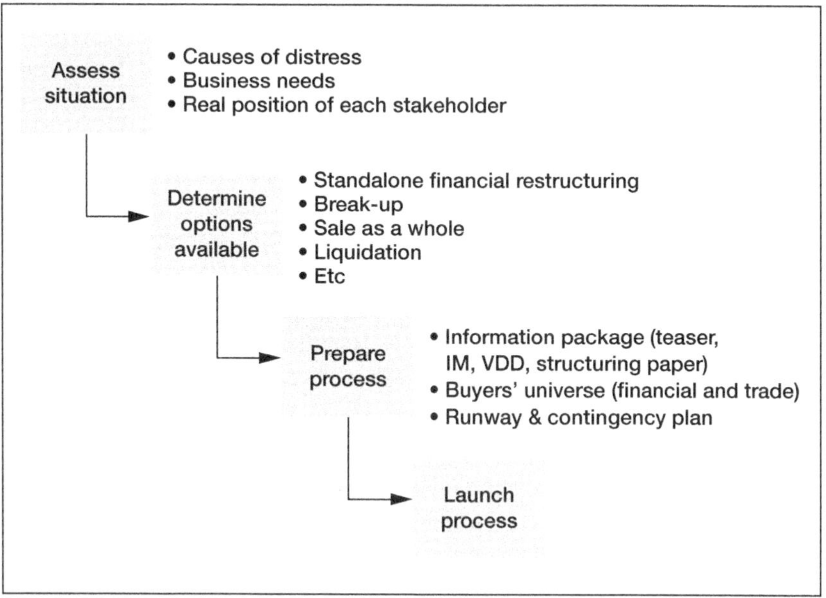

6. Investor perspective

Investing in distressed assets is an investment strategy that is becoming increasingly popular. According to Prequin, at the end of 2017 distressed debt funds were sitting on $83 billion worth of "dry powder", in addition to more than $150 billion of unrealised value from previous investments, four times higher than at the beginning of the last financial crisis in 2007. This capital has been raised with the belief that markets are getting closer to their peak and are due for a correction.

The strategy is attractive because it is countercyclical and can provide significant returns. Distressed investors can usually invest across the capital structure and are generally sector-agnostic, but only a subset are well equipped to take control of distressed assets. While some funds might end up seeking control in the absence of a better outcome, it may not be their preferred strategy.

Distressed debt investors that focus on owning directly distressed assets tend to be more specialised. The most successful ones focus on sectors they know well in order to leverage previous experience, operational know-how, and access to specialist turnaround management teams. This is notably evident in the retail, industrial and financial services sectors. Other investors can cover a variety of sectors, often leveraging their large private equity platforms to gain privileged access to deal flow and specific industry insights.

An investment in a distressed asset requires more due diligence than a normal investment. The investor cannot take anything for granted and will need to second-guess the information available. For this reason, the quality of the advisers involved, including consultants and experts, can make a real difference in getting the process off on the right foot.

Depending on the economic cycle, investors will be flooded with opportunities, and will have limited time to dedicate to each one, so will look for ways to discern between a real opportunity and a waste of time. When the opportunities are scarce, more investors will be willing to invest time and participate, but the financial adviser involved should always be wary of letting too many parties into a process, especially if they will not be able to offer real value. This gatekeeper role is a key value-add input from an adviser and will avoid distracting management from running the business.

The investor analysis will start with understanding the cause of distress: is it balance sheet driven or is it operational? The ideal scenario for investors is a good business with a bad balance sheet. However, in most situations, the distress is caused by a combination of different issues.

The investor then needs to develop a plan to manage the turnaround. This requires a clear view of what can be done differently to restructure the business and generate a positive return:

- Will the existing management team participate in the turnaround?
- Were they the cause of the problem?
- Does the business need significant investment?

In some situations, such as the Yellow Pages directories businesses, the investment strategy for some of the funds involved in the various restructurings has not entailed growing the legacy business again. Instead, these investors have focused on managing industry-wide decline in order to generate a positive return on the investment.

As part of the plan to manage the turnaround, the investment professional will also identify the perimeter of the acquisition. Restructuring proceedings, in and out of court, provide very powerful tools that can facilitate the reorganisation of an existing business, shedding, for example, contracts and leases with relative ease. The recent restructuring of a british department store is an example of the capabilities and attractiveness of a UK administration to implement a restructuring. In this transaction, after the majority shareholder walked away from an agreed recapitalisation that would have reduced the number of stores through a company voluntary arrangement (CVA), but kept significant financial liabilities in place, administrators were quickly appointed to preserve the going concern and sell the company. The business was ultimately sold to its minority shareholder for a total consideration worth less than 10% of its outstanding liabilities, with the purchaser retaining the ability to cherry pick any remaining assets and leases.

Managing turnarounds requires a different set of skills to running a normal business – hence the proliferation of professionals specialised in turnarounds. Most distressed investors will rely on one of these specialist teams in order to free up investment professionals from the day-to-day activities involved in managing an acquired asset.

The investor will also need to identify how best to acquire control of the target asset. A number of actions will need to be implemented for a successful operational restructuring, and without the ability to influence these actions the investor would remain at the mercy of other parties. Control can be shared – for example, where cutting a deal with the entrepreneur can make a difference in getting a transaction completed – but it has to be effective and meaningful.

Most financial investors, as with private equity firms, will also look to the potential exit strategy prior to investing. This could be a sale to a non-distressed investor once the turnaround is complete, or to a trade buyer that could not get comfortable during the ongoing restructuring, or even a listing/IPO. As in the Yellow Pages example discussed earlier, it could also be running the business for cash until its useful life expires.

Once this assessment is completed, the investor should be in a position to outline to the seller what it brings to the table:

- Capital: on its own, capital is likely not enough due to the widespread availability of distressed capital out there.
- Sector expertise: depending on the quality of the management team in place this can be quite critical, not only to assess the opportunity, but also to create value.
- Turnaround expertise: this is a real value-add and can significantly improve the chances of acquiring the asset.
- Synergy: this is often hard to realise, and if available, such synergy is generally related to portfolio companies already controlled by the investor.

7. Corporates acquiring distressed assets

Corporates are often overlooked as potential buyers for a distressed asset, but can be a very interesting proposition.

Most corporates shy away from distress for a variety of reasons. Notably, it is more difficult to assess value and sell it internally to the board and externally to shareholders, especially for public companies. Dealing with the complexity of a restructuring can also be time consuming, and most corporates are not used to dealing with this specific complexity. Furthermore, some distressed sales need to be implemented in a tight time frame, which collides with normal corporate decision-making processes. In addition, a corporate might see an opportunity in a competitor going out of business and therefore see limited benefit in buying them out, waiting instead for the opportunity at the very end to cherry pick selected assets out of a liquidation.

For all of these reasons, having an adviser that can cover both M&A and restructuring can be extremely helpful in both navigating the prospective opportunity and avoiding missing opportunities to extract significant value from the process.

When active, corporates can outbid financial investors and still pay a very attractive price. They can cherry pick assets, which may not be possible in a normal context. The potential value creation could be significant, but so are the risks. It is important to have a clear plan to mitigate potential risks, identifying how to implement the acquisition, avoid contaminating the existing business, and manage internal and external communications. This last point is particularly important for public companies, which will be focused on managing any negative press.

In terms of implementation, there are two main approaches. The corporate can work directly with the target and the ultimate owners (not necessarily the shareholders) to agree a sale. Alternatively, it can wait for a change of control and then implement a transaction with the new financial investor(s). Both approaches have their merits and shortcomings, as can be seen in Table 1, below.

8. Investing in a company in distress

Different investors will have very different approaches. Financial investors interested in taking control can use a variety of strategies, which can generally be narrowed down into three approaches, with various pros and cons, as shown in Table 2, below.

Corporates usually shy away from an investment lacking the certainty of control, and thus avoid options 2 and 3.

If there is a clear difference in value expectation between fulcrum security – where the value breaks – and investor willingness to pay, the investor needs to be creative and provide instruments to bridge that gap (eg, out-of-money warrants or earn-outs), sharing the upside with creditors and sometimes even shareholders, and facilitating the implementation of the transaction by reducing overall cost and friction.

If the seller does not have a credible contingency plan, it should expect investors participating in the process to chip at the price offered until a viable alternative can be presented.

9. Valuing a distressed company

"Price is what you pay. Value is what you get." Warren Buffett's well-known advice for value investing is all the more relevant in the context of valuing a distressed company, as the different methodologies used to calculate its intrinsic value will also be used as reference to determine the transaction value (ie, the price).

"What you get" can be calculated using a number of valuation methodologies, as below.

Table 1: Distressed acquisitions by corporates

	Direct approach	**Indirect approach**
Approach	• Engage directly with the target and the ultimate owner • Take into account real position of each stakeholder in order to engage with relevant parties (not necessarily shareholders) • Explore various implementation options	• Wait for the company to be taken over by creditors, then agree/implement transaction • Potentially have dialogue in the background with stakeholders that will take control, in order to have effective implementation mechanics post-change of control
Advantages	• Speed of execution • More certainty and control over the process • Potentially implementable under court supervision	• No involvement with the restructuring • Easier PR
Disadvantages	• Need to participate in the restructuring process and manage PR, especially if implementation is controversial (eg, treatment of trade creditors) • Significant engagement from corporate development team	• Slower than direct approach • Execution risk – more competitive if other trade buyers come to the table after the restructuring • Reduced leverage *vis-à-vis* creditors

Table 2: Options for investing in a distressed company

	Option 1 *Make an offer for the asset*	**Option 2** *Acquire control through a debt-for-equity swap*	**Option 3** *Provide new money for the asset*
Approach	• Direct approach to an acquisition • Implement-ation in or out of court	• Acquire control through the debt • Build up a position large enough to drive the restructuring and prevent alternatives from being implemented (ie, acquire a blocking stake)	• Company could be looking for alternatives to a sale, including raising new money • If new investment is compelling it provides a way to get a foot in the door and get to know the company better from a more secured position
Advantages	• Does not require a significant initial investment (solely time and advisers' fees) • Allows for due diligence	• Can potentially force an outcome • Can minimise the overall cost of the investment	• Foot in the door – protected investment with fixed return
Disadvantages	• Cannot force an outcome • Risk of becoming a stalking-horse	• Requires an initial investment, likely looking from the outside in • No certainty of outcome	• Limited control • No ownership – unless subsequent default and acceleration

9.1 Income-based approach (DCF)

The discounted present value of the company's future cash flows is the most common valuation methodology in distressed situations. However, as distressed companies have to deal with declining financial performance, an uncertain future and depleting liquidity, the forward-looking assumptions required to compute sensible discount rates and realistic cash flows can make this exercise difficult and imprecise.

9.2 Asset-based approach

An alternative to the income-based approach is to consider the value of the assets. While this methodology has the benefit of using historical accounting data, which can be easily sourced and verified, the results of this technique can be misleading. The book value of an asset may significantly differ from its fair market value, or its replacement cost, and will need to be estimated. The circumstances in which these assets are going to be sold also affect the valuation. However, the asset-based approach is helpful to assess the liquidation value of the company and usually provides a valuation floor.

9.3 Market-based approach

Trading and transaction multiples can be used to get a better sense of the target's fair market value in a given market. However, while this technique is often relevant for going concern entities, as it provides a framework for relative valuation versus its peers and through the cycle, forward multiples (such as EV/Sales or EV/EBITDA) carry a higher degree of uncertainty for distressed companies.

Furthermore, in the case of cyclical industries, a company may be distressed when the entire industry is also in distress, making trading multiples hard to assess and transaction multiples less relevant, because they would not necessarily reflect the new industry dynamic and the pressure to sell.

In summary, the uncertainty resulting from distress impacts all three commonly-used valuation methodologies. However, to paraphrase Winston Churchill, DCF is the worst methodology to value a distressed company, except for all the others. In fact, valuing a distressed company using a DCF eliminates any noise associated with imperfect market data or outdated accounting values. Instead, although the methodology relies on a number of assumptions, an acquirer can form its own views on a target's business, its recovery plan, and the potential synergies to be realised, with a certain level of precision and granularity.

The other approaches might be used to complement the DCF analysis. The asset-based approach can provide a valuation floor, while the market-based approach provides a sanity check for the DCF.

10. Implementing a transaction

A distressed M&A transaction can be implemented as a normal sale, but this requires consent from many parties, potentially with unanimity.

Each country has certain restructuring tools to implement disposals under various forms of court supervision, in order to facilitate the sale and cut out out-of-the-money hold-out stakeholders or creditors trying to delay or prevent the transaction in order to extract value.

Familiarity with the various procedures and understanding the pros and cons of each relevant jurisdiction can make a very meaningful difference and create substantial value for both the seller and the acquirer, with a particular focus on re-cutting the business being sold and preserving tax assets accumulated by the corporate during years of underperformance.

The United States is very advanced in this regard. A distressed sale can be implemented during a Chapter 11 process either through a 363 sale or as a plan of reorganisation. The Chapter 11 sale process is used so frequently and comes with so much case law that it is familiar to financial and trade buyers alike. It allows a tailored sale process to run under court supervision, with all the advantages associated with the Chapter 11 proceeding. The sale process can even be run prior to filing, using a pre-pack to implement the transaction.

The United Kingdom also has powerful – and less expensive – tools that have been used successfully in order to implement distressed M&A transactions. A scheme of arrangement – which is not an insolvency proceeding – can be used to quickly execute a compromise between the company and its creditors. If coupled with a pre-pack administration, it can be used to transfer assets to a newco, shedding liabilities, including pension obligations, that in some circumstances present a real impediment to a consensual sale transaction.

Continental Europe has played catch-up, with most of the major countries (including Italy, Spain, France and Germany) recently reforming their bankruptcy law in order to provide effective restructuring tools to corporates, including asset sales.

11. Conclusion

Restructuring is a team effort and requires the ability – and the patience – to mediate among parties with very different interests. M&A in a distressed context can be incredibly frustrating at times, but if well executed it results not only in the preservation of financial value for the stakeholders of a company, but also in a healthier corporate for the benefit of its employees and the surrounding community.

This chapter has attempted to provide a brief overview of distressed M&A, the main actors, processes and tactics. It will hopefully be a stimulus for practitioners to take a step back before starting an all-encompassing process, and to think about what the company needs to thrive as a going concern and how the restructuring process can help achieve that objective and maximise value.

Each situation will be different and will require a different solution, with the right combination of method and creativity to preserve value. In the words of Sun Tzu, "Do not repeat tactics just because they have gained you one victory. Let your methods be regulated by an infinite variety of circumstances."[1]

The author would like to thank Charles Pontvianne for his contribution in writing this chapter.

1 Sun Tzu, *The Art of War*, Pax Librorum, 2009.

Shipping and offshore restructurings

Stephan Chischportich
Matthew Whiting
Evercore

1. Introduction

Companies operating in the shipping and offshore oilfield services sectors (together 'the maritime sector') have been the subject of much focus over the last decade and have provided ample business opportunities for restructuring advisers, restructuring counsel and distressed debt investors alike. The industry (and its various subsectors) has, by nature of its high volatility and cyclicality, been prone to recurrent financial challenges, driven primarily by over-investment in newer and more efficient vessels during cyclical highs, declining demand for maritime services during cyclical lows and resultant supply/demand imbalances across time.

During cyclical downturns, this supply/demand imbalance has put significant pressure on maritime companies' top-line performance, driven by a combination of lower utilisation and lower contract rates, and has consequently put downward pressure on both cash flows and underlying asset valuations. The resultant combination of insufficient cash flows to cover debt service obligations and (in many cases) operations, and asset valuations troughing at levels which are at, or below, the value of outstanding debt has resulted in cyclical financial distress across the sector over the past ten years and has prompted a number of restructurings.

As is the case in most restructurings, when a company faces financial difficulties achieving a successful outcome generally requires:

- a stable platform to allow for productive discussions amongst stakeholders; and
- consensus amongst stakeholder groups to address seemingly conflicting objectives and perspectives – particularly as they relate to the fundamental restructuring building blocks of business plan, valuation and debt capacity.

However, in maritime restructurings, the potential for divergent views and objectives is often magnified by the complexity of companies' financing structures, the varying quality of underlying collateral and the diverse composition of stakeholder groups.

In light of these complexities, successful maritime restructurings, in line with many other restructurings, have generally required a principles-based approach that seeks to incorporate the following key tenets into the underlying framework of a transaction:

- The framework must be viewed by all stakeholders as equitable and objective.
- The framework must respect underlying collateral positions and expected recoveries.
- In many instances, the framework will provide a menu of available options (even for similarly situated stakeholders) to manage divergent views and interests and to increase support.
- The framework will often make use of contractual and/or jurisdictional mechanisms to bind (minority) dissenting creditors, cram down stakeholders, and/or forge consensus.

In this chapter, we will examine in more detail:

- the market dynamics that have led to cyclical financial challenges in the maritime sector;
- the issues that arise in assessing and developing the building blocks of restructuring discussions;
- the complexity resulting from maritime companies' financing/stakeholder structures; and finally
- the tried and tested framework for successful financial restructurings in the sector.

2. Market dynamics

While there are numerous subsectors within the maritime industry, each with a subset of its own underlying operational and financial drivers, there are nonetheless a number of overarching similarities which have directly or indirectly impacted the wider industry's susceptibility to cyclicality and to the recurring financial challenges that have come with it:

- Their assets are usually mobile (allowing supply to physically move to where demand is located).
- Their fleets can comprise any number of individual assets and/or asset types.
- The evolution of their fleet composition is largely a function of market dynamics, the desire to remain competitive and technological advances.
- They have high operational gearing and the key drivers of their profitability are generally revenue-related (ie, freight rates, charter rates and/or utilisation rates, often embodied in medium- to long-term contracts which may incorporate rates above current market).

The combined implication of these factors has been that, historically, when demand has exceeded supply and revenues have been high, maritime companies have sought to capitalise on their (newfound) underlying profitability and to grow and/or modernise their fleets expeditiously. The pace of such growth has been hastened by the availability of relatively inexpensive asset-level (LTV-based) financing, which in turn has allowed maritime companies to expand their fleets quickly during boom times without regard to the underlying quality of, or implications for, the remainder of the company's fleet (or the global fleet more generally).

While such growth/modernisation would be prudent in the context of steadily increasing demand, the fact is that demand for maritime services is anything but steady. In fact, drivers of demand across the sector are inherently unpredictable, uncontrollable and volatile as they are linked primarily to

- global and regional GDP growth rates;
- geopolitical trends (global trade agreements, sanctions, OPEC production targets, taxation, etc); and/or
- changing trading patterns driven by inventory levels, changes in production capabilities, shifts in consumption behaviour and changes in infrastructure (port expansion, expansion of the Panama Canal, etc).

This resultant combination of rapid fleet growth and volatile/unpredictable demand patterns has proven time and again to lead to market distress, and has created cyclical supply/demand imbalances which have often led to financial challenges across the industry.

3. Restructuring building blocks

The complex industry dynamics that are a feature of the maritime sector introduce significant complications in agreeing and structuring a transaction to resolve a company's financial difficulties. Specifically, given the potential for a high degree of uncertainty and/or divergent views surrounding future supply and demand dynamics, achieving consensus amongst stakeholders as to the fundamental building blocks of a restructuring transaction – business plan, valuation and debt capacity – can prove exceptionally challenging.

3.1 Business plan

At the heart of any financial restructuring is the company's business plan, which provides management's best estimates of the projected financial performance and cash flow trajectory of its operations, and which is based on a number of underlying drivers and operating assumptions. The business plan, to the extent it is credible, informs stakeholders' perceptions and views on potential opportunities and the fundamental requirements of a successful restructuring. In particular, the business plan provides the basis for discussions and negotiations regarding:

- the extent to which new money may be required;
- the valuation of the enterprise (and in some cases, individual assets); and/or
- the potential debt capacity of the business post-restructuring.

In less cyclical industries, in which the medium- to long-term trajectory of a company's operations is less volatile, preparation of a business plan is often non-contentious, as the views held by management and stakeholders on future performance are more easily aligned. However, in the maritime sector, where uncertain supply and demand dynamics are commonplace, the development of an objectively defensible set of business plan assumptions can prove difficult.

For that reason, when developing a business plan it is prudent for maritime companies to seek independent views from industry experts and other experienced market participants. Their views often facilitate a more informed dialogue between the company and its various stakeholder groups, as in many cases they are perceived to be more objective and less likely to be biased towards a specific outcome or business trajectory.

Nonetheless, as part of restructuring discussions, and even when a business plan is robust and defensible, the risk of a significant divergence of opinion amongst the company's stakeholder groups can remain. The potential for divergence amongst a maritime company's stakeholders is often further exacerbated by the implications of the company's business plan for its valuation and debt capacity and by the associated impact on specific stakeholders' expected long-term recoveries.

3.2 Valuation and debt capacity

In a restructuring context, valuation and debt capacity are critical components for determining and assessing:

- stakeholders' economic interests and/or expected recoveries; and
- long-term capital structure requirements.

An understanding of each allows for discussion and negotiation surrounding the potential treatment of various stakeholders' claims as part of a restructuring, and often dictates the need for (and terms of) any potential impairment of creditors' claims and shareholders' interests. Given that successful restructuring transactions require support from a majority (if not all) of a company's stakeholders, it is important that such treatment be viewed as equitable and, in turn, that underlying valuation and debt capacity work be conducted in an objective and transparent manner, supported by a sufficient majority of stakeholders.

Because maritime companies generally finance their assets with a combination of secured LTV-based debt (often including parent guarantees), asset-level leases and/or unsecured debt at the parent (see the section on structural complexities below); and because restructuring dynamics are heavily impacted by collateral coverage and expected recoveries of each specific creditor group, valuation in a restructuring context generally involves a combination of both asset-level/sum-of-the-parts valuation analysis and group-level valuation analysis. In practice, this has generally meant conducting valuation work through one or a combination of the methods in the following table:

Table 1: Valuation in a restructuring context

Valuation type		**Summary**
Asset/vessel level (sum-of-the-parts)	Broker appraisals	• Fair market value of assets, as appraised by reputable brokers • Generally based on recent asset sales (when available) and/or informed by broker estimates of the wider market trajectory • Incorporates age of assets and useful life
	Business plan valuation	• Asset-level bottom-up valuation • Generally based on business plan's asset-level earnings and/or cash flow projections • Common methodologies include discounted cash flow (DCF), comparable company and/or comparable transaction approaches
Group level		• Includes 'platform' value • Generally based on business plan's consolidated earnings and/or cash flow projections • Common methodologies include DCF, comparable company and/or comparable transaction approaches

The combination of these and other approaches allows each stakeholder group to assess its likely recoveries on account of both secured (asset-level) and unsecured (parent-level) claims and, in theory, facilitates constructive dialogue amongst stakeholders. However, the potential for varied results and the fact that stakeholders' views and objectives in a restructuring (ie, whether to extend debt, take ownership of assets or some other outcome) are often informed by their own underlying collateral package and/or their position in the corporate structure, creates further complexity in the restructuring of maritime companies.

For example, in a situation where the business plan valuation of assets exceeds that of broker appraisals on a sum-of-the-parts basis, and the group-level valuation exceeds the sum-of-the-parts analysis, assessing the platform value of the parent entity and its subsidiaries may be contentious among creditors. In such a scenario, and based on the (simplistic) assumption that the value of a maritime company is equal to the sum of its asset-level value and the platform value itself, the views of creditors may well be influenced by their relative positions in the capital structure. Those creditors who have a secured interest in the company's assets may contend that the higher business plan asset valuation has most merit (as this will minimise the imputed valuation of the parent/platform itself) and those creditors whose claims rely primarily on the value of the parent for recovery may adopt the opposite position.

Herein lies a further difficulty of maritime restructurings – namely, that the structural complexities of the industry, and specifically stakeholders' relative positions in the capital structure, can have wide implications for stakeholders' views as to the most appropriate valuation and debt capacity methodologies (and even the underlying business plan supporting such analyses).

4. Structural complexities and intercreditor considerations

Given the nature of the industry, and in particular the underlying market dynamics of the sector, maritime companies have historically financed and grown their fleets across time and at the asset level. In practice, this has meant that the corporate structures of companies active in the space have evolved to become quite complex and generally include the following:

- a complex financing structure based on a combination of individually financed collateral 'silos' and/or parent financing;
- disparate quality and value of underlying assets (sometimes with a significant gap between the best and worst assets);
- varied financing models (eg, bank debt, institutional term loans, bonds, alternative capital and preferred stock – with both primary and secondary holders);
- complex cash pooling/cash management arrangements; and

- separate management entities that operate the company's assets and which are often the counterparty to customer contracts and relationships.

These structural complexities bring with them a host of challenges in aligning the interests of stakeholders in restructuring discussions.

4.1 Collateral structure

Historically, as maritime companies have expanded their fleets, they have done so through the bolt-on of additional vessels using vessel-owning special purpose vehicles (SPVs) beneath an existing parent entity. This growth has generally been funded through the procurement of new secured financing at the asset/subsidiary level, with such debt benefiting from both a secured interest at the vessel-owning SPV level (mortgages, share pledges, assignments of earnings, etc) and an unsecured interest at the parent level (generally a guarantee). When credit markets have proven to be particularly robust, maritime companies have in some cases further augmented their financing structures by the issuance of additional unsecured debt or preference stock at the parent level.

As a result, maritime companies' corporate structures have generally evolved to include a web of vessel-owning SPVs (each with its own separate financing) sitting below a parent entity which, in its own right, may act as a guarantor under the SPV financings and/or have acquired additional debt. In essence, such companies have become a collection of individual assets (or groups of assets) operating under a corporate brand or umbrella.

This fact has far-reaching consequences in the context of maritime restructuring discussions. Specifically, the underlying corporate structures mean that maritime companies can be easily dismantled, with each secured creditor group maintaining the ability to take control of its collateral through a relatively straightforward enforcement process which may not directly impact the remainder of the company's assets (barring the potential implications of parent guarantees and/or potential cross-defaults). Therefore, as part of restructuring negotiations, each creditor group will generally weigh the relative pros and cons (from a recovery perspective) of either taking ownership of its collateral or facilitating a going-concern restructuring – bringing into sharp focus the perceived value of the parent and/or platform, and often begging the question whether or not there is incremental value in keeping the group together.

4.2 Disparate quality of assets

The answer to the question of whether keeping the group together is a value-maximising strategy is not a simple one – and it is further complicated by two factors:

- maritime companies often comprise a heterogeneous fleet of vessels of varying age, quality and value; and
- each creditor group, by virtue of the nature of its collateral (or lack thereof), may ultimately weigh the attractiveness of available restructuring outcomes differently.

Those creditors who benefit from a combination of easily marketable collateral and/or relatively robust collateral coverage may be inclined to crystallise the associated value expeditiously – foregoing potential long-term value appreciation – to avoid any downside risks associated with a prolonged restructuring. Conversely, those creditors with less marketable collateral and/or inadequate coverage may be more disposed to preserve the going-concern status of the corporate in the hope of a long-term market turnaround, the improvement or retention of value associated with the corporate guarantee, and the potential to improve their recoveries over time.

The possibility of such divergent stakeholder interests is at the forefront of any maritime restructuring and needs to be carefully managed and addressed through an objective and equitable transaction framework (see section 5 below).

4.3 Types of financing/stakeholders

Compounding the potential for divergent stakeholder views is the fact that the nature of maritime financing has changed in recent years, bringing new types of stakeholders. While historically maritime companies have relied primarily on relatively inexpensive bank debt to finance growth, the increasing prevalence of institutional term loans, high-yield bonds and alternative capital has crept into the maritime space. Despite the commercial benefits of pursuing varied financing options, the introduction of a new group of creditors has also brought with it disparate stakeholder perspectives and objectives which have informed the nature of restructuring discussions in recent years, as illustrated by Table 2.

Varied perspectives of a company's stakeholders can create significant challenges in reaching broad consensus for a restructuring transaction, and an understanding of the diverse composition of a company's creditor groups is therefore critical when developing and assessing available restructuring options and arriving at a consensus (see section 5 below).

Table 2: Financing perspectives

Institution	Financing type	Restructuring perspectives/objectives
Banks	Bank debt	• Low cost of capital and return requirements • Aims to maximise face value of debt post-restructuring, frequently at least in line with collateral value • Less receptive to debt impairment; more disposed towards amend & extend transactions
Investment funds and CLOs	Institutional term loans and high-yield bonds	• Mark-to-market across time • More inclined to trade in and out of securities • Behaviour driven, in large part, by trading prices at the time of deal discussions
Hedge funds	Trading/ alternative capital	• Generally purchase debt at a discount to par • Inclined to maximise economic returns • Receptive to and sometimes prefer equitisation (even when holding secured debt) and/or alternate return-maximising structures including asset ownership

4.4 Intercompany cash management

A maritime company's cash management practices can have far-reaching ramifications for stakeholders' expected recoveries and, in turn, for developing an equitable restructuring transaction (ie, one that respects the underlying collateral positions of creditors).

Because many maritime companies have grown through the amalgamation of additional vessel-owning SPVs beneath a parent entity, the way in which cash is moved around the corporate structure is critical to ensuring that each entity remains adequately capitalised. At times, funds can flow on the basis of dividends and/or equity contributions. However, in practice, central cash management procedures are generally put in place that rely on a complex web of intercompany loans (whether formal or simply by virtue of book entries) to move cash freely throughout the group.

The relative positioning of these intercompany loans at each entity (quantum, payable or receivable, ranking, etc) can have significant implications for the allocation of value across a maritime company, and consequently can significantly impact expected recoveries of various creditor groups when financial challenges begin to mount. It is therefore of paramount importance to appropriately assess a company's cash management practices and – where possible – to conduct a full analysis of intercompany loans and their relative size and ranking.

4.5 Management company

A further complication in maritime restructuring transactions is the fact that a maritime company's operating assets are often managed by a separate company, which may sit within or outside the corporate structure.

Such a management company may be perceived to be of critical importance to the underlying operations of the business and/or the value of the company. Many maritime companies derive significant value from the cash flow associated with existing customer contracts and relationships – which may provide long-term revenue opportunities at rates above the current market level. A full understanding of how these dynamics, the implications for expected stakeholder recoveries, and the risks that may be associated with potential change of control provisions are embedded in customer agreements with the management company, is critical to the development and implementation of a balanced and objective restructuring transaction.

5. Putting it all together – the restructuring framework

In light of the aforementioned complexities, successful restructurings in the maritime sector have generally relied upon a principles-based approach which seeks to ensure an objective, transparent and equitable framework designed to balance the (potentially) competing objectives of all stakeholders.

A tried and tested approach has evolved over time and generally involves a series of steps designed to

- ensure an objective and equitable process;
- align stakeholder interests; and
- achieve broad consensus as the basis for a restructuring transaction.

The steps are as follows:

1. Stabilisation of the platform
2. Development of a credible business plan
3. Preparation of an objective valuation and debt capacity analysis
4. Detailed review of stakeholder objectives and perspectives

5. Development of a preliminary (equitable) transaction framework
6. Utilisation of consensus-building tools and tactics to maximise support and facilitate implementation

5.1 Stabilisation of the platform

A priority in maritime restructurings is to provide adequate time and financial stability to develop and agree a transaction framework amongst the company's stakeholders. While this is true of all restructurings, it is of particular importance in the maritime sector given that – upon an event of default – secured creditors have the ability to seize assets (ie, vessels) and can dismantle the company. Stability can be achieved in myriad ways, though the most common approach is to seek a standstill arrangement (either consensually or through a mechanism like the automatic stay in US Chapter 11) which provides a window of time for the company and its stakeholders to negotiate and evaluate various restructuring alternatives without the threat of enforcement or vessel seizure.

5.2 Credible business plan

It is imperative as part of a maritime restructuring that the company's management team take the time that is required to develop a credible business plan, ideally in advance of restructuring negotiations.

The plan will necessarily be based on underlying views and assumptions regarding evolving market dynamics which can be difficult to predict given the uncertain supply and demand patterns typical of the sector. For this reason, and to ensure that the business plan is viewed by all stakeholders as sufficiently robust and defensible, it is common practice (and advisable) for management teams to solicit independent third party views on the trajectory of the industry, which can then inform the underlying assumptions and drivers of the plan.

5.3 Objective valuation and debt capacity

Given the unique financing structures of maritime companies discussed above, and because restructuring discussions are generally driven by stakeholders' underlying economic interests and expected long-term recoveries, asset-level and group-level valuation and debt capacity analyses are key to any transaction negotiations.

Companies, then, should approach negotiations with stakeholders equipped with an objective valuation methodology which

- relies upon both the aforementioned credible business plan and independent broker estimates; and
- assesses both asset-level/sum-of-the-parts valuation analysis and group-level valuation analysis.

Adopting such an approach

- enhances the transparency of transaction discussions;
- facilitates stakeholders' review of possible recoveries;
- informs stakeholder perspectives as they approach deal negotiations; and
- increases the likelihood of achieving a transaction structure that balances the objectives of all stakeholders.

5.4 Stakeholder perspectives

Armed with these building blocks of a maritime restructuring, it is essential that a company and its stakeholders engage in active discussions with one another to better understand the potentially divergent interests of all parties.

It is advisable for a company to present its work directly to all stakeholders in the first instance – either individually or as a group – and then to develop a process in which varied opinions can be expressed openly amongst all parties. During this process, and to facilitate subsequent deal negotiations, it is imperative that all stakeholders gain an understanding of the views, perspectives and ultimate objectives of all parties. This can only be achieved through assiduous analysis and frequent dialogue. Of particular importance at this stage is an understanding of the relative collateral positions (where relevant) and the rights and remedies of each stakeholder and/or stakeholder group, and of the relative attractiveness of their exercise of these rights and remedies compared to a potential consensual transaction.

The views and perspectives of stakeholders can have significant implications for the progress of deal negotiations, and for the structure of any supportable transaction framework.

5.5 Equitable transaction framework

Companies should develop a restructuring framework that

- respects underlying collateral positions as well as expected recoveries; and
- equitably allocates deal consideration (and value) on that basis.

Where possible, such a transaction structure should take account of the potentially divergent views of all stakeholders which can result not just from stakeholders' underlying recovery expectations, but also from the heterogeneity of institutional types which is prevalent in the sector.

5.6 Consensus-building tools & tactics

Achieving consensus in a maritime restructuring can prove exceptionally challenging and often requires creative deal structuring designed to

- bridge stakeholders' potentially competing objectives; and

- incorporate binding mechanisms designed to limit the risk of holdouts and build consensus towards an agreement.

(a) *Bridging objectives – the menu approach*

Maritime restructurings have increasingly made use of a menu approach designed to increase support for a transaction. Similarly situated stakeholders are generally provided with a suite of two or more options from which they can choose – all of which can be perceived as equitable and all of which are developed to address specific differences in the underlying objectives of key stakeholders.

Table 3 illustrates the effectiveness of such an approach by using a (hypothetical) company with a single secured loan of $100 million, two underlying creditors and no other stakeholders in interest:

Table 3: Perspectives of similarly situated stakeholders

	Holder 1	**Holder 2**
Amount of loan	$50 million	$50 million
Institution	Bank	Hedge fund
Key objective of the restructuring	Maximise residual debt on balance sheet	Maximise economic return, regardless of 'form'
View on sustainable debt capacity	$50 million	$50 million
View on current value of collateral + platform	$75 million	$75 million
View on future value of collateral + platform	$75 million	>$100 million

In such a circumstance, aligning the interests of the two parties may prove challenging given asymmetric goals and expectations as they relate to both the key objectives of the restructuring and the perceived future value of the company. Offering the parties an identical deal is unlikely to address their divergent expectations, and achieving the support of more than one of the holders will therefore be unlikely. However, by offering each party a different form of consideration (but nonetheless on an equitable basis) it may be possible to bridge competing objectives in a manner that garners sufficient support.

Taking this example further, and starting with commonality of views, each party would agree that its baseline expected recovery is $75 million (being the current value of the collateral and platform) and that not more than $50 million of debt should remain on balance sheet (being the sustainable debt capacity of the company). Neither party is therefore likely to support a transaction if it results in a recovery which is less than 75 cents on the dollar, and neither party is likely to support a deal that includes in excess of $50 million of residual debt.

Because Holder 1's key objective is to maximise its residual debt on balance sheet, and because it believes that the future value of the company is unlikely to exceed $75 million, it will likely be inclined to support only a transaction that either monetises the value today (ie, through a sale of the company) or that reinstates 75 cents of debt as part of the deal (the latter not being possible given views on sustainable debt capacity). Holder 2, on the other hand, may approach discussions differently as – given its own incentive to maximise economic return as well as its view that significant upside value exists – it will likely want (and value) the retention of its interest in the company and the equity upside that such an opportunity presents.

While these divergent objectives may appear irreconcilable at first glance, the use of a simple menu approach may facilitate a transaction – for example, by offering debt/equity to each party as follows:

Table 4: The menu approach

	Holder 1	Holder 2
New debt	$50 million	–
Equity (%)	–	100%[1]
(Perceived) equity value	–	$50+ million

Such a structure would allow each party to achieve its underlying objectives; it would offer a recovery that is preferable to the no-deal alternative; and, ultimately, it would allow unanimous support to be achieved despite seemingly contradictory deal objectives and expectations.

1 In practice, it is likely that a portion of the equity would need to be reserved for a management incentive plan and/or existing shareholders.

While this example is simplistic, similar logic can be applied to far more complex situations and developed to include other forms of consideration. It has been used to great effect in maritime restructurings to allocate combinations of cash, debt, equity and/or other consideration to similarly situated creditors, and possibly some form of equity to existing shareholders – in varying proportions designed to address stakeholders' expectations and maximise support towards an agreeable transaction.

(b) Limiting holdouts – developing binding mechanisms

Because a restructuring requires the unanimous support of all stakeholders to be implemented outside of a courtroom, the risk of holdouts remains high and can increase the challenges associated with achieving an implementable transaction. While the use of a menu approach can often alleviate this tension and further align stakeholders' interests, it is sometimes insufficient to achieve the support of all parties. To avoid the risk that a dissenting minority can thwart progress towards a deal that is supported by an overwhelming majority, maritime restructurings have made use of creative binding mechanisms that provide a path towards implementation even if unanimity is ultimately not achievable. These include:

- contractual binding mechanisms, where voting provisions within existing debt documentation are utilised; and
- judicial binding mechanisms, where local or international court processes are used to 'drag' minority stakeholder groups into a transaction and/or to 'cram' stakeholders vertically.

Given the international nature of the maritime sector, the latter has proven particularly effective as companies can typically make use of court processes in numerous jurisdictions. For example, a company with a parent entity in the Cayman Islands and subsidiaries in, say, the US, UK and Singapore (a situation not uncommon in the maritime sector) may be in a position to 'forum shop' – that is, to avail itself of court procedures in one or more of these jurisdictions (eg, a UK scheme of arrangement or a US Chapter 11).

Being aware of the different regimes available, and understanding the potential implications of each, can significantly increase the likelihood of a achieving a consensual outcome, as the risk of holdouts is mitigated.

6. Conclusion

While the restructuring of maritime companies – whether as advisers, investors, or otherwise – is not for the faint of heart, those who understand the underlying market and stakeholder dynamics of the sector and its numerous subsectors will undoubtedly find attractive restructuring opportunities in which to participate in the future. To quote Sun Tzu, "In the midst of chaos, there is also opportunity."

Retail restructurings

Mark Firmin
Richard Fleming
Vanessa Rudder
Alvarez & Marsal

---

1. Introduction

Is the UK retail sector in crisis?

The simple answer is yes. The increasing number of challenges facing the UK retail sector were of particular interest to restructuring professionals, government and key industry stakeholders during 2018. Profit warnings, store closures and insolvencies of some big-name retailers have been flooding the newspapers.

In fact, the Insolvency Service, which publishes statistics on company insolvencies across the UK, has cited retail as one of the key industries with the largest rise in insolvencies. In the 12 months ending Q3 2017, the sector had 2,144 new company insolvencies, an increase of 2.2%. This trend has continued into Q1 2018, with retail remaining in the top three sectors for new company insolvencies.

The Centre for Retail Research released statistics in June 2018 further substantiating this trend, with retail insolvencies increasing consistently over the last three years and the 2018 outlook suggesting more of the same.

Table 1: Retail insolvencies

Period	Companies failing	Stores affected	Employees affected
2018 (6 months)	23	1,851	20,891
2017 (12 months)	44	1,383	12,225
2016 (12 months)	30	1,504	26,110
2015 (12 months)	25	728	6,845

Source: Centre for Retail Research, Who's Gone Bust in Retailing 2010–18. Available at: www.retailresearch.org/whosegonebust.php.

Given this trend, the key questions are as follows:

- What is driving the challenges?
- How can businesses best respond when things go wrong?
- Who are the winners and losers?

2. What is causing the crisis?

Whilst the UK retail sector appears to be suffering more recently compared to previous years, not all the challenges are new. There are some fundamental sector dynamics which leave the industry vulnerable to stress, and these have existed for decades. However, whilst many of them are well known, not all are easy to defend against, and those that are capable of being defended against have sometimes been ignored, with some retailers being in denial for decades.

2.1 Issues impacting sales

(a) Mature market and declining consumer spend/confidence

Many businesses enter the mature phase of their industry lifecycle with no real defensive strategy and therefore find themselves quickly slipping down the demise curve when new challenges materialise. Retail businesses are no different. The UK bricks and mortar retail sector is in the mature phase of its lifecycle and operates in an increasingly competitive environment; as such, retailers need to be able to adapt their product offering and shopping experience based on quickly moving consumer demands.

Operating in a mature phase isn't all bad if consumer spending and confidence remain stable. However, the OECD predicts that the UK's Gross Domestic Product (GDP) growth rate will continue to slow, going from 1.8% in 2017 down to 1.4% in 2019 (see https://data.oecd.org/gdp/real-gdp-forecast.htm#indicator-chart). Given GDP is a good indicator of consumer spend, when GDP declines it is fair to deduce that stress on the retail market will increase. Couple this with declining consumer confidence (clearly being impacted by Brexit, rising rates, employee costs and even the aftermath of the global financial crisis), and it can be seen that retailers have had a lot to contend with.

The question is, has there been a tangible impact on retailers? Many retailers, including House of Fraser, have cited an overall reduction in consumer spend and lower consumer confidence as issues affecting their businesses. In 2017, who would have thought that John Lewis would be posting break-even results?

Challenges such as aggressive competition are not new. For example, competition was a key contributing factor in the insolvency of Threshers, the UK's largest off-licence retailer, over which Richard Fleming and colleagues were appointed administrators back in 2009. Part of the demise of Threshers was attributed to a poorly managed business but it was also down to strong competition from supermarkets. Whilst big supermarkets may not have intentionally targeted Threshers, offering beer and wine at heavy discounts as a loss leader to drive increased footfall had the effect of stealing customers from Threshers and leaving it unable to compete profitably, the net result being the closure of around 1,300 stores and the loss of around 6,500 jobs.

(b) ***Increasing pace of consumer change***

A key feature of success in the retail market is the ability to respond quickly to consumer trends. However, with a fickle customer base, which changes its needs and wants at speed, the retailers who thrive are those who able to react to these trends as quickly as they appear. Recently have we seen examples of big retailers admitting their product offering is wrong; for example, M&S's fashion lines have been struggling season after season (arguably due to a lack of understanding of their customer demographic) and have, in the last quarter, put a number of their fashion lines under review (eg, Per Una). Other less recent examples include Austin Reed, which went into insolvency in 2016, and Jane Norman (2014) which both had clothing lines that were neither high-end/luxury nor low end/discount products – they failed to effectively identify their target market and respond to a shift away from middle-market ranges. By contrast, businesses like Zara, which have been able to adapt to trends and offer a seamless multi-channel experience at the right price, have performed better.

(c) ***Online shopping***

The fickle nature of consumers is not limited to fashion trends and crazes, but also the way in which they shop and the type of experience they demand. There has been much commentary on the shift towards online shopping, with the likes of Amazon, ASOS, Boohoo, Net-A-Porter, AO.com and others reaping the rewards. Many bricks and mortar stores have succumbed to complacency, relying too much on the traditional in-store shopping approach rather than investing in their online proposition.

Analysis released by the Office of National Statistics highlights the increasing importance of internet sales. As a percentage of the total, internet retail sales have quadrupled over the last decade, from around 4% in May 2008 to around 17% in May 2018 (see www.ons.gov.uk/businessindustryandtrade/retailindustry/timeseries/j4mc/drsi). With online sales coming at the expense of in-store sales, retailers need to invest in their online strategy and potentially reconsider their often 'over-rented' store footprint to remain competitive.

The rise in popularity of online shopping is primarily driven by consumers' demand for convenience. Consumers want to be able to make purchases or compare products and prices from their lounge, or from their mobile devices while on the go. This trend in convenience shopping stretches to speed of product delivery, with customers demanding next day (or in some cases same day) delivery. If retailers don't have the right mix of online shopping and an efficient distribution network, they will invariably lose customers to retailers who do.

The UK Toys "R" Us restructuring was a prime example of where the move to online was too little, too late, especially in the toys category, where up to 50% of sales are made online. Trying to compete with the likes of Amazon Prime, whose entire business model revolves around online selling supported by excellent logistics, means a competitor's online offering needs to be as dynamic, price-competitive, efficient and easy to use in order to be credible. Simply having an online offering is no longer enough. Trying to move away from a bricks and mortar, towards an online model has left some retailers discovering they lack the skill-set required to drive online sales. Staples, which closed 106 UK stores in 2016, was a retail failure which cited online competition as a critical factor affecting its sales and ultimately its solvency.

(d) In-store experience

It is not just the shift to online purchasing that has troubled retailers in recent years. The customer's preference for an in-store experience – so-called 'destination shopping' – has also become increasingly important in shaping efforts to attract and retain consumers. Again, Toys "R" Us is an example of having missed the boat. Its lack of an in-store experience, where families could interact and play with the product, left it vulnerable to competitors, in contrast to the likes of Lego, which sees families head to strategic flagship stores to experience (and not just purchase) its offering. Consumers have changed in the way they want to shop. Other examples include Lululemon, which offers in-store yoga classes; IKEA, which hosts dinner parties to showcase its kitchen ranges; Selfridges and Harrods, who host huge store-wide events to drive footfall; and Tesco, which has introduced the upmarket coffee shop Harris & Hoole.

This desire for an experience, rather than just products, is further reinforced by recent trends which have seen younger buyers choosing to spend an increased proportion of their disposable income on leisure activities and experiences rather than just traditional retail products. With retailers now having to compete with leisure providers for discretionary spend, the destination shopping and convenience offerings are of increasing strategic importance for retailers.

2.2 Issues impacting cost base

Whilst retailers have desperately been trying to maintain top line sales, they have also been hit with some significant cost pressures.

(a) Increasing rent and large store portfolios

Unsurprisingly, one of the biggest issues facing bricks and mortar retailers is rental cost and the increasing number of unprofitable stores in their portfolios. Many mature retailers will have legacy store leases on long-term tenures with upward-only rent reviews linked to the retail price index (RPI) as standard. As such, in the current environment of declining sales density and contractual rent on longer-term leases often significantly above market rent levels, it doesn't take long for these factors to shine a light on loss-making stores.

Having such a rigid rent structure has clearly been working in landlords' favour as they have, for years, been capitalising on rising RPI and built-in downside protection against shifts in market rent. However, it cannot come as a surprise to anyone, including landlords, that this structure will not continue indefinitely. Given the trajectory of the UK's declining consumer spend and confidence, it is very surprising that many landlords do not have access to retailers' store-by-store trading data. The UK is an outlier in this regard compared to continental Europe.

Even the commercial real estate consultancy firm Colliers has called for reform on leases in response to the sector's structural challenges, suggesting leases be reduced to a standard five years (down from c. 25+ years), and rents based purely on turnover in each store. A move to rent based on turnover is not a novel idea, with many leases in continental Europe already following this structure; and although change is occurring slowly, the increasing popularity of the landlord CVA (discussed below) as a means to compromise lease obligations, may be the catalyst required to bring about a fundamental, but necessary, change in lease structures in the UK.

(b) Rising business rates

Business rates are also putting significant pressure on retail profitability.

Business rates are charged by the government on all shops, offices, warehouses and factories and are linked to both the value of a property and inflation. Like rent, business rates are not new, but have become an increasingly large proportion of retailers' cost base, and despite substantial lobbying (in particular from the British Retail Consortium), the government has continued to increase business rates. To give some idea of scale, some commentators have suggested that the April 2017 rates rise will cost UK businesses an additional £1 billion per annum, around £270 million of which is likely to be borne by retailers.

Whilst the level of rent gets a lot of media air time, major retailers such as Tesco, whose CEO has said business rates are the biggest tax his company pays, at £700 million a year, are also highlighting business rates as a major issue contributing to stress in the sector. We have seen many retail stores where the rates bill is as high as the rent bill. Whilst continued lobbying may yield some relief, business rates are likely to continue to put pressure on margins and potentially push retailers to take a more focused look at contracting their physical store portfolio in an attempt to mitigate these ever-increasing costs.

(c) ***Brexit***

Many people have pointed fingers at the potential pitfalls of Brexit, but the negative effects are becoming all too real. In early 2018, the CEO of the failed electronics retailer Maplin cited a weak pound due to Brexit as a cause of its demise. Maplin's CEO is not alone; Poundworld (which also went into insolvency in 2018) quoted its lack of buying power resulting from a declining pound as a cause of its failure.

Whilst we still don't have a clear picture of what life will be like post-Brexit, there is little doubt that Brexit is having, and will continue to have, a negative impact on the ability of UK businesses to recruit enough living wage unskilled labour. For retail, think not just shops but also warehouses and distribution networks. Secondary school economics lessons tell us that a shortage of labour can only result in an increase in wages and the cost of doing business.

3. What is the best insolvency process? It depends who you ask ...

3.1 Administration

Over the 30 years up to and including the global financial crisis, a UK administration was the go-to process for retail restructurings; then the company voluntary arrangement (CVA) debuted in 2009 with JJB Plc and Blacks Leisure Plc.

An administration allows for the sale of the business (in its current or a reduced form) to another party, or it can facilitate a wind-down of operations. Particularly in the latter scenario, there are only a few winners and the landlords and unsecured creditors are rarely among them.

From the perspective of insolvency practitioners (IPs), a trading administration will almost always result in higher fees compared to a CVA (or a pre-pack administration) due to the level of skilled resource required to facilitate the sale/closure of the business to realise value. Nevertheless, for a number of reasons stakeholders have historically preferred administration to CVA:

- Lenders have generally had a better understanding of the administration process.
- There was an element of certainty in recoveries when closing down businesses and liquidating assets via a pre-packaged sale.
- Lenders were reluctant to risk launching a CVA (which is a public process and involves soliciting votes from all unsecured creditors, that is, employees) without having a high degree of certainty as to delivering a successful vote at the CVA meeting.

In addition, it could be argued that the restructuring profession as a whole added to the perceived uncertainty of outcome by its lack of experience with larger company CVAs. Whilst the CVA itself is governed by legislation, at its roots it is a commercial proposition.

Other parties preferring administrations were distressed investors and savvy retailers who were interested parties but outside the process. They saw administration as an opportunity to cherry pick assets for a bargain price. They knew that the administrator would be looking to sell assets quickly (whether the business as a whole or part of it), and that the alternative would often be a value-destructive fire sale of assets.

Whilst administrations and pre-pack sales have retained their popularity through the global financial crisis and beyond, the biggest challenge has always been extracting value. Asset values diminish significantly (stock is often only recovered at cost or below) as a result of the insolvency appointment, and an administrator does not have the power to compel landlords to enter into an agreement with the purchaser. Instead they can only give the purchaser a licence to occupy for a limited period while negotiations take place.

Another important consideration in choosing an administration over a CVA is the ability of management to remain *in situ*. On appointment, and contrary to a CVA, in an administration the day-to-day running of the business passes from management to the IP. If a sale is achieved, management may retain their positions post-transaction or, as is more often the case, the purchaser might have its own management team ready to drop in and the incumbent management may be terminated.

3.2 Company voluntary arrangement

Depending on your interest in the company, your views on administration versus CVA may differ considerably. However, there is no denying that the CVA is becoming an increasingly popular choice for retailers to restructure their store portfolio and use this as an anchor point to develop and execute the other essential ingredients of any turnaround plan, such as a revamped customer proposition, improved management team and additional financial backing.

When the 'retail' or 'landlord' CVA was introduced in 2009, many doubted it would succeed. Many stakeholders, and indeed some IPs, failed to fully appreciate the benefits a CVA could provide to a business where the turnaround was in part dependent on the need to shrink the geographical footprint. But with greater understanding of the process and the consequent rise in its popularity, many opinions have now been swayed, and for good reason.

(a) Benefits of a CVA

A CVA provides a mechanism which allows the business to be restructured by compromising certain unsecured creditors, whilst allowing the company to continue to trade and remain under the control of the existing management team. Leaving the business in the hands of management is not something that is available in an administration and as such, arguably results in less business disruption. Whether this shift in control is a good thing or a bad thing will depend on your views as to how the company came to be in distress in the first place.

A CVA is always a lower cost restructuring option than a trading administration. This is clearly beneficial for the company and financial stakeholders, including unsecured creditors, given they are in effect meeting those costs.

A CVA is also very flexible. A company can use it to compromise any class of unsecured creditors, meaning that some creditors can be paid in full, whilst others can be compromised.

Rent is one of the most onerous liabilities retailers have and for this reason in particular CVAs have become popular. A CVA allows the cost base (ie, rent) to be restructured, thereby potentially enhancing future earnings potential.

Use of a CVA to renegotiate or terminate onerous contracts and facilitate an accelerated, but orderly, property portfolio rationalisation strategy is tempting in the current environment. IPs are being approached more frequently by shareholders, management teams and lenders alike, all curious to understand if the CVA mechanism might be available to them.

However, the CVA white knight is not available to everyone. A CVA can only be proposed in circumstances where the alternative is likely to be another form of insolvency, typically administration. Accordingly, companies are unable to use it purely as a strategic tool to rationalise a large and expensive store portfolio if insolvency is not a real risk. This scenario is exactly what some commentators are implying certain retailers are doing, and is territory that every restructuring professional should take steps to avoid.

In reality, this use of a CVA as a strategic tool has not been in evidence. More often than not, retailers have simply been unable to grow their top line sales at the same rate as the increase in rent, and it doesn't take long for a large retail store portfolio to become unable to generate sufficient revenue to remain cash generative (after absorbing central and fixed costs).

In addition, given that rent reviews are often upwards only, at some point the rent costs will exceed the true market value of a lease, and among various recent CVAs on which Alvarez & Marsal has advised, the average portfolio has shown between 15% and 30% of its properties as over-rented. This is clearly not sustainable, and again, given the current challenging sales environment, without a restructuring of the property portfolio more retailers are likely to fall into insolvency.

Whilst onerous leases have been around for a long time, one of the first landlord CVAs was in 2008/9, for JJB Sports. JJB Sports was a listed UK sports retailer with significant cash flow issues (primarily due to rent on several non-trading retail stores) and was facing insolvency. In 2009, the directors proposed a CVA to compromise lease claims (both rent costs and contingent claims) on around 140 stores and to move rental obligations from quarterly to monthly.

No other unsecured creditors were compromised under the CVA. Whilst this was controversial at the time, at the CVA meeting the company's creditors (including landlords) voted overwhelmingly in favour.

Another important component of the JJB Sports CVA restructure was that the company retained its listing status and, more importantly, attracted new money from shareholders via a £100 million rights issue. This substantial cash injection, combined with a new management team and a revamped customer proposition, formed the basis of the turnaround plan. The ability to launch a rights issue and raise new equity alongside the CVA was truly ground-breaking at the time. The business ultimately failed, but the CVA was an extraordinary success in the circumstances, failure arguably having more to do with management's execution of the turnaround plan.

Even with the controversy that surrounded the JJB Sports landlord CVA (and similarly the Blacks Outdoor Retail CVA) over a decade ago, others have recently started to replicate the structure. The CVAs proposed by Carpetright Plc and Mothercare are each a case in point, the CVA being used to implement a store rationalisation programme in conjunction with a rights issue.

As the above examples make clear, CVA and rights issues are often inter-conditional. Without the rationalisation programme, the rights issue would not be attractive and without the capital injection from the rights issue, it is unlikely that the CVA alone would have generated sufficient savings to rescue the businesses.

(b) The size of the prize

A typical retail landlord compromise CVA is represented by the table on the follwoing page.

Developed properly (and as long as it sits alongside other necessary operational and financial restructuring) a CVA can:

- make a business more attractive to investors, increasing prospects of raising new money;
- provide a mechanism to return a business to profitability by rationalising the cost base;
- provide a platform for the wider turnaround;
- preserve value for both creditors and shareholders; and
- potentially avoid administration or liquidation.

Table 2: A typical landlord compromise CVA

Green rating (stores retained unaltered) Typically 25–50% of portfolio	**Amber rating (stores retained, rent reduced)** Typically 25–50% of portfolio	**Red rating (stores exited)** Typically 25–33% of portfolio
• Profitable leases where no compromise is required or proposed. • May include Amber stores that are strategic to the portfolio or are subject to cross guarantees. • Proposal: no compromise, except a move to monthly (as opposed to quarterly) rent payments.	• Marginally profitable or leases that only become profitable if a rent reduction can be achieved. • Proposal: rent reduction of 15–35% for the period of the CVA (typically 3+ years).	• Unprofitable stores that are not viable even if a rent reduction is achieved. • Proposal: lease termination after a planned wind-down period; rent reduction during the wind-down period typically 45–50%; dilapidations liability compromised.

(c) ***Negatives of a CVA***

Whilst a CVA has many benefits and is very flexible, it is not a cure-all. As mentioned, a standalone CVA may not solve all a business's problems. For example, whilst the rent burden can be addressed, if the business needs a more fundamental turnaround plan, even with a CVA it may not be sustainable. This was seen in the UK Toys "R" Us scenario, where even though the CVA was voted through and lease obligations were compromised, Christmas sales did not materialise as forecast, partly due to problems sourcing the latest stock items. As a result, the business was unable to generate sufficient operating profit to continue trading.

The other disadvantage is that, unlike an administration, the CVA process does not provide a moratorium from creditor action (save for small company CVAs). As such, there is a risk, particularly as the CVA is a very public process (all creditors are notified and required to vote) that certain creditors may take enforcement action. This risk, whilst real, can be managed. If the development of the CVA terms are appropriate and therefore compelling, and the CVA launch and communication plan is managed effectively, creditors should behave rationally and support the CVA (though of course there are always exceptions, some of which are discussed below).

Whilst there is no moratorium available to large companies launching a CVA, the government in 2016 proposed the introduction of a statutory pre-insolvency moratorium.[1] The aim of the moratorium would be to provide businesses with time to negotiate and develop proposals and seek creditor approval. If the moratorium becomes law, it will be interesting to see whether this protection entices more businesses to use a CVA as a rescue procedure.

(d) Who doesn't like CVAs?

Landlords: Given that landlords have been the main unsecured creditor class targeted by the recent wave of CVA proposals, their dislike is understandable. Whilst there may be some sympathy for landlords, there are various reasons why this sympathy has been qualified, including the following:

- A CVA can only pass if 75% by value of unsecured creditors who vote, vote in favour. This includes the landlords, who can choose to vote against. However, experience shows that the clear majority of compromised landlords vote in favour.
- If landlords feel the CVA is unjust, they can challenge it during the 28-day challenge period. In practce, however, if the CVA is drafted appropriately there are unlikely to be sustained challenges from landlords, particularly given that the alternative is administration.
- A typical CVA provides the landlords of sites being terminated with a notice period of a number of months during which rent is paid in full. This gives landlords a head start to find and secure a new tenant. This head start is not available in an administration.
- One of the reasons a company proposes a CVA in the first place is that it has cash flow issues due in part to paying over-market rent on sites. As such, landlords have potentially been collecting inflated rent on properties for years, during a time when other stakeholders may have suffered; for example, finance providers who have been asked to take haircuts.

This should not be interpreted as landlords having no bargaining power. The CVA has been around for over a decade, so landlords have arguably had plenty of time to coordinate and be represented during its currency and indeed before it is launched, in much the same way as have every other stakeholder group.

1 Company Voluntary Arrangements: Evaluating Success and Failure. Paper issued May 2018 by R3.

Was anyone surprised when House of Fraser finally launched a CVA? It had been coming for years. However, other than very public media campaigns, which criticise CVAs but provide limited alternative solutions, there has been minimal coordinated activity from the landlord community.

The British Property Federation (BPF) has recently started to voice concerns and has called on government to conduct a review of the CVA process on the basis that it is being misused by companies to drive through property restructurings. The concerns raised include:

- a lack of transparency;
- unfair discrimination between different creditors; and
- a lack of regulation to ensure CVAs are used appropriately and drive good practice.

The BPF has called for changes, including:

- implementing a process for CVAs similar to that of the administration pre-pack pool, where CVAs would be referred to an independent body for review;
- the insolvency profession and the BPF working together to codify good practice in terms of voting rights and voting structures for CVAs; and
- insolvency professionals following BPF best practice guidance on engagement with property owners as early as possible in the CVA process.

All that being said, it appears the that these actions may have been a little tardy, as we are starting to see examples of retailers looking to take advantage of the recent landlord CVA momentum by including CVA-related clauses in new lease agreements. For example, Next has started requesting clauses be included which effectively reduce rents to a level comparable to that of adjoining tenants who have implemented a successful CVA achieving rent reductions. The BPF has condemned Next, and how this plays out will depend on the leverage of each party – will landlords choose to find alternative tenants, and do retailers really need the store?

Pension trustees/the Pensions Regulator (TPR)/Pension Protection Fund (PPF): The other stakeholders becoming increasing important and influential are the pension creditors. The value of the pension claim (which is calculated based on the section 75 Pensions Act 1995 buy-out deficit) will often have a material influence on whether the CVA will reach the requisite voting thresholds. Therefore, early engagement with the pension creditors is critical. Recent experience – notably with Toys "R" Us – has shown that the pension trustee is a sophisticated creditor, often advised by restructuring professionals (unlike the landlord community), who will not take its CVA voting decision lightly.

The PPF is concerned about the implications of an increasing number of CVAs for defined benefit pension schemes and has released a guidance note.[2] The guidance suggests that the PPF assessment period will commence as soon as a CVA is proposed and the PPF will acquire the right to vote on the CVA (from the trustee). Importantly, the guidance also provides that the PPF will vote either in favour of or against the CVA, rather than simply abstaining. These points reaffirm the notion that the PPF will be an active participant in a CVA restructuring and should be consulted early to ensure its support.

There are also implications for the PPF in circumstances where the CVA ultimately fails and the company ends up in administration, thus exacerbating the problems of 'PPF drift' (a forecast increase in PPF exposure due to more members being above the national retirement age and therefore exempt from the PPF caps). In this area, we are seeing increasing activity from pension trustees and the PPF.

4. Conclusion

It is clear that the retail sector has suffered, and continues to suffer, from significant structural challenges that are edging poorly managed retailers closer to insolvency. However, with the increasing popularity and success of the CVA as a mechanism to restructure costs, and thereby attract new investment, all hope is not lost.

The question is, will landlords continue to be the main creditor targeted and impacted by retail CVAs? The answer will depend on how the dynamics continue to evolve. Retailers are becoming less dependent on landlords, given the recent sector shift towards online provision. As such, landlords may need to accept that the good years are behind them and find new ways of restructuring their own business models.

With support for CVAs now coming not only from companies but from IPs, lenders, funders and shareholders, we will likely see more landlord CVAs in the future.

Finally, it is a key point that landlords invariably achieve a better outcome in a CVA than they would in a liquidation.

---

2 Pension Protection Fund Restructuring & Insolvency Team, Guidance Note 4: Company Voluntary Arrangements, 1 June 2018. Available at: www.pensionprotectionfund.org.uk/DocumentLibrary/Documents/Pre%20pack%20guidance%20note%20revised%20June%2018.pdf.

France

Alexandra Bigot
Lionel Spizzichino
Willkie Farr & Gallagher LLP

---

1. Introduction

The French restructuring system is among the most efficient and mature in the European Union. The aim of the French system is to facilitate consensual restructurings. Recent statistics show a high success rate for out-of-court proceedings like *conciliation homologuée*, with over 75% of cases resolved in this way and insolvency proceedings initiated in less than 25% of cases.

France is considered an attractive jurisdiction for foreign distressed investors. A number of successful debt-to-equity swaps have been carried out over the years, from Autodistribution's purchase by Towerbrook in 2009 and SGD's purchase by Oaktree in 2010, to recent deals like the acquisitions of Vivarte by Oaktree, Goldentree, Alcentra and Babson; SAUR by BNPP, Natixis and Attestor Capital; Latécoère equity by Apollo and Monarch; and, of course, CGG, with US$1.95 billion of debt converted into equity.

France is also an attractive market for investors seeking opportunities from insolvency proceedings, which allow them to cherry pick assets and workforce. Significant transactions to date involving foreign investors or foreign trade buyers include the investment by Algerian Cevital in Fagor Brandt; OpenGate in Kem One; Lone Star in Coeur Défense; Peaked Hill Partners in Arc International; and, most recently, the Swiss company Schmolz + Bickenbach in Ascometal.

In the context of insolvency proceedings, a debtor-in-possession process has been in place for more than 30 years and French law favours the recovery of businesses in difficulty and the preservation of jobs. In 2017, recovery proceedings were favoured by 'significant' debtor companies (that is, companies with a turnover exceeding €51 million), with 63 reorganisation proceedings, compared to 15 safeguard proceedings and 14 judicial liquidations.

Law No. 2015-990, also known as the Macron Law (promulgated 12 March 2014 and 6 August 2015), created 18 specialised commercial courts with jurisdiction to handle restructuring and insolvency proceedings for large and medium-sized companies and as such develop a specific and professional expertise in dealing with complex cases.

The aim of the current chapter is to provide an overview of the legal framework for restructuring in France, and to offer practical guidance.

2. Out-of-court proceedings

Debtors facing economic difficulties may, under certain circumstances, request the commencement of out-of-court proceedings, either *mandat ad hoc* or conciliation proceedings, the aim of which is to conduct informal negotiations between the debtor's main creditors and stakeholders in order to reach an agreement; for example, to reduce or reschedule its indebtedness.

A mediator (*mandataire ad hoc* or *conciliateur*), who may be nominated by the debtor, is appointed by the president of the court at the request of the debtor. His or her mandate is determined by the debtor under the direction of the president of the court. The debtor's auditors must be notified of the order appointing the mediator. The debtor's works council or employees' representatives do not need to be notified.

Proceedings are voluntary, confidential and flexible. Statutory confidentiality obligations imposed on all stakeholders party to (or even aware of) such proceedings are key, providing valuable protection for the debtor's business by limiting both the potential loss of confidence of commercial counterparties and operational disruption, and ultimately preserving value for all stakeholders. In this amicable framework, management retains control of the business, no creditor can be forced into a restructuring agreement, and any agreement between the parties must be fully consensual.

The proceedings will not trigger any automatic moratorium on claims. However, it is common practice that creditors involved in a negotiation under the aegis of a mediator commit not to take any action against the debtor during the negotiations, resulting in a full standstill period in practice. In addition, any contractual provision adversely affecting the rights and/or obligations of the debtor as a direct consequence of requesting the opening of proceedings (eg, an event of default trigger) is deemed null and void. Any contractual provision requiring the debtor to bear more than three-quarters of the fees of the professional advisers retained by creditors in connection with these proceedings is also deemed null and void.

The mediator does not have coercive powers, but rather keeps the president of the court informed of progress through various reports. When an agreement is reached, the mediator is usually directed by the court, at the request of the debtor, to ensure and monitor the proper implementation of the agreement (*mandataire à l'exécution de l'accord*).

2.1 *Mandat ad hoc* proceedings

Mandat ad hoc proceedings are used by debtors facing any kind of difficulty, without being insolvent.

Under French law, a debtor is considered insolvent when it is in 'cessation of payments' (*cessation des paiements*). Essentially this means it is unable to pay its debts as they fall due with its immediately available assets (cash, cash equivalents), taking into account available credit lines, existing debt rescheduling agreements and moratoria – basically it fails a cashflow test. A debtor will not be insolvent if it can demonstrate that it has sufficient cash available to meet its payment obligations, regardless of the fact that due debts may remain unpaid.

Mandat ad hoc proceedings are less formal than conciliation proceedings: there are no time constraints and there is complete flexibility in framing the scope of the mandate. In practice, a *mandat ad hoc* is often opened prior to conciliation proceedings. If reaching an agreement under *mandat ad hoc* proceedings seems likely, they may be converted, upon the debtor's request, into conciliation proceedings.

2.2 Conciliation proceedings

(a) Overview

Conciliation proceedings may be opened only if the debtor faces economic, financial or legal difficulties (whether actual or foreseeable) and is not or has not been in cessation of payments for more than 45 calendar days. Opening conciliation proceedings during this 45-day period absolves the debtor's management from the mandatory filing for bankruptcy that would otherwise be required at the end of the period.

The proceedings are carried out under the guidance of a court-appointed conciliator for a period not exceeding four months but that can be extended, through a reasoned order, by up to one month.

The main purpose of conciliation proceedings is to promote the conclusion of an amicable agreement between the debtor and all or some of its creditors and/or trade partners to end the debtor's difficulties, for example, providing for the restructuring of its indebtedness.

Upon request of the debtor and after consulting the participating creditors the conciliator may also be instructed to organise a partial or total sale of the business (known as pre-pack proceedings) which may be implemented in the context of further insolvency proceedings. This hybrid tool creates a link between confidential proceedings and insolvency proceedings and was introduced by an ordinance dated 12 March 2014 for use in situations where the only solution for the company appears to be a sale of its assets as a going concern.[1]

Although no automatic stay on claims applies, a debtor may seek extensions of payment periods where a creditor files a claim or attempts to enforce its rights against the debtor during the conciliation proceedings (pursuant to article L.611-7 of the French Commercial Code and 1343-5 of the French Civil Code).

1 Ordinance No 2014-326 of 12 March 2014 reforming out-of-court and insolvency proceedings.

The judge who appointed the conciliator can impose a moratorium of up to 24 months on one or several dissenting creditors (whether involved in the proceedings or not). The moratorium may be terminated in the event no conciliation agreement is reached.

As with *mandat ad hoc* proceedings, no coercive measures can be applied. There is also no cram-down mechanism for dissenting parties – only a fully consensual agreement may be reached. Creditors not willing to take part cannot be bound by the agreement nor forced to accept it. However, note that where an agreement cannot be reached with all parties to the conciliation proceedings due to dissenting creditors, the debtor has the option to pursue two types of expedited judicial proceedings to impose a plan on dissenting creditors (see below).

(b) Consensual agreement

Where an agreement (*protocole de conciliation*) is reached by all parties it may be acknowledged (*constaté*) by the president of the court. Once acknowledged, the agreement is binding on the parties and enforceable without further recourse to a judge (*force exécutoire*). The existence of conciliation proceedings and the subsequent agreement remains completely confidential.

Alternatively, the conciliation agreement may be homolgated (*homologué*) by the court at a hearing. The agreement may be homolgated only if the following conditions are met:

- The debtor is not in a state of cessation of payments or the agreement terminates such a situation.
- The terms of the agreement ensure the sustainability of the debtor's business.
- The agreement does not breach the interests of non-signatory creditors.

The consequences of approving a conciliation agreement are as follows:

- *New money privilege:* Providers of new money, goods or services to ensure the continuation of the debtor's business during conciliation proceedings and/or pursuant to the conciliation agreement will take priority over all pre-petition and post-petition claims in the event of subsequent insolvency proceedings. This excludes certain pre-petition employment claims and procedural costs. Furthermore, this privilege does not apply to share capital increases subscribed to shareholders (but does apply to shareholder loans meeting the above conditions). Rights attached to this new money privilege have been significantly clarified and reinforced since the 2014 reform. In addition, security interests granted to secure such new financings may also benefit from protection against hardening period-related risks (which could otherwise result in such security being voided).
- *Public judgment:* The works council or employees' representatives must be informed by the debtor of the content of the conciliation agreement and

are invited to attend the court hearing ruling on such agreement. The court's decision to approve the agreement will be published in the French legal gazette and therefore subject to third-party opposition (within 10 days from its publication) or appeal by the public prosecutor (within 10 days from receiving the notice of the decision by the court registrar) or the contracting parties (within 10 days from the formal notification of the judgment by the court registrar). However, the content of the agreement remains confidential (except for disclosure of the guarantees securing the agreement and the terms of the new money privilege granted to creditors).

The conciliation agreement itself and any prior agreement will not be subject to avoidance actions if reorganisation or liquidation proceedings are opened with respect to the debtor company at a future date, since the clawback period (*période suspecte*) cannot be backdated by the court to a date earlier than the date of court approval of the agreement, except in the case of fraud.

If the debtor breaches the terms of the conciliation agreement, any party to it may petition the president of the court (if the agreement was acknowledged) or the court (if the agreement was approved) for its termination. If such termination is granted, grace periods granted in relation to the conciliation proceedings may be revoked.

(c) Potential cram-down

If no agreement can be reached with all parties to the conciliation proceedings, due to dissenting creditors, two specific judicial proceedings may be opened by the debtor before the end of the conciliation proceedings to impose a plan on those dissenting:

- accelerated safeguard proceedings (*sauvegardes accélérée*); or
- accelerated financial safeguard proceedings (*sauvegardes financière accélérée*).

Both allow the court to expedite the adoption of a plan approved by a two-thirds majority of the creditors' committees which can then be imposed on the dissenting minority (see below).

3. Judicial proceedings

3.1 Safeguard proceedings

Under French law, there are three types of safeguard proceedings:

- standard safeguard proceedings;
- accelerated financial safeguard proceedings; and
- accelerated safeguard proceedings.

All are voluntary in-court pre-insolvency proceedings that can only commence at the debtor's request.

The key features of safeguard proceedings are the same as those of reorganisation proceedings (*redressements judiciaire*).

(a) Standard safeguard proceedings

The objective of standard safeguard proceedings is to facilitate the reorganisation of a company at an early stage, ensuring the continuation of the business, the protection of employment and the payment of creditors.

Eligibility: Safeguard proceedings are only available to solvent debtors (ie, debtors who are not in cessation of payments under the solvency test described above) who are facing difficulties – financial, commercial, operational or otherwise – that cannot be overcome. Following the 2011 Supreme Court *Coeur Défense* case[2] debtors do not need to demonstrate that the difficulties faced are operational difficulties in order to be eligible for safeguard proceedings. The mere potential of an event of default requiring the renegotiation of the terms of the finance documentation may constitute a difficulty allowing the debtor to petition for safeguard proceedings.

Opening proceedings: On the debtor's petition, the court judgment opening safeguard proceedings appoints the following (as under reorganisation proceedings):

- a supervisory judge (*juge commissaire*) who oversees the proceedings and the protection of the parties' interests. The supervisory judge is notably in charge of reviewing, approving and/or rejecting proof of claims filed by creditors, as well as authorising the payment of creditors benefiting from retention of title over assets necessary for the debtor to operate. He or she may also oversee and approve management decisions that fall outside the scope of the ordinary course of business (see below).
- one or two court-appointed administrator(s) (*administrateur judiciaire*), depending on the size of the business, to supervise the debtor's management operations and assist the management in preparing a draft safeguard plan to propose to the creditors. For smaller companies, no judicial administrator is appointed at the commencement of safeguard proceedings.
- one or two creditors' representative(s) (*mandataire judiciaire*), depending on the size of the business, to represent the creditors' interests and assess proofs of claim. The creditors' representative can be assisted by up to five

2 Decision of the commercial chamber of the French Supreme Court, 8 March 2011, No 10-13988, No 10-13989 and No 10-13990.

creditors appointed as supervisory creditors (*contrôleurs*), at the sole discretion of the court.

Although they are pre-insolvency proceedings, safeguard proceedings are not confidential and the opening judgment is both disclosed in the commercial register and published in the French legal gazette (*Bulletin officiel des annonces civiles et commerciales*). Creditors do not attend the opening hearing; however, they may still challenge the opening judgment. The opening judgment may also be appealed by the debtor and the public prosecutor. All appeals and challenges must be brought within ten days of notification of the judgment in the case of the debtor or public prosecutor, or its publication in the legal gazette, in the case of third parties (creditors being considered as third parties).

The observation period: Safeguard proceedings begin with an observation period (*période d'observation*) of up to six months for the purpose of assessing the financial position of the business. The observation period may be renewed once at the request of either the debtor, the court-appointed administrator or the public prosecutor for a further period of six months. In exceptional circumstances the public prosecutor may renew the observation period a second time for an additional six months. The observation period will therefore not exceed 18 months in any case. In practice, the duration will primarily depend on the ability of the debtor to finance its operations throughout the period.

The debtor retains control of the management of the business with the assistance of the judicial administrator. Management decisions that fall outside the scope of the ordinary course of business, as well as decisions considered to be important under statute, require the prior approval of the supervisory judge. Examples of such decisions include granting security interests or settling disputes. Where such a decision is likely to have an impact on the outcome of the proceedings, the supervisory judge must consult with the public prosecutor prior to approval.

Automatic stay on pre-petition claims: Once a safeguard has been ordered there will be an automatic stay on legal actions against the debtor,[3] with a couple of notable exceptions as detailed below. This protection extends to individuals acting as guarantors and is intended to encourage the debtor's management, who may be acting as personal guarantors, to seek court assistance to address difficulties at an early stage. This individual protection in safeguard proceedings is not available in judicial reorganisation proceedings.

In addition, interest, whether statutory or contractual, as well as interest

3 Such as actions seeking payment of pre-petition claims arising prior to the date of the opening judgment, or the rescission of a contract due to payment default.

arising from late payment and surcharges, will not accrue and is stopped from the date of the opening judgment, with the exception of interest on loans with a term of one year or on payments deferred for more than one year.

There are a few exceptions to the prohibition of payment of pre-petition claims:

- *Set-off:* Payments by way of set-off against mutual claims are authorised provided the relevant claims are deemed sufficiently connected (*créances connexes*) which, according to case law, would in particular be the case for mutual claims arising out of one or several agreements relating to a single economic transaction.
- *Assets necessary to operate:* The supervisory judge may authorise payment of a pre-petition creditor to secure the surrender of an asset which is pledged or held by a third party, where the asset is necessary for the pursuit of the debtor's business. Similarly, payment may be approved to recover goods or rights transferred into a fiduciary estate (*patrimoine fiduciaire*) or to enable the exercise by the debtor of a purchase option in respect of assets under a finance lease by paying unpaid rental amounts.
- *Claims secured by a retention of title:* Claims for restitution may be filed with the administrator where the debtor is in possession of movable property to which a third party holds the legal title, for example in the case of unpaid goods sold to the debtor but subject to a retention of title clause. If a claim is filed within three months of the publication of the opening judgment, and if it is proven that the property was held by the debtor on the opening judgment date, the property may be returned to its legal owner or payment made of the purchase price. Where the property in question has been sold to a third party after the opening judgment date, the legal owner's right to restitution may be subrogated to the receivables held by the debtor against the purchaser of such property.

Certain post-petition claims will also be considered subject to the automatic stay if they relate to expenses that are:

- not necessary for the debtor's business activities during the observation period;
- not incurred for the requirements of the proceedings; or
- not in consideration for services rendered or goods delivered to the debtor during this period.

All other post-petition claims must be paid as they fall due. If they are not paid they will be given priority over pre-petition claims subject to certain limited exceptions (such as the new money privilege described above).

Creditors (excluding employees) must file proof of their claims with the creditors' representative within two months of the publication of the opening judgment in the French legal gazette. The deadline for creditors located outside France is four months. Creditors holding a registered security or contract (eg, finance leases that must be registered publicly) will be individually notified of the opening judgment and the timeframe for filing proofs of claim will begin with this notification and not with publication in the gazette.

Failure to submit a claim in time will render a claim unenforceable, both during the performance of the safeguard plan and after the full performance of the plan. As a result of a reform introduced in 2014, however, claims disclosed by the debtor upon filing for safeguard proceedings are deemed to have been filed in time (for the amount stated by the debtor).[4] Creditors may still file a revised proof of claim in such circumstances.

The creditors' representative will verify all statements of claim. If the debtor does not challenge a claim, it will be submitted to the supervisory judge who may then admit the claim, ultimately allowing the holder to participate in subsequent distributions in accordance with the safeguard plan. Decisions of the supervisory judge can be challenged before the court.

Regime of executory contracts – rejection of *ipso facto* provisions: The protection of executory contracts is provided for under safeguard proceedings to protect the ability of the debtor to operate during the observation period. *Ipso facto* clauses triggering an event of default or enabling an acceleration of debt due to the commencement of safeguard proceedings are deemed null and void. This allows the debtor to continue to benefit from the repayment term agreed initially. Similarly, any contractual provisions enabling early automatic termination of a contract or increasing the burden on the debtor solely by reason of the debtor entering safeguard proceedings are deemed null and void.

In addition, due to the automatic stay, contracting parties must continue to perform their obligations under executory contracts despite any payment default of the debtor prior to the commencement of safeguard proceedings.

The court-appointed administrator may apply to the supervisory judge to request the performance of executory contracts, or for their termination, provided that doing so would not excessively prejudice the interests of the contract counterparty. The agreement may be terminated on approval of the supervisory judge. A specific exception applies to employment contracts and trust agreements entered into by the debtor as settlor; these contracts cannot be terminated. Costs or penalties arising from termination of any contract are treated as pre-petition or ineligible post-petition claims. This allows the administrator to cherry pick the debtor's contracts and terminate overly onerous contracts at a limited cost. Contract counterparties may also initiate

4 Ordinance No 2014-326 of 12 March 2014 reforming out-of-court and insolvency proceedings.

the process by notifying the appointed administrator, indicating their preference for either the performance or the termination of the contract. If there is no response from the administrator within one month following notification, the contract will be deemed terminated.

Claims arising out of the performance of contracts during the observation period are treated as eligible post-petition claims paid as and when they fall due (or benefiting from statutory privilege as above). However, failure to pay any sums due in accordance with the terms of a contract that is continued during the observation period will result in the termination of the contract (subject to exceptions such as commercial leases which benefit from additional protections against termination).

(b) Restructuring through a safeguard plan

The purpose of safeguard proceedings is to reorganise the debtor through the agreement of a safeguard plan. This may be achieved through a debt restructuring (rescheduling, write-offs) or capital reorganisation (including by way of debt-for-equity swap). Alternatively, a partial sale of the business, limited to one or more changes of activities if the debtor operates several distinct branches (so that at least one type of activity remains with the debtor) may be implemented in safeguard proceedings under the terms of an asset sale plan (see section 3.3 f) below).

A draft safeguard plan is prepared by the debtor, with the assistance of the judicial administrator, and submitted to the creditors and then to the court for approval. Creditors (with the notable exception of bondholders) may also submit a competing draft plan to creditors. The creditor consultation process varies according to the size of the business.

French law provides for the formation of two classes or committees of creditors for debtors that employ more than 150 employees or have an annual turnover of more than €20 million (or with specific authorisation of the supervisory judge):

- a committee of credit institutions or similar entities as well as creditors which have entered into credit transactions with the debtor (including holders of shareholder loans), whether secured or not and irrespective of their contractual seniority; and
- a committee of major trade creditors, that is, those with more than 3% of the total trade claims.

Creditors that have acquired claims initially held by previous trade creditors or credit institutions will be considered members of the credit institutions committee as regards those claims *ipso jure*.

The plan must be approved by a two-thirds majority of the value of debt claims held by the members of each voting committee. As a result of the 2014 reforms, subordination agreements, intercreditor voting arrangements and/or hedging agreements under which the claim of a creditor can be repaid (in whole or in part) by a third party are "taken into consideration" for the calculation of votes (which does not mean that their provisions will be strictly applicable). Creditors shall disclose the existence of any such arrangements to the judicial administrator who will decide on the voting rights and procedure. Should a creditor disagree with the voting rights procedure, the creditor or the court-appointed administrator may bring summary proceedings before the president of the court under expedited procedural rules up to two days prior to the date of the vote. Creditors who are not affected or repaid in full upon adoption of the plan are not consulted on the draft plan. Creditors benefiting from security over an asset transferred to a trust *(fiducie sûreté)* will only be consulted in respect of the portion of their claim not covered by the value of the collateralised asset transferred into the trust.

Once the draft plan has been approved by the two creditors' committees, bondholders, if any, will be consulted at a single bondholders' meeting comprising all bondholders, irrespective of each bond indenture. The bondholders' meeting must approve the proposals by a two-thirds majority as with the creditors' committees.

Finally, if the draft plan provides for a modification of share capital or the articles of association of the debtor (as, for instance, in a debt-for-equity swap), these modifications must be approved prior to submitting the draft plan to the court for approval by the shareholders and, where required, assemblies of holders of securities that may give access in the future directly or indirectly to the capital or voting rights of the company (eg, holders of convertible bonds/warrants). Although safeguard proceedings do not allow for cram-down of shareholders, the 2014 reform makes provision for the court to reduce the majority applicable to shareholder meetings convened on first notice to a simple majority of the shareholders present or represented (usually two-thirds or 75%) with a quorum of 50% of the voting shares.

If approved by both committees, and as the case may be by the bondholders' single assembly and/or the shareholders' assemblies, the draft plan is submitted to the court for approval. Approval is subject to the court being satisfied that the interests of all creditors are sufficiently protected (including those that did not vote in favour of the plan or were not members of the committees). The plan may, however, provide for differential treatment amongst creditors to the extent justified by their different situations/positions, and subordination agreements entered into amongst creditors can be taken into consideration as noted above. Any disputes regarding the vote of the creditor committees will be settled by the court approving the plan.

On approval, the plan becomes binding on all members of the creditors' committees and can be effectively crammed down on minority dissenting creditors (save for certain exceptions such as claims benefiting from new money privilege, which cannot be deferred or written off without the express consent of the creditor concerned).

The two-thirds majority vote (compared to the maximum 75% majority recommended by the EU draft directive) combined with the various options that can be proposed as part of the safeguard plan have shown their efficiency. More generally, the constitution of these committees, in terms of their organisation and the consultation process, is far simpler and more flexible than the reorganisation within impaired classes that exists in the US.

If the committee consultation process is not required because the company does not meet the relevant thresholds, or where creditors are not members of the committees or of the bondholders' assembly, the judicial administrator will consult individually with them. This consultation process is also applicable in circumstances where the draft plan has been rejected by one of the creditors' committees or the bondholders' assembly. If the judicial administrator conducts this process in writing, creditors must respond within 30 days from receipt of the consultation document. Failure to respond within this time will be deemed consent to the proposal contained in the document. Conversely, where the proposal provides for a conversion of all or part of the creditor's claim into equity it will be deemed rejected if the relevant creditor does not respond within 30 days.

The court may impose on all non-consenting creditors (excluding members of the committees) a uniform rescheduling of debt (up to ten years) on equal terms for all creditors and subject to a maximum repayment holiday period of one year and to a minimum annual repayment of 5% of the outstanding claims as from the third year. The court cannot impose a debt cancellation (or debt-for-equity swap) on dissenting creditors. In addition, certain specific claims may not be termed out by the court, such as claims secured by new money privilege.

Where claims are owed to public creditors (namely tax administrations and social contribution organisations) these may also be restructured under a safeguard plan. However, this class of creditor must be consulted on debt waiver proposals in accordance with a different set of rules.

If a safeguard plan is approved, the court appoints an insolvency practitioner as *commissaire à l'exécution du plan* who supervises the implementation of the safeguard plan and will allocate the yearly dividend paid by the debtor amongst the creditors. In practice, the court-appointed administrator or the creditors' representative, appointed during the safeguard proceedings, will often assume this role.

The judgment ruling on the plan, whether adoption or rejection, may be appealed by the debtor, the administrator, the creditors' representative, the employees' representative or the public prosecutor. Creditors who have challenged the vote of the creditors' committee (or as the case may be of the bondholders' assembly), may also appeal the judgment approving the plan. Challenges in this respect will be limited to the vote of the committee – creditors cannot challenge the plan on other grounds and cannot do anything if they have not challenged the vote previously.

The court can convert safeguard proceedings into recovery or liquidation proceedings if it is obvious that the business cannot be restructured because a debtor is in cessation of payments or is obviously unable to obtain a safeguard plan, which inability would rapidly result in the debtor being in cessation of payments. This conversion must be on the request of the debtor, the court-appointed administrator or the public prosecutor.

(c) Pre-packaged safeguard proceedings: expedited proceedings

Under French law, there are two types of accelerated proceedings:

- accelerated financial safeguard proceedings; and
- accelerated safeguard proceedings.

These hybrid proceedings bridge the gap between conciliation proceedings and standard safeguard proceedings. Their principal purpose is to allow large companies facing difficulties to implement a restructuring plan in a very short timeframe with the consent of a two-thirds majority of their creditors. The plan can be imposed on the dissenting minority.

While infrequently used in practice (with only two having taken place in 2017), fast-track safeguard proceedings have proven to be efficient threats against minority dissenting creditors, enabling a fully consensual restructuring agreement to be secured in conciliation once sufficient support has been obtained (close to the two-thirds majority provided for under safeguard proceedings), and balancing the absence of coercive measures available under such amicable proceedings.

Eligibility for expedited proceedings: A debtor company will only be eligible to apply for the accelerated safeguard procedure where it:

- is subject to ongoing conciliation proceedings at the time of application;
- faces difficulties which it is not in a position to overcome;
- has prepared a draft safeguard plan during the conciliation proceedings to ensure the continuation of the business as a going concern (it must be likely the plan will receive sufficiently wide support from the creditors taking part in the proceedings); and
- publishes accounts which are certified by a statutory auditor or established by a certified public accountant, the debtor having:
  - more than 20 employees; or
  - a turnover greater than €3 million (excluding VAT); or
  - an aggregate balance sheet that exceeds €1.5 million; or

- publishes consolidated accounts in accordance with article L 233-16 of the French Commercial Code.

In contrast to standard safeguard proceedings, expedited proceedings may be opened by a debtor that is in cessation of payments, provided the cessation of payment occurred less than 45 days prior to the opening of the conciliation proceedings.

Duration of proceedings: The debtor must compile a list of claims of each creditor who participated in the conciliation and who is eligible to file a proof of claim, within ten days of the commencement of the expedited proceedings. Certification of the list by the statutory auditor or the accountant will constitute the filing of proof of claims on behalf of each creditor until and unless they decide to make their own filing.

Most of the standard safeguard proceedings legal regime is applicable to expedited proceedings where compatible with the shorter timeframe.

Accelerated safeguard proceedings can last up to three months. Accelerated financial safeguard proceedings can only last one month with a possible further extension by the court of one month.

The safeguard plan: The main distinction between the two expedited proceedings relates to the class of creditors involved in the consultation process:

- In accelerated financial safeguard proceedings, only the debtor's financial creditors will be consulted, that is, members of the creditors' committee and/or the bondholders' assembly.
- In accelerated safeguard proceedings, members of the suppliers' committee will be consulted in addition to the creditors' committee and/or the bondholders' assembly.

The draft safeguard plan may provide for debt rescheduling, debt cancellation and/or conversion of debt into equity capital of the debtor, with the relevant shareholders' consent. Creditors' committees and the bondholders' assembly are required to vote on the proposed safeguard plan within 15 days of its notification in case of accelerated safeguard proceedings or within eight days in case of accelerated financial safeguard proceedings. The plan must be approved by a two-thirds majority of creditors before it can be adopted.

If the plan is not adopted by the creditors and approved by the court by the applicable deadline, the court shall terminate the proceedings. As a result, the debtor will most likely become insolvent and will have to file for reorganisation or liquidation proceedings.

In practice, companies rarely seek expedited proceedings, but the threat of proceedings provides an incentive for the unanimous consent of all creditors during conciliation proceedings. They have proved to be very useful in that respect.

3.2 Reorganisation proceedings (*procédures de redressement judiciaire*)

Reorganisation or liquidation proceedings must be opened once a debtor becomes insolvent (ie, is in cessation of payments in accordance with the cashflow insolvency test described above).

(a) Opening of reorganisation proceedings: an insolvent debtor with a chance of recovery

The representative of the debtor company must file for bankruptcy (reorganisation or liquidation proceedings) within 45 days of the debtor entering a state of cessation of payments, provided that conciliation proceedings are not pending. Failure to do so will expose him or her to personal liability.

In practice, the representative of an insolvent company will petition for reorganisation proceedings when the insolvent company has sufficient liquidity to continue operating and where rescue seems ultimately possible, although the assessment of the prospects for such a rescue is made by the court at its own discretion.

Unlike the *mandat ad hoc*, conciliation or safeguard proceedings outlined above, reorganisation proceedings may also be initiated at the request of the public prosecutor or by any unpaid creditor, regardless of the nature of its claim. The court may also convert reorganisation proceedings into liquidation proceedings at any time, upon request of the debtor, the administrator, the creditors' representative, a supervisory creditor or the public prosecutor, if the rescue of the company does not seem possible.

(b) Continuation of the business during reorganisation proceedings

The consequences following upon the court's opening judgment are the same as under safeguard proceedings.

The same procedural bodies are appointed and the observation period commences in the same manner. Note, however, that under reorganisation proceedings the administrator may be tasked with assisting the debtor in making management decisions (*missions d'assistance*) in which case the debtor remains in possession but the administrator may also be empowered by the court to take over management (*mission d'administration*). In practice, this latter option occurs rarely.

In addition, the opening judgment determines (generally on a preliminary basis) the date on which the debtor actually became insolvent. The date of insolvency is generally deemed to be the date of the court's judgment unless the court specifically sets an earlier date.

The rules regulating reorganisation proceedings are largely the same as those that apply to safeguard proceedings. The debtor company is under the same protection during the observation period to enable it to prepare and implement a viable solution for the future without increasing its liabilities or reducing the value of its assets.

There will be an automatic stay of any legal action against the debtor as under safeguard proceedings and subject to the same exceptions; and interest, whether statutory or contractual, as well as interest owing on late payment and surcharges, will not accrue from the date of the opening judgment (except in respect of loans for a term of at least one year or in respect of contracts providing for a payment which is deferred by at least one year).

Asset disposals made during the observation period outside the ordinary course of business, or any mortgage, pledge or lien granted by the debtor, or settlement agreed by the debtor, must be authorised by the supervisory judge.

With very minor exceptions, the rules are the same as those applicable to safeguard proceedings in the following areas:

- the proof and verification process for creditors' claims;
- the property claims process (*actions en revendication*), for example in respect of retention of title claims;
- the payment of post-petition claims; and
- the organisation of creditors within committees and the consultation process for such creditors.

Finally, there are a few notable differences between safeguard and reorganisation proceedings:

- *Redundancy:* Under reorganisation proceedings, the administrator must seek the approval of the supervisory judge before actioning any redundancy plan. The judge will only approve a redundancy plan where it is urgent, inevitable and essential during the observation period.
- *Simplified dismissal:* A simplified dismissal process, differing from the process under safeguard proceedings or under general French labour law,[5] can be implemented in order to enable the company to adapt quickly and to keep operating as a going concern while it searches for a viable continuation or sale solution. Subject to certain conditions, the information/consultation process with employees' representatives is shortened, with only one mandatory meeting taking place.[6]
- *Simplified timeline:* The timeframe for the validation and homologation of the agreement by social authorities is reduced to 8 days, compared to

5 Safeguard proceedings follow the general rules provided by French labour law.
6 Compared with two meetings at least 14 days apart under general French labour law rules.

15 and 21 days respectively under safeguard proceedings, such delay being even shorter under liquidation proceedings (4 days).

- *Employee claims insurance:* In contrast to safeguard proceedings, the debtor company is insolvent and may therefore not be able to pay its employees' wages. Unpaid wages or indemnities accrued from up to 60 days prior to the opening judgment will be paid to the employees directly by the employees' claims insurance institution (known as the AGS) which in turn will possess a claim against the debtor that will have to be taken into account when preparing the plan (see below).
- *Executory contracts:* Executory contracts performed by the administrator during the observation period described above give the counterparty the right to immediate cash payment unless the parties reach an agreement in this regard. Prior to 2014, this regime was aligned with safeguard proceedings; however, the 2014 reform removed this obligation from safeguard proceedings, allowing the administrator additional flexibility – reorganisation proceedings are more restrictive on this point.

(c) ***The clawback period (*****période suspecte*****)***

One of the main differences with safeguard proceedings due to the insolvency of the company is that any transaction entered into, and certain payments or transfer of rights over assets made, by the debtor during the so-called clawback period, can be challenged by the court-appointed administrator, the creditors' representative or the public prosecutor and then voided by the court.

The clawback period is the period between the date on which the company actually became insolvent and the date of the opening judgment. The insolvency date can be backdated by the court to up to eighteen months prior to the insolvency judgment. However, where reorganisation proceedings are preceded by conciliation proceedings and an agreement approved and confirmed by a judgment (*jugement d'homologation*), the insolvency date cannot be backdated to before the homologation judgment, except in the case of fraud.

As a result of the debtor's insolvency, certain transactions it enters into, payments made and transfers of rights over assets, during the clawback period, can be challenged by the court-appointed administrator, the creditors' representative or the public prosecutor and subsequently voided by the court.

French law provides for a distinction between automatically void and voidable transactions depending on the gravity of the transaction, payment, or transfer of rights made by the debtor during the hardening period:

- *Automatically void transactions:* Under French law, certain specified transactions will be automatically void if entered into during the hardening period. A request may be submitted to the court by the administrator, the creditors' representative, the public prosecutor or the *commissaire à l'exécution du plan* to have the transaction voided. The specified transactions include:

- the transfer of movable or immovable assets without consideration;
- disproportionate agreements where the obligations of the debtor materially exceed those of the other party;
- payments in any form related to debts that have not fallen due or made by abnormal means;
- encumbrances perfected over the debtor's assets to secure pre-existing debts; and
- precautionary and protective measures, for example, seizure of assets, subject to certain specific conditions.

- *Voidable transactions:* Operations that are not listed as automatically void may be voided by the court at its own discretion. Such transactions include payments related to debts that have fallen due or agreements entered into for consideration, provided that such transactions were initiated or entered into while the other party knew that the company was insolvent. A request must be submitted to the court by the administrator, the creditors' representative, the public prosecutor or the *commissaire à l'exécution du plan.*

These mechanisms are important as they allow for the restitution to the insolvency estate of assets that were encumbered, disposed or sold at a time where the company was already insolvent and therefore required the protection of insolvency proceedings.

(d) *Objectives behind reorganisation proceedings*

The objectives of reorganisation proceedings are, as set by law, to ensure:

- the sustainability of the debtor's business;
- the preservation of employment; and
- the settlement of the debtor's liabilities.

The court will have regard to these criteria in any ruling it makes on any potential exit solution.

During reorganisation proceedings, the court-appointed administrator will assist the debtor with drawing up a continuation plan, similar to a safeguard plan. Should the court consider that there is no viable continuation plan, the administrator will be empowered by the court to organise the sale of the company's business as a going concern.

(e) *Continuation plan (***plan de redressement par voie de continuation***)*

If a continuation plan is proposed in competition with an asset sale plan, the continuation plan must be preferred by the court, provided the proposed continuation plan is sustainable.

The continuation plan can provide for debt rescheduling, debt write-offs, equity reconstitution, debt-for-equity swaps, partial sale of the business or change of ownership.

The same procedure applies to agreeing a continuation plan as under safeguard proceedings.

Since 2014, the draft restructuring plan prepared by the debtor may compete with one or more alternative draft continuation plans proposed by one or several creditors who are members of the creditors' committees (noting that this option is not extended to the bondholders who are members of the bondholders' general assembly). In the absence of creditors' committees, or if the creditors' committees or bondholders' assembly do not vote in favour of the proposed continuation plan, creditors are then consulted individually on the draft plan.

As with safeguard, shareholders must be consulted in reorganisation proceedings; however, there are a number of additional mechanisms in place that enable the court to deal with dissenting shareholders during reorganisation proceedings.

A new mechanism was introduced in 2015 in the context of reorganisation proceedings that allows the French court to push through a debt-for-equity swap in circumstances where shareholders refuse to vote on the share capital proposals contained in the continuation plan.[7] The court may order either:

- the appointment of a proxy (*mandataire*) to vote in lieu of the shareholders; or
- the compulsory sale of their shares.

French courts therefore have the power to dilute or compel divesture of shareholder interests. Note however that only the court-appointed administrator or the public prosecutor may request the implementation of this mechanism, which is subject to other quite restrictive conditions. In practice, owing to its complexity this mechanism has rarely been implemented. It applies more as a threat to dissenting shareholders during amicable proceedings or safeguard proceedings than a genuine alternative to reaching a consensual agreement.

Where the debtor's net equity is below half of its share capital[8] and the continuation plan provides for an increase to the share capital in favour of parties committing to perform the plan, the court may appoint a proxy to convene the required shareholders' meeting and vote on behalf of a dissenting shareholder in order to increase the share capital in favour of persons committing to perform the plan (creditor or third party). Until November 2016,

7 Law No 2015-990 of 6 August 2015, also known as the Macron Law.
8 The minimum provided by French corporate law.

this power was limited to the amount required to recover net equity; however, this is no longer the case. Since most distressed companies have already lost half of their equity by the time they file for reorganisation proceedings, we expect to see this new provision become more widely used in practice.

In circumstances where the debtor's shareholders and management are the same person or entity, the court may impose a condition to its confirmation of the continuation plan, requiring the replacement of *de jure* or *de facto* management. The court may also require the sale of shares held by such management. The court will only pursue such a course of action on request of the public prosecutor and if it is necessary for the recovery of the company. This has proved useful in family-owned businesses where the shareholders also manage the business.

Finally, the main weapon against dissenting shareholders is the court's power to order the sale of the debtor business as a going concern, as shareholders will be fully disenfranchised in such an eventuality.

(f) *Asset sale plan (*plan de cession*)*

The court may empower the administrator to organise the sale of the company's business as a going concern.

Bid submissions and procedure: A public and competitive bid process must be conducted by the administrator with a view to receiving offers from third parties for all or part of the company's assets and activities. The debtor company, the *de jure* or *de facto* managers of the debtor company, and the supervising creditors (appointed as controllers) are not allowed to submit a bid offer to the administrator unless they obtain a specific authorisation from the public prosecutor. The administrator must also inform the employees of their ability to submit offers.

The administrator will set and publish a deadline for submission of bids. If bids received by such deadline are not satisfactory or not sufficiently binding, the administrator may extend the deadline one or even several times. Bidders may only propose improvements to their offer during the process. All bids submitted to the administrator must set out the details of what is to be acquired, since the acquirer may wish to cherry pick certain assets out of the business. This entails listing all assets, rights, contracts and the number of jobs (set out by professional category) to be acquired or transferred. Bidders will be required to finance the rebuilding of the working capital of the business once acquired since all receivables, cash and cash equivalents will remain subject to the proceedings. No improvement to their offer may be proposed by the bidders after their last offer, which must be submitted at least two business days before the court adjudication hearing. Any condition precedent stated in their final offer (including antitrust or administrative approvals, waiver of preemptive rights, financing, etc, as the case may be) must be satisfied or waived at the latest during the adjudication hearing. The court's only options are to implement or reject an offer; it cannot amend a bid in any way by the addition or withdrawal of any asset or contract.

Where ongoing contracts are deemed useful for the continuation of the business (eg, financial leases, leases and property/services supply agreements) the court can unilaterally assign such contract without the contracting party's consent. This is the case even where the contract contains provisions contrary to this – for instance, a lease agreement can be assigned to the purchaser despite the landlord's right to termination as a result of unpaid rent. Although the consent of the contracting party is not required it will be entitled to give its opinion during the hearing.

As a matter of principle, there is no transfer of the liabilities of the debtor to the purchaser in an asset sale plan. Limited statutory exceptions provide, however, for a transfer of specified liabilities, notably:

- the indebtedness secured over a transferred asset where such debt pertains to the financing of the encumbered asset; and
- the debt due to a creditor who holds a retention right over an asset which is included in the scope of the asset sale plan.

Following consultation with the debtor, the administrator, the creditors' representative, the public prosecutor and the works council, the court will select the offer most likely to satisfy the three objectives of reorganisation proceedings – sustainability, preservation of employment and settlement of liabilities.

Unlike asset sales implemented under Section 363 of Chapter 11 of the United States Bankruptcy Code, French courts have significant discretion and will decide between competing bids in light of several criteria, among which the maintenance of employment and the sustainability of the debtor's business will predominate, rather than the purchase price proposed by the bidder. Accordingly, an offer may be upheld by the court despite a low monetary consideration. It must also be noted in this respect that credit bids are not available under French insolvency law (see further below).

In practice, this has helped save thousands of jobs while allowing for deep operational restructuring at the same time (not just a balance sheet restructuring at holding company level).

Bids following *mandat ad hoc* or conciliation: Since the 2014 amendments, the sale process may also be initiated and pre-packaged in the context of prior *mandat ad hoc* or conciliation proceedings. The bid solicitation process is organised at an earlier stage by the mediator and conducted confidentially in keeping with the nature of these proceedings. The sale is then implemented under subsequent insolvency (generally reorganisation) proceedings as set out above but within a few weeks since the administrator may be excused by the court from running a public competitive bid process. In such case the court sets the date of the final hearing convened to adjudicate on the bids in its opening judgment.

The purpose of this fast-track sale process is clearly to reduce as much as possible the period during which the debtor will remain under insolvency proceedings, in order to preserve the value of the business, while benefiting from the regime applying to purchases of assets under insolvency proceedings. Note that even though such a regime appears advantageous, there are still a few constraints with respect to calendar and publicity that need to be complied with when considering this hybrid procedure, and the court can always decide to relaunch a bid process if it considers it necessary.

Bid selection: The court will issue a judgment selecting the purchaser. The judgment:

- may set a time period during which the transferred assets cannot be disposed of or sold by the purchaser without the court's prior authorisation;
- determines the date on which the purchaser will take possession of the transferred assets (*entrée en jouissance*), contracts and employees, although not yet taking legal ownership. This date is generally the date of the judgment itself or the day after; and
- empowers the administrator to take all necessary measures and execute all agreements with a view to regularising the purchase agreements.

Transfer of ownership occurs on the signature date of the purchase agreements, generally a few months after the purchaser has taken possession. As long as the agreements are not executed, the legal ownership of the assets is not transferred and as a consequence no asset can be sold, pledged or rented out by the bidder for the purpose of obtaining finance.[9]

The court's judgment can be challenged through appeal by the debtor, the public prosecutor, the purchaser itself (only to the extent the judgment imposes undertakings beyond those made by the purchaser in its bid), or the assignee of a transferred contract (but only for the section of the judgment relating to such assignment) within 10 days of the issuance of the judgment or the notification of such judgment to the relevant party, as the case may be.

Specificity of secured creditors and employee super privilege: Under French bankruptcy law, credit bidding is not permitted. In France, any creditor

9 Except upon court authorisation. The court will rule pursuant to a report from the liquidator and after having heard the employees' representatives.

intending to acquire assets under an asset sale plan must propose a price in cash, as is the case with any third party, notwithstanding any lien such creditor may have on all or part of the assets.

Usually prices paid by bidders are low and do not match the market value of the assets or the face value of the liens on the collateral. If the collateral is secured by a lien, the court will allocate a portion of the purchase price paid by the (preferred) bidder to the collateral in order to exercise the preferential rights of the secured creditor. The payment of this portion of the purchase price shall bar creditors from exercising their rights attached to the collateral against the preferred bidder. The full payment of the purchase price by the preferred bidder thus triggers the release of liens on the collateral, even though the price does not match the face value of the secured claim.

In addition, under French labour law, employees' claims benefit from a priority rank (a super privilege up to the value of €79k per employee in 2018) and a general privilege (for excess amounts) on the movable and immovable assets of the debtor. Employee claims are defined broadly under labour law to include any sum unpaid by the debtor in relation to labour contracts, including, for instance, lay-off indemnities and social contributions.

The claims outlined above are secured by law over the debtor's assets generally, and can be repaid from the first proceeds distributed irrespective of which asset was sold to generate such proceeds. As a result of the French ranking system, a creditor secured on the most valuable asset may not be repaid on the proceeds generated by the sale of that asset if the employees' claims exceed the asset value and no other asset can be sold.

In practice, given the rather high cap on the amount for super-privileged claims, the broad definition of employees' claims, and the fact that purchase prices for asset sale plans can be very low, the proceeds will usually only repay the employees' claims. This effectively means that security held by creditors does not guarantee repayment (with the exception of claims benefiting from new money privilege or operational post-petition claims).

As a result, most French security interests are not bankruptcy-proof and the secured creditors are generally not fully repaid.

However, as briefly mentioned above, certain specific security interests can be efficient against the purchaser of an asset sale plan:

- *Assets financed by a loan secured over them:* Where such assets are incorporated into an asset sale plan, the purchaser will be compelled to repay the remainder of such loan as it becomes due and payable. Any amount unpaid prior to the transfer of the asset shall remain the liability of the insolvent estate.
- *Assets subject to a retention of title right:* Any creditor holding a retention of title claim can request full repayment before releasing his right over an asset incorporated into an asset sale plan.

- *Assets granted as collateral but retained for use by the debtor through a trust:* Such assets cannot be incorporated into an asset sale plan without the agreement of the trust beneficiaries. Generally full repayment is requested in this scenario.

3.3 Judicial liquidation proceedings

Where a debtor is in cessation of payment and it does not seem possible to turn around its operations, judicial liquidation (*liquidation judiciaire*) proceedings shall be opened.

(a) Grounds

Liquidation proceedings can be opened (with or without any prior safeguard or reorganisation proceedings) at the request of the debtor, or upon petition of the public prosecutor[10] or any unpaid creditor (whether secured or unsecured and regardless of the amount of its claim). As liquidation proceedings are generally a last resort, courts prefer that reorganisation proceedings are initiated first. In the event no turnaround solution can be found these can then be converted into liquidation proceedings.

(b) Impact on creditors and debtor

All creditors must file their claims within the same timeframes as under safeguard and reorganisation proceedings. The opening judgment triggers an automatic stay of proceedings against the debtor and of payments of any pre-petition claims. By exception, secured creditors benefiting from a pledge can enforce their security interest under strict conditions by requesting the court to transfer the ownership of the pledged assets (*attributions judiciaire* – see below).

Unlike all other proceedings, the debtor is automatically discharged from the management of its operations as from the opening judgment and cannot deal with any asset of the company as long as liquidation proceedings are ongoing. This is not a sanction against the debtor or the management but rather aims to preserve the interests of creditors.

(c) Objective of liquidation proceedings

The aim of judicial liquidation proceedings is to organise the sale of the debtor's business or assets through either of the following:

- an asset sale plan – all or part of the debtor's business is sold as a going concern; or
- a sale of assets individually (piecemeal sale) – assets will be sold at public auction or by private sale.

---

10 If no conciliation proceedings have been opened.

The court appoints a liquidator (*liquidateur judiciaire*) to act in both the debtor's and the creditors' interests. Where safeguard or reorganisation proceedings have been converted into liquidation, this will usually be the former creditors' representative. The debtor's assets are sold with a view to maximising the proceeds of sale. Proceeds will be allocated towards repayment of the creditors according to the ranking of their claims, to the extent that funds are available.

Operation of the debtor business generally ceases shortly after the opening of the liquidation proceedings. In exceptional circumstances, where the court considers the business is likely to be sold as a going concern rather than via a piecemeal sale of its assets, it may also authorise a temporary continuation of the operations for up to six months. Where this is the case, the court will appoint an administrator in addition to the liquidator, and the rules applicable to the continuation of operations under reorganisation proceedings will apply. The administrator will then launch a competitive public auction process for the assets of the company, similar to the bid process under reorganisation proceedings.

(d) *Duration and termination*

The duration of liquidation proceedings is not set out by law. However, any creditor can request that the court order the liquidator to close liquidation proceedings after two years following the opening of judicial liquidation proceedings.

The court will end proceedings when:

- no liabilities remain;
- the liquidator has sufficient funds to repay all the claims;
- the interest of continuing liquidation is disproportionate to the difficulties faced in selling the assets; or
- more generally, the continuation of liquidation proceedings becomes impossible due to a shortfall of assets (which may then trigger management liability – see below).

(e) *Outcome of liquidation proceedings*

As mentioned above, the aim of liquidation proceedings is to sell the assets of the company (either through an asset sale plan or a piecemeal sale) to allocate the highest amount of proceeds to creditors in their order of priority.

Since one of the main aims of French insolvency law is to safeguard jobs, the sale of the business as a going concern is preferred over the sale of assets individually wherever possible. Therefore, individual asset sales will generally occur in practice where it has not been possible to sell the debtor's business as a going concern.

In the event assets are sold individually, the liquidator may request the authorisation of the supervisory judge to sell the real estate by means of either:

- judicial auction (*vente par adjudication judiciaire*);
- amicable auction before notary (*vente par adjudication amiable*); or
- private sale (*vente de gré à gré*).

The supervisory judge will determine through an order:
- the asset price;
- the main terms of the sale; and
- the terms and conditions of publication.

Movable assets can only be sold by auction or privately.

Creditors holding a security interest over an asset can seek the enforcement of their rights against the debtor should the liquidator fail to sell the relevant assets within three months of the opening judgment.

Moreover, the pledgee can request the supervisory judge, prior to the sale of the asset, to authorise the judicial award to it of the debtor's asset (*attribution judiciaire*) even if its claim has not been verified and admitted yet. This is similar to a foreclosure on the asset. If the pledgee's claim is rejected in whole or in part, it must return the asset or its value to the liquidator, subject to the admitted amount of its claim.

Where the continuation of operations is authorised, creditors will not be able to seek such enforcement or foreclosure.

3.4 Settlement of liabilities

Creditors must be repaid according to the statutory order of priority set out below, with certain preferred creditors taking priority (including, for instance, employees, post-petition legal costs, creditors who benefit from a new money privilege).

As in safeguard and reorganisation proceedings, post-petition claims (ie, claims arising after the opening of liquidation proceedings) are usually paid at their due date. However, in the event such claims cannot be repaid at their due date, they will benefit from a priority ranking.

The proceeds of sales must be allocated in order of the following ranking:

1. super-privileged employees' claims;
2. post-petition legal costs (essentially court officials' fees);
3. creditors benefiting from the new money privilege;
4. claims secured by security interests over immovable property, and/or specific security interests over moveable property, in particular security interests to which a retention right is attached;
5. post-petition claims, the incurrence of which was necessary for the continuation of proceedings;
6. claims secured with other security interests than those mentioned at 4 above; and
7. other claims.

3.5 Super-privileged employees claims

Under French law, employees' claims are granted a general privilege on the movable and immovable assets of their employer. Moreover, should insolvency proceedings commence, a substantial part of the employees' claims will benefit from super priority for payment, known as super privilege of employees' claims.

Super privilege covers unpaid salaries for a period of up to 60 days prior to the commencement of either reorganisation or liquidation proceedings. Claims for super privilege are capped by statute and updated annually. For 2018 the cap per employee is €79k. Super-privileged claims are granted priority ranking, ahead of any other claims irrespective of their security or privilege.

To prevent situations where this privilege becomes ineffective as a result of a lack of assets, the creation of an insurance organisation (*assurance de garantie des salaires – AGS*) was mandated in 1973 to cover employee claims in case of insolvency proceedings.[11] This system is based on principles of collective responsibility, where each *in bonis* employer must make annual contributions to the AGS, who in turn will pay employees' claims, up to the capped amount, as they become due on behalf of the debtor, with the AGS replacing the employees as the creditor of the debtor.

4. Liability and sanctions

4.1 Management liability

Directors and officers may be held liable, as a result of mismanagement, for all or part of the debtor's outstanding debts where there are insufficient liquidation proceeds to make repayment (*insuffisance d'actifs*).

Actions against management can only be brought in the context of liquidation proceedings (noting, however, that any asset sale plan decided under reorganisation proceedings will require a subsequent conversion of reorganisation proceedings into liquidation proceedings). It must be proven that the shortfall of assets (calculated at the commencement of the liquidation proceedings) is a result of mismanagement, albeit a direct causal link need not be demonstrated. As long as mismanagement has contributed to the insufficiency of assets, there is no requirement to prove that it is the main or sole cause of the asset shortfall. Furthermore, it is not necessary to show that the directors had a personal interest in particular transactions. Mismanagement may arise through their direct actions or their failure to act.

This liability extends to both *de jure* directors and officers (formally appointed directors or managers with representation powers), and *de facto* management (any individual or entity that is not officially a director or officer but has repeatedly influenced the company's management or strategic decisions).

---

11 Law No 73-1194 of 27 December 1973.

An action for an asset shortfall may be brought by the liquidator, prosecutor or the majority of the supervising creditors (who can demand that the liquidator commence proceedings if the liquidator has failed to act) and must be brought within three years from the date of the opening of liquidation proceedings.

The court may decide that all or part of the asset shortfall must be repaid by one or several managers collectively.

Moreover, directors' and officers' liability may be sought for certain specific breaches such as:

- carrying out loss-making operations while being aware that it would lead to insolvency;
- conducting the debtor's operations for their own benefit or using its assets as their own;
- distorting the debtor's assets or credit to its personal interest or to favour another entity in which it has a direct or indirect interest; or
- fraudulently misappropriating or concealing assets or increasing the debtor's debts.

Individuals held liable by the court may be prohibited from managing any business for up to 15 years, and holding any public office for up to five years. Individuals subject to actions for liability can negotiate with the liquidator and agree a settlement, but only if their liability has not yet been definitively confirmed by a court.

4.2 Creditors' liability

The liability of creditors is limited under French bankruptcy law. Pursuant to Article L 650-1 of the French Commercial Code (as interpreted by case law), where safeguard, reorganisation or judicial liquidation proceedings have commenced, creditors may only be held liable for any loss suffered as a result of facilities granted to the debtor, where granting such facilities was wrongful, in the case of:

- fraud;
- improper interference with the management of the debtor; or
- disproportionate security or guarantees in respect of the amount of the facilities (ie, if the value of the granted asset exceeds the amount of the facilities).

If the creditor is found liable it will likely be required to pay damages. Any security or guarantees taken to support facilities can be cancelled or reduced by the court. It may be possible for creditors to be found liable on other grounds under the Civil Code but such actions are rarely successful.

5. Conclusion

French insolvency law has continued evolving since the major reform of 2005, and is now recognised as one of the most efficient in Europe, largely inspiring the latest developments at the European level and more specifically the draft European directive of 22 November 2016 (as amended on 11 October 2018), with a European Parliament vote foreseen for early 2019.

The efficiency of the system is evidenced by the statistics, with the tremendous success rate of amicable proceedings (around 60% in 2017)[12] and fewer liquidation proceedings compared to other main European countries. This can be explained by the debtor-friendly culture which since 1985 has promoted rescue of the distressed company as the main objective. The creation and further improvement of pre-insolvency amicable proceedings, the development of fast-track proceedings and the involvement of management in the preparation and implementation of viable solutions are key in this respect.

As a consequence, French distressed groups, unlike most continental European corporate groups, do not feel the necessity to shift their COMI to the UK in order to benefit from a scheme of arrangement to deal with complex corporate and financial restructurings. The recent restructuring of CGG, led in France and implemented in parallel through French safeguard proceedings and US Chapter 11 (and Chapter 15) is a good example of the attractiveness of the French legal system.

French rescue culture has helped pioneer a strong debtor-in-possession approach which has increasingly been followed in other jurisdictions. Under French proceedings (except liquidation), the management of the debtor remains in place and is generally presumed to be more likely to deliver a long-term and sustainable restructuring solution than creditors, whose interests are generally more focused on short-term returns. Close involvement of the court alongside the insolvency practitioners – who are appointed by the court rather than by creditors – provides sufficient comfort for independent action and the development of even complex long-term solutions that avoid the need for rapid disposal of the business as a going concern in order to limit potential liability.

It is anticipated that future reforms will continue to balance the various stakeholders' interests and reinforce, at least in some areas, the role and powers of creditors. This has already begun with, for example, the ability of creditors (other than bondholders) to be members of a creditors' committee to propose alternative restructuring plans. One avenue of improvement will be to create creditors' committees that take account of the ranking as well as the value of claims.

12 See: Altares/Deloitte report for 2017.

Spain

Ignacio Buil Aldana
Sandra Gómez San Esteban
Javier Segura Valero
Cuatrecasas

1. Introduction

The Insolvency Act (22/2003) regulates all material aspects of Spanish insolvency procedure for both companies and individuals. The procedure is designed to satisfy creditors' interests and to reorganise and preserve viable companies that have become insolvent.

The insolvency and restructuring regime has been subject to several amendments introducing significant reforms. Amendments passed from 2014 to 2016 have followed the path initiated by the 2009 and 2011 reforms, together ensuring that the Spanish regime is in a better position to provide effective solutions to handle financial and operational distress. A set of effective refinancing tools, similar to those available in other EU jurisdictions, foster out-of-court (or with minimal judicial intervention) refinancing workouts in the form of an expedited and efficient regime to restructure highly leveraged debtors and secure their viability in the medium term.

Companies and debtors rely on these Spanish workouts as a way to restructure their debt, rather than turning to refinancing schemes governed by other creditor-friendly jurisdictions. For example, since the introduction of court-sanctioned refinancing agreements in Spain in 2011, over 1,700 debtors in distressed situations have resorted to the pre-petition workout as a way to restore their financial viability in the long term. Benchmark examples of corporate groups that have embraced this workout include big names in the Spanish distressed market such as Natra, Comsa, Abengoa, Celsa, Eroski, FCC and Bodybell.

There remains room for further improvements and developments in the Spanish workout process to ensure a more efficient restructuring market. For example, some participants in the Spanish market have suggested adjusting the scheme to broaden its 'crammable' effects to include debtor changes and security cancellations, as well as introducing equity cram-down. However, given the prevailing political and economic climate, additional amendments to the insolvency and restructuring legal regime in the medium term are unlikely. On top of that, the Spanish legislature has left a degree of uncertainty on key issues regarding out-of-court restructurings; close attention will have to be paid to case law trends and game-changing court decisions, as indeed has already been the case in high profile cases such as *FCC* and *Abengoa*.

2. Filing for insolvency

Insolvency proceedings are triggered only if the debtor is in a state of insolvency (whether actual or imminent). Specifically, a debtor is deemed insolvent when it is regularly unable to meet its obligations as they become due (the so-called 'cash-flow test').

Pursuant to Section 2.2 of the Insolvency Act, insolvency shall be determined based on the following three general criteria:

- There must be payment default; that is, the debtor must be unable to meet its payment obligations. This inability is understood not strictly as assets minus liabilities, but more broadly as the inability or impossibility of regularly meeting payment obligations. Consequently, it is irrelevant whether payment default is caused by a lack of assets or liquidity, or by an excess of liabilities over assets.
- Default must be in respect of due and payable obligations. If the obligations are not due and payable, there may not be actual insolvency.
- Default must be regular. Insolvency must involve an ongoing inability to comply with various obligations (ie, not a minor or isolated late payment or a single unpaid credit).

Pursuant to Section 3 of the Insolvency Act, the debtor (for companies, the board of directors or, if the debtor started an out-of-court liquidation and subsequently filed for insolvency, the liquidators) and any of its creditors are exclusively entitled to file a petition for insolvency.

In terms of Section 5 of the Insolvency Act, the debtor is obliged to file a petition for insolvency within two months of the date on which it becomes aware or should have become aware of the state of insolvency. Further, Section 5.2 of the Act establishes a presumption, unless otherwise proved, that the directors become aware of the company's state of insolvency when any of the following circumstances provided for in Section 2.4 of the Insolvency Act take place:

- The debtor defaults generally on its current payment obligations.
- Attachments due to pending enforcements affect the debtor's aggregate assets.
- The debtor removes assets or liquidates them hastily or at a loss.
- There is a general breach of certain obligations (eg, payment of taxes due during the three-month period prior to the petition for insolvency; social security contributions; wages; indemnities; or other remunerations payable due to employment relationships).

Insolvency proceedings may be initiated either by the debtor (voluntary insolvency) or by any of its creditors (mandatory insolvency). Whether proceedings are voluntary or mandatory will affect the debtor's management capacity during insolvency (ie, supervision or intervention).

Although the debtor is obliged to file a petition for a declaration of insolvency within two months of the date when it becomes aware or should have become aware of its insolvency, there is an exception to that general rule.

Pursuant to Section 5 *bis* of the Insolvency Act – by the so-called 'pre-insolvency' or 'Section 5 *bis*' petition – the debtor can assert that negotiations are being pursued with creditors either to enter into an out-of-court refinancing agreement pursuant to Section 71 *bis* of the Insolvency Act (individual and collective refinancing agreements) and the Fourth Additional Provision of the Insolvency Act (court-sanctioned refinancings), or to obtain the necessary support from creditors to file a pre-pack or advanced composition agreement. In such case, an extra four-month period applies.[1] This comprises three months to reach a refinancing agreement or gather enough support from creditors, plus one month to file the petition for insolvency. (In the event negotiations are unsuccessful, the debtor must file a petition for insolvency once the four-month period has expired.)

During this four-month period, any petition for a declaration of mandatory insolvency filed by creditors will not be admitted. Additionally, the 5 *bis* notice shall stay any enforcement proceedings

- against collateral necessary for the continuity of the debtor's business activity; or
- commenced by creditors holding financial liabilities when creditors holding at least 51% of the financial liabilities have expressly supported the commencement of negotiations to enter into a refinancing agreement.

This stay in the enforcement proceedings shall continue until one of the following events occur:

- a refinancing agreement, pursuant to the terms of Section 71 *bis* of the Insolvency Act, is formalised;
- the petition for the *homologación judicial* of a refinancing agreement is admitted;
- an out-of-court agreement on payments is adopted;
- the necessary support for an early composition agreement has been obtained; or
- insolvency proceedings are opened (insolvency declaration).

1 This allows the company's directors to extend negotiations with their creditors by up to six months (two months from becoming aware of the insolvency, plus three months to negotiate after the 5 *bis* notice, plus one month to file the petition in the event that the negotiations are unsuccessful).

Once the debtor has filed a 5 *bis* notice, it is not entitled to file another one until one year has elapsed.

For a voluntary petition, the debtor must file the following documents, among others:

- an application for insolvency;
- a special power of attorney to request insolvency proceedings;
- a report providing information on the debtor's most relevant legal and economic factual background, as well as information on the economic and legal transactions that it has carried out within the previous three years;
- a schedule of liabilities (ie, list of creditors);
- a schedule of assets and rights;
- a list of employees and labour representatives; and
- specific financial information (annual accounts from the previous three years).

If a creditor petitions for a debtor's insolvency (mandatory petition), it must show evidence of the debtor's insolvency. Such evidence might include:

- generalised default on payments by the debtor;
- the existence of multiple seizures over the debtor's assets;
- hasty or loss-making liquidation of assets; or
- multiple defaults on certain tax, social security or employment obligations during the applicable statutory period (three months).

3. Insolvency procedure

The insolvency proceedings set forth in the Insolvency Act apply to all types of debtors (whether companies or individuals) and consist of a common phase (to determine assets and liabilities), which may be followed by a composition phase and/or a liquidation phase (if the debtor requests it, or if the composition agreement is not approved, is rejected by the court or is breached by the debtor).

An abbreviated insolvency procedure applies in simpler cases involving relatively small amounts – that is, when the list submitted by the debtor includes fewer than 50 creditors, liabilities do not exceed €5 million, and the aggregate value of assets and rights is less than €5 million. However, the insolvency court has absolute discretion as to whether to apply the abbreviated procedure. Abbreviated procedures may also apply where a debtor files a proposal for an early composition agreement or for a composition agreement that includes a structural modification whereby all the debtor's assets and liabilities are transferred as a whole. Abbreviated procedures must apply if the debtor files a liquidation plan together with the petition for insolvency that contemplates a binding offer to acquire the debtor's business unit, or indicates that the debtor has ceased its business activities and no employee contracts are currently in force.

Under the abbreviated procedure, common deadlines are considerably shortened (eg, the trustee's deadline to file the inventory of assets and the report including the list of creditors is shortened to 15 days).

4. Effects on the debtor

As previously indicated, the effects of a declaration of insolvency on the debtor depend on whether insolvency is filed voluntarily and/or declared mandatorily.

If the insolvency is voluntary, the debtor usually retains the power to manage and dispose of its business, albeit under the supervision of the trustee. All actions carried out by the debtor in breach of the required supervision of the trustee may be declared null and void.

Where the insolvency is mandatory, the debtor is removed from office (suspension) and its assets are managed by the trustee.

Notwithstanding this, the regime of supervision or intervention of the trustee may be modified by the insolvency court at any time.

As a precautionary measure, when the debtor is a company and insolvency proceedings have been declared, the insolvency court may grant injunctive relief over the assets and liabilities of its directors (*de jure* or *de facto*), or liquidators (appointed directors who conduct the debtor's liquidation) and attorneys with general powers (including all who have held these positions in the preceding two years) when there are sufficient grounds to believe that any of these parties might be obliged to cover the insolvency deficit arising out of the proceedings as a result of their personal contribution to the aggravation of the debtor's insolvency. Such injunctive measures serve to secure the potential personal liability of directors, imposing a duty on them to assume and pay part or all of the insolvency debt remaining after the debtor is liquidated, provided that the insolvency has been qualified as culpable (see section 11 below).

5. Insolvency court and trustee

The insolvency procedure is conducted by the commercial court of the jurisdiction where the debtor has its centre of main interests (COMI). For companies, a legal presumption arises that this COMI is the debtor's registered office. Attempts to move the debtor's registered office within the six months preceding the declaration of insolvency are deemed to be null and void for these purposes.

The insolvency court has sole and exclusive jurisdiction in specific matters, in particular over the following:

- matters of civil jurisdiction affecting the debtor's assets;
- actions to amend, terminate or collectively suspend employment agreements and/or to suspend or terminate senior management agreements;
- liability actions against directors, liquidators and auditors; and

- generally, all executory and injunctive relief that affects the debtor's assets.

In addition, the insolvency procedure is managed by a trustee, who may be an attorney, an auditor or an economist with expertise in insolvency – no specific qualifications apply, although trustees should generally have at least a five-year expertise in insolvency and a postgraduate or relevant qualification in insolvency.

In broad terms, the essential functions of the trustee consist of:

- completing or replacing the debtor's capacity to run its business (if the debtor is under an administration, suspension or substitution regime as a result of the insolvency declaration); and
- drafting the trustee report, which must be accompanied by the inventory of assets; the list of creditors; the assessment of any proposals for a composition agreement or the liquidation plan, as the case may be; and the valuation of the company and its production units under the hypothesis of continuity of operations and liquidation, respectively.

Pursuant to Section 48 *bis* of the Insolvency Act, which was introduced by the 2011 amendments, the trustee is exclusively empowered to bring corporate liability actions against shareholders during insolvency proceedings.

The trustee's fees, which are categorised as 'administrative expense priority claims' (see below) are calculated on the basis of specific criteria described in Royal Decree 1860/2004 (applying a varying percentage, which ranges from 0.003% to 0.6% of the debtor's net assets and liabilities, disregarding equity).

6. Effects on creditors

Creditors have a duty to file their claims in a timely manner. Indeed, creditors are required to communicate to the trustee (either in writing or electronically) their identification details and the origin, amount, nature, acquisition and due dates of the debt owed by the debtor, plus the requested classification, within one month following the day after publication of the declaration of insolvency in the Spanish *Official Gazette*.

Where the claim communicating the debt is submitted late, the claim may, in certain circumstances, be classified as subordinated debt (ie, junior to all other classes of claim). All creditors shall be classified as privileged, ordinary or subordinated. Privileged creditors are senior to ordinary creditors, which in turn are senior to subordinated creditors.

Creditors' ranking determines not only the order of payment, but also their potential mandatory subjection to a composition agreement with creditors. Specifically, privileged creditors are bound by a composition agreement only if they accept it voluntarily, or if they are crammed down provided certain qualified majorities are reached (see section 8 below), without losing their right to preferential payment with respect to ordinary and subordinated creditors.

There is a special and prioritised category of debts – so-called 'administrative expense priority claims'. These are debts that arise after the declaration of insolvency (eg, expenses generated by the procedure itself). These expenses are not subject to ranking and are required to be paid as they fall due. The trustee may alter the order of payment for expenses if this is in the best interests of the insolvency proceedings, where there are sufficient assets to cover these expenses in full, and the reordering does not affect employee, public tax or social security claims.

Privileged debts can have a special or general privilege, depending on whether the security is created over a specific asset (special privilege) or over all of the debtor's assets (general privilege). Special privilege debts generally include those for which collateral consists of specific property or rights (eg, mortgages or pledges) or equivalent rights (eg, a financial lease agreement for the leased property).

Debts with general privilege consist of:

- debts relating to salaries (subject to a limit) and indemnities for termination of employment agreements, and occupational health and safety claims, provided that these were incurred prior to the insolvency;
- tax and social security withholdings;
- debts for individual work by independent contractors and those owed to authors for the assignment of licensing rights over intellectual property accrued during the six months prior to the declaration of insolvency;
- tax debts, other debts of public entities and social security debts – up to 50% of their value;
- debts arising from tort liability;
- 50% of debts arising from cash injections that have been granted as part of a refinancing agreement, pursuant to Section 71 *bis* of the Insolvency Act and the Fourth Additional Provision of the Insolvency Act (see below); and
- 50% of debts held by the creditor requesting a mandatory declaration of insolvency (unless such debts are subordinated claims).

Subordinated debts include those where notice is given late, debts classified as subordinated under contractual covenants, surcharges and/or interest (except those with *in rem* guarantees), penalties, fines, and debts held by parties that are 'specially related' to the debtor (see below), or parties that have carried out bad-faith actions that are detrimental to the insolvency proceedings or that obstruct the regular process of such proceedings.

Where the debtor is a company, a specially related party may be:

- any partner with unlimited personal liability for corporate debts;

- an individual or entity that holds a significant stake in the debtor's share capital at the time the debt is created (at least 5% if the company has securities admitted to trading on an official secondary market or 10% if the company does not have securities or other instruments admitted to trading);
- a *de jure* or *de facto* director or receiver; or
- a company belonging to the debtor's group and its common shareholders (if they exceed the thresholds provided in the second point above – ie, if they hold at least 5% of the subsidiary's share capital if such subsidiary has securities admitted to trading on an official secondary market or 10% if the subsidiary does not have securities or other instruments admitted to trading).

In the event any specially related party transfers its debt to a third party within the two years prior to the insolvency declaration, such third party shall also be considered as a specially related party, unless there is evidence to the contrary.

However, any creditors who, in compliance with the terms of a refinancing agreement pursuant to Section 71 *bis* or the Fourth Additional Provision of the Insolvency Act or in compliance with the terms of an out-of-court agreement on payments or a composition agreement, have capitalised, directly or indirectly, all or part of their debts (debt-for-equity swap), shall not be considered as specially related parties, even if they have assumed the status of directors of the debtor.

The declaration of insolvency also has the following effects on debts:

- *Interest:* The declaration suspends the accrual of interest on debts, whether legal or contractual, except for debts with *in rem* guarantees, which will continue accruing interest up to the amount of the guarantee. Although the accrual of interest is a controversial issue among commercial courts, certain regional courts (hierarchically superior to commercial courts) indicate that pursuant to Section 59.1 of the Insolvency Act, the continued accrual of interest in respect of privileged credits (with *in rem* guarantees) affects only remuneration interest, according to the interest rate agreed between the parties, but not default interest.[2] Notwithstanding this, recent rulings stipulate that privileged claims enjoy special treatment within insolvency proceedings, similar to that regarding separate enforcement, and therefore the accrual of remuneration interest shall continue once the insolvency is declared and, where the facilities agreement is terminated and the credit falls due,

2 Among others, rulings from the Salamanca Regional Court, 25 November 2008, JUR 2009/104066; and the Zaragoza Regional Court, 4 December 2008, JUR 2009, 144439.

default interest shall also continue accruing. Thus, remuneration and default interest arising from a privileged credit are both covered by the guarantee and shall be classified as part of the privileged credit up to the value of the guarantee.[3,4]

- *Set-off:* The debtor's credits and debts before the declaration cannot be set off against the debts and credits entered into afterwards (ie, the set-off conditions must exist before the insolvency is declared). Set-off is possible only where the legislation governing the main obligation, other than Spanish law, allows it.
- *Guarantees:* Creditors holding joint additional guarantees granted by third parties that have not voted in favour of a composition agreement are not affected by the agreement in their right to claim against the guarantor, which means that they may continue to claim 100% of their debt from the guarantor.
- *Foreclosure of* in rem *guarantees:* Actions involving the enforcement of assets belonging to the debtor's estate, including mortgages and pledges, will be suspended until a composition agreement is approved, liquidation has commenced, or one year has elapsed from the date of the declaration of insolvency (except if the insolvency court rules that certain assets are not necessary for the debtor to conduct its whole business or a given production unit).

With respect to those assets which the insolvency court has declared not necessary for the debtor's activity, it is worth highlighting that the relevant creditor will be entitled to commence an enforcement proceeding during the common phase even if such proceeding was not initiated prior to the insolvency declaration.

Once the liquidation phase has commenced, if the enforcement proceeding was initiated prior to the opening of the liquidation phase, such enforcement proceeding may continue, unless the relevant asset is part of a business unit which is being sold.[5] On the other hand, if the enforcement proceeding was not

---

3 Among others, rulings from the Cordoba Regional Court, 16 February 2009 (JUR 2009, 323048); and the Madrid Commercial Court 6, 30 September 2010 (JUR 2011, 37196) and Barcelona Regional Court 19 June 2014 (JUR 2014, 228257).

4 The value of the guarantee for these purposes is the lower of:
- the maximum secured liability set out in the relevant security agreement; and
- the value of the collateral, which, for the purposes of insolvency proceedings, is calculated as 9/10 of the collateral's reasonable value.

5 In such case:
- Secured creditors shall receive a portion of the purchase price equal to the proportion that the value of the relevant secured asset (calculated as 9/10 of the asset's reasonable value) represents in proportion to the total value of the relevant business unit.
- If the purchase price to be received is lower than the value of the relevant secured asset, the sale shall require the support of 75% of the secured creditors belonging to the same class (public law creditors, labour creditors, financial privileged creditors or other privileged creditors – see below) that is affected by the sale.

commenced prior to the opening of the liquidation phase, the enforcement of the asset may only be conducted pursuant to the terms foreseen in the liquidation plan.

7. Effects on contracts

Pursuant to Section 61.3 of the Insolvency Act, all clauses that entitle a party to terminate an agreement based solely on the other party's declaration of insolvency are deemed void (although it is still usual practice to insert these so-called '*ipso facto*' clauses in contracts), with a few exceptions (eg, agency contracts). This rule does not apply to the liquidation phase (in which the counterparty will be entitled to terminate an agreement which includes the liquidation as a termination event).

As a general rule, the declaration of insolvency does not affect executory contracts – that is, agreements with reciprocal obligations where either the debtor or the other party has not yet performed their obligations. However, the trustee may request that the insolvency court terminate a contract on grounds of convenience for the insolvency proceedings and in the best interests of creditors.

8. Composition agreement with creditors/composition phase

The Insolvency Act encourages creditors to settle on a composition agreement. This may be proposed either by the debtor or by creditors (depending on the stage of insolvency proceedings), and sets forth how and when creditors are to be paid. Once executed, these agreements must be honoured by the debtor and respected by all creditors.

From the filing of the petition for insolvency until the deadline for creditors to submit their claims, the debtor is exclusively entitled to file a proposal for an anticipated composition agreement. This must be presented with the support of creditors whose aggregate claims represent over one-fifth of the liabilities declared by the debtor at the start of the proceedings (or one-tenth of such liabilities if the proposal is filed alongside the insolvency petition). Once the proposal is filed, the debtor must seek the support of the remaining creditors in order to obtain the necessary support to approve the proposal. If the support is insufficient, the debtor may request the opening of the composition phase or apply for liquidation. In the event that it decides to request the opening of the composition phase, the debtor may maintain or amend the initial composition plan or it can submit a new proposal.

A proposal for an anticipated composition agreement may be beneficial for the debtor in terms of time, as it may be submitted along with the petition for voluntary insolvency or before the expiry of the deadline for creditors to submit their claims, allowing for it to be accepted before the composition phase, and approved by the court upon conclusion of the common phase.

From the expiration of the deadline for creditors to submit their claims until the expiration of the deadline to file objections to the trustee's report (or, if objections are filed, up to the date when the final report is filed), the debtor and/or creditors whose claims represent at least one-fifth of the total claims listed on the final creditors' list (which is included in the trustee report) may submit proposals for a composition agreement.

Finally, the debtor and/or creditors whose claims represent at least one-fifth of the total claims listed on the final creditors' list may also propose a composition agreement from the date that the creditors' meeting is called until 40 days prior to the date scheduled for the meeting of creditors (in the event that no proposal for an anticipated composition agreement has been filed and liquidation has not been requested).

Composition agreements must include a payment schedule as well as proposals for a write-off and/or a grace period. In those cases where the implementation of the composition agreement depends on the continuation of the debtor's business activity, the composition agreement must also include a business plan. In addition, the composition agreement may contain alternative proposals for all or any of the creditors (except public creditors), including debt-for-equity swaps, conversion of debt into convertible bonds, subordinated loans, profit-participating loans (PPLs), loans with payment-in-kind (PIK) interest, or the conversion of the debt into other debt instruments. The composition agreement may also include structural changes (mergers, spin-offs, etc) and proposals for the transfer of all assets or business units to a specific person, with a commitment from the acquirer to continue the activity and to pay off the debt in accordance with the payment schedule set out in the composition agreement.

The majorities required to approve the composition agreement depend on its content as shown in Table 1 on the following page.

Therefore:

- A simple majority of the ordinary claims and 60% of each class of privileged claims – public law creditors, labour creditors, financial privileged creditors and other privileged creditors – is necessary if the proposal includes a payment in full of the ordinary claims within a maximum term of three years or a write-off of less than 20%.
- At least 50% of the ordinary claims (and 60% of each class of privileged claims) is necessary if the proposal includes a write-off up to 50%, a grace period of up to 5 years and the conversion of the debt into PPLs for a term no longer than 5 years.
- At least 65% of the ordinary claims (and 75% of each class of privileged claims) is necessary if the proposal includes a write-off over 50%, a grace period of up to 10 years, the conversion of the debt into PPLs for a term no longer than 10 years, or any other alternative set forth in Section 100 of the Insolvency Act.

Table 1: Majorities required to approve composition agreement

Content of composition agreement	Ordinary creditors threshold	Privileged creditors threshold (per class)[6]
• Immediate payment of ordinary claims and write-off < 20% • Full payment of ordinary claims within 3 years	Portion of liabilities voting in favour greater than portion of liabilities voting against	60%
• Write-off ≤ 50% • Grace period < 5 years • Conversion of debt into PPL with a term < 5 years	50%	60%
• Write-off > 50% • Grace period from 5 to 10 years • Conversion of debt into PPL with a term from 5 to 10 years • Other alternatives provided for in Section 100 of the Insolvency Act	65%	75%

The effects of a composition agreement approved with the above ordinary majorities are binding on the debtor, the ordinary creditors and the subordinated creditors. The subordinated creditors are affected by the same write-offs and grace periods as the ordinary creditors, although the grace period for the subordinated creditors shall commence once the grace period foreseen for the ordinary creditors has elapsed.

Once the composition agreement is approved by the ordinary creditors, it will

6 According to Section 94.2 of the Insolvency Act, there are four classes of privileged creditors: (i) public law creditors; (ii) labour law creditors (excluding the part of the senior management staff's claims that exceeds the amount with general privilege); (iii) financial creditors (holders of any privileged financial indebtedness, regardless of whether they are subject to financial supervision); and (iv) the remaining creditors (mainly commercial creditors and other creditors not included in the other classes).

not be binding on privileged creditors except those who voted in favour of the composition agreement or those who decide to accede to it once it has been approved by the insolvency court. Notwithstanding this, all the privileged creditors in a certain class (public law creditors, labour creditors, financial privileged creditors or other privileged creditors) will be crammed down if the majorities referred to above (ie, 60% or 75%) are reached within the relevant class.

If the composition agreement foresees preferential treatment for certain creditors or groups of creditors, it shall be necessary to obtain, in addition to the above-mentioned majorities, a favourable vote, in the same proportion as the applicable above-mentioned majorities, of the claims not affected by the preferential treatment.

The holders of subordinated debts and, in particular, specially related parties who have acquired their debts by means of *inter vivos* transactions subsequent to the declaration of insolvency, are not entitled to vote.

9. Liquidation

Liquidation is an alternative outcome to the insolvency procedure. It takes place where no composition is reached, or in circumstances when the composition agreement is rejected by the insolvency court or not implemented in full by the debtor. The debtor may also decide to file for liquidation at any time during the insolvency proceedings. This petition by the debtor is compulsory if, during the period when the effects of the composition agreement are still in force, the debtor becomes aware that it will be unable to meet payment commitments undertaken in the approved composition plan.

The trustee must prepare a liquidation plan, that is then approved by the court considering the aim of the Insolvency Act, which is to preserve companies or production units through their transfer as a single business unit, unless it is in the best interests of the proceedings to divide said units up or sell some or all of the elements separately. Preference is given to alternatives that allow the business to continue.

If the debtor is a company, its dissolution will be declared, and the trustee will act as the liquidator and will be obliged to report quarterly on this. In this regard, the directors of the debtor will be removed from office *ex lege*.

The main effects of liquidation are that deferred debts fall due and non-cash liabilities are converted into cash debts.

As previously mentioned, under the Insolvency Act the court must apply the rules governing abbreviated insolvency proceedings if the debtor files a liquidation proposal along with the petition for insolvency. The proposal must include a binding purchase offer (in writing) from a third party in respect of the debtor's business unit. Further, a liquidation proposal may also be filed where the debtor can evidence to the insolvency court that its business has ceased and no employee contracts are in force.

As previously indicated, deadlines are shortened in abbreviated proceedings, the more so when a liquidation proposal is filed together with the petition for insolvency. Under the current regime, the possibility of selling part of the business as a going concern becomes more realistic, considering the usual length of insolvency proceedings and the diminution of value of the company's assets during the process.

If the insolvency court approves the liquidation proposal, it can also approve the resolution of all contracts where both parties are yet to perform their respective obligations, except those that may affect the binding offer to purchase the debtor's business submitted alongside the insolvency petition.

The Insolvency Act grants a greater degree of discretion regarding the rules and content of liquidation plans than is the case with composition agreements.

However, although the liquidation plan can be adapted to maximise the value of the estate and to provide maximum recovery for creditors, the overriding principle is to preserve companies or production units, treating them as a whole, except where it is more protective for purposes of the insolvency proceedings to divide them up or sell some or the elements separately, with preference given to any option which facilitates the continuation of the business. Among other measures, the Insolvency Act contemplates the assumption by the acquirer of the production unit of any administrative authorisations or licences the insolvent company holds (unless the acquirer states its intention not to so benefit); and exemption from liability for certain claims not paid by the insolvent company prior to the transfer.

Once the liquidation phase has finished and all the assets of the company have been liquidated, the insolvency will be closed and the company will be dissolved. However, where the estate of the debtor was insufficient to satisfy all its debts, these debts will survive. If further goods and assets of the debtor subsequently come to light, the insolvency proceedings will be reopened in order to liquidate such assets and repay the residual outstanding debts.

10. Claw-back period

During insolvency proceedings, it is possible to challenge those actions deemed detrimental to the debtor's estate that took place before the declaration of insolvency. Such challenges are subject to the following rules:

- Actions carried out in the two years preceding the declaration of insolvency may be rescinded, even in the absence of fraudulent intent.
- The actions must be "to the detriment of assets", which will be presumed:
  - without admission of evidence to the contrary (non-rebuttable presumptions), in the case of dispositions for no consideration or payments or other acts cancelling obligations with a due date after the declaration of insolvency (except those having an *in rem* guarantee); and

    - with admission of evidence to the contrary (rebuttable presumptions), in the case of dispositions for valuable consideration carried out in favour of any related party; the granting of security covering pre-existing debts or new debts incurred to cancel pre-existing debts; or payments or other actions cancelling obligations that are secured by an *in rem* guarantee and with a due date after the declaration of insolvency.
- Otherwise, damage to the debtor's estate must be proved by the person seeking rescission.
- Safe harbours in this context will be:
    - actions carried out in the debtor's ordinary course of business and under customary market conditions; and
    - refinancing agreements entered into between the debtor and its creditors pursuant to the terms of Section 71 *bis* of the Insolvency Act and the Fourth Additional Provision of the Insolvency Act – these are protected from claw-back actions, as further explained below. With respect to the former, protection only relates to claw-back claims filed by other dissenting creditors, so the trustee (appointed in an eventual insolvency of the debtor) will still be entitled to challenge the refinancing agreements if any of the applicable statutory requirements have been breached. Conversely, court-sanctioned refinancing agreements pursuant to the Fourth Additional Provision are fully shielded from claw-back actions and under no circumstances can such transactions be subject to claw-back.
- Good-faith third-party acquirers of the debtor's assets will enjoy the protection and immunity provided by the public registry regulations.

Only the trustee is permitted to take claw-back actions, although exceptionally a creditor seeking rescission will be entitled to do so if the trustee has not challenged the detrimental action within two months of the creditor's written request to do so.

It is important to note that intent of fraud is not required to bring a claw-back action under the Insolvency Act. In circumstances of fraud, Spanish civil law provides an additional action to challenge fraudulent conveyance transactions, for which the enforceable period is extended to four years. This civil rescissory action is known as '*acción pauliana*'. It cannot be filed if there are any other recovery mechanisms available, and it can be brought, in contrast to claw-back actions, even if the insolvency proceeding has not yet been declared, and by any interested person (not just the trustee). The above-mentioned safe harbours do not apply for an *acción pauliana*.

Where rescission occurs (either as a result of a claw-back action or an *acción pauliana*), both parties must return or exchange both the asset or service provided (if possible) and the price or consideration paid for it. If, pursuant to that return, the debtor owes a debt, this shall be deemed a claim with administrative expense priority. In the event that bad faith on the part of the creditor is shown, its debt shall be subordinated.

11. Qualification of insolvency proceedings

Qualification is an optional process within insolvency proceedings. It allows for the imposition of civil liability on directors who have negligently or culpably contributed to the creation or aggravation of the situation which led to the initiation of insolvency proceedings. The effects are strictly civil and are not binding for the purposes of criminal jurisdiction.

The qualification process is not mandatory and depends upon the final outcome of the insolvency proceedings:

- Where the debtor ends up in liquidation, insolvency proceedings must be qualified when the liquidation phase is declared open.
- Where a composition agreement with creditors is reached, insolvency shall be qualified only if the composition agreement is particularly onerous. In particular, qualification will proceed when the write-off exceeds one-third of the amount of debts or when a grace period of more than three years is agreed for all creditors. In cases where the composition agreement is not particularly onerous, qualification will not apply unless the composition agreement is breached.

The aim of the rules governing commencement of the qualification process is to encourage directors of insolvent companies to petition for insolvency proceedings while there is still a reasonable possibility of paying off creditors.

Insolvency proceedings may be qualified as fortuitous (non-liable) or culpable (liable). Fortuitous insolvency refers to a case where the insolvency or its aggravation is not attributable to a particular person, so there is no liability. If the trustee's report, and, if applicable, the report by the public prosecutor's office, qualifies the insolvency as fortuitous, the process is completed with an order for dismissal.

Pursuant to the Insolvency Act, three elements are required to qualify insolvency proceedings as culpable:

- There was wilful misconduct or gross negligence on the part of the *de jure* or *de facto* directors, or any person who had that status in the two years prior to the declaration of insolvency.
- The company's insolvency was created or aggravated.
- There is a causal link between the first and second points.

The Insolvency Act stipulates certain circumstances where the insolvency is always qualified as culpable (for which no evidence to the contrary is admitted) and certain cases in which wilful misconduct or gross negligence is presumed (for which evidence to the contrary is admitted). These are set out in turn below.

11.1 Automatically culpable scenarios (non-rebuttable presumptions)

The following circumstances constitute non-rebuttable presumptions so that the insolvency will be qualified as culpable in all cases:

- substantial breach or significant irregularities in keeping the accounts;
- serious inaccuracy or misrepresentation in the documents presented in the insolvency proceedings;
- the *ex officio* commencement of liquidation due to a breach of the composition agreement, attributable to the insolvent party;
- cases of concealment of assets or of removal of some or all assets, which damage the creditors; or delay or obstruction to any enforcement that has been commenced or is likely to be commenced;
- the fraudulent disposal of assets or rights from the debtor's estate during the two years before the declaration of insolvency; and
- the carrying out of any legal transaction aimed at faking the debtor's assets and its financial situation.

11.2 Rebuttable presumptions

Similarly, the rebuttable presumptions consist of wilful misconduct or gross negligence that aggravates the insolvency situation, unless proved otherwise, by breaching any of the following duties imposed by the Insolvency Act:

- breach of the duty to file a petition for insolvency in due time;
- breach of the duty to cooperate with the insolvency court and the trustee, failure to furnish necessary or appropriate information or failure to attend (whether in person or through an attorney) the creditors' meeting when attendance at the meeting would have been crucial for the approval of the composition agreement;
- breach of the duty to draft annual accounts, submit them for audit (if necessary) and, once approved, deliver them to the commercial registry in the three years prior to the declaration of insolvency; and
- frustration of a refinancing agreement or of an out-of-court agreement for payment caused by the refusal, with no reasonable cause, by shareholders or directors of a debt-for-equity swap or of an issuance of convertible instruments provided for in such an agreement.

Where the court qualifies the insolvency proceedings as culpable, the qualification ruling gives rise to important effects for the directors (whether *de jure* or *de facto*) who – culpably or negligently – contributed to the debtor's insolvency. The ruling must specify the reasons for the culpable qualification and identify the affected directors and the specific effects for those directors.

The primary effect for directors is a ban from:

- administrating the property of others for between two and 15 years;
- acting on behalf of or being empowered by any person for the same term;
- operating any business activity; and
- holding an equity stake in any trading company.

Directors of an entity affected by such a ban are dismissed automatically from office. If their dismissal hinders the functioning of the governing body, the trustee might call a general shareholders' meeting to appoint replacement officers.

In the scenario of a composition agreement, the qualification ruling might, as an exception, authorise a banned director to remain in control of the business or as director of the debtor if the trustee so requests.

A further effect for directors is the loss of any rights that they might hold as creditors in the insolvency proceedings or against the insolvency estate, and the return of any assets or rights that they may have obtained wrongly from the debtor's assets or received from the insolvency estate, as well as the obligation to provide an indemnity for the damage caused.

Pursuant to the most recent amendments to the Insolvency Act, where the qualification procedure has been started or reopened due to the start of the liquidation phase, the insolvency court may order all or some of the directors or liquidators – whether *de jure* or *de facto* – or those with general powers of attorney for the debtor who have been held to be subject to the qualification to personally assume all or part of the debtor's deficit.

Where several persons have been found culpable, the insolvency court shall specify the amount to be paid by each person affected, in accordance with their relative contribution to the culpable acts.

This third effect for directors is also known as the 'liability insolvency action', through which the Spanish legislature has offered creditors access to the directors' assets (as a further guarantee in addition to the debtor's assets) to ensure that, under certain circumstances, those assets can be used to pay the amount of their debts not covered by the liquidation of the estate.

Pursuant to the Insolvency Act, three tests must be met for the liability insolvency action to apply:

- The qualification procedure must have started due to the liquidation phase being started or reopened. This means that an order for payment cannot be made if the insolvency ends with a composition agreement, even if the qualification procedure has begun and the insolvency is found to be culpable. However, an order for payment may be made if the composition agreement is subsequently breached, as this would lead to the start of liquidation and the reopening of the qualification procedure.
- The insolvency must have been qualified as culpable (ie, where the

situation of insolvency has been caused or aggravated by wilful misconduct or gross negligence by the company's *de jure* or *de facto* directors, as described above, including, as potentially liable parties, directors that held office during the two years prior to the date of the declaration of insolvency).

- The insolvency estate's inability to pay the debts held by creditors must have been shown.

In these circumstances, the insolvency court may order all or some of the directors to be held subject to the qualification and accordingly required to cover all or part of the debtor's deficit. The Spanish legislature drafted the provision concerning the court ruling with a wide margin of discretion regarding not only the order itself, but also the amount of the order, which may cover all or part of the total amount of the debts.

If several people are affected by the qualification, the ruling shall specify the amount payable by each director, depending on his or her relative contribution to the acts that resulted in the insolvency being qualified as culpable. This is an interesting and practical aspect relating to the defence of directors, because it may avoid the joint (and insufficiently reasoned) orders for payment often found in some rulings.

The reforms fail to resolve the controversial question of whether the qualification procedure is designed to repair the damage caused, or instead to punish certain actions taken, by the debtor's directors. However, the reforms do resolve the issue of who is the beneficiary of the proceeds resulting from such liability, by providing that all amounts obtained by enforcing the qualification ruling will be added to the insolvency estate.

12. *De facto* directors

The fact of being considered a *de facto* director has key implications in the context of an insolvency scenario. For instance, *de facto* directors will be considered as specially related parties to, and therefore subject to subordination of their claims against, the debtor. In addition, these persons may be subject to civil liability if they are considered directly responsible for the debtor's culpable insolvency, as explained above.

However, the Insolvency Act does not provide a definition for the legal concept of a *de facto* director. This is only defined in the Spanish Companies Act (1/2010), as any person who performs the task and role of director without being validly appointed, as well as any person under whose instructions the company's directors act.[7]

7 This definition was introduced in the Spanish Companies Act by virtue of the amendment effected by Law 31/2014, dated 3 December 2014.

Despite the lack of definition in the Insolvency Act, the concept of a *de facto* director is well rooted in the Spanish legal system and is commonly dealt with in civil cases, although most precedents arise from first instance civil courts and there are relatively few precedents within insolvency case law. According to the prevailing doctrine and the few case law precedents available, definitions of '*de facto* director' might include:

- directors whose appointment has lapsed;
- directors whose appointment is in force, but invalid (ie, because it contravenes a legal provision);
- those who hold themselves out as directors before third parties and who control the management and the administration of a company, despite not having been formally appointed to that role; and
- those who do not hold themselves out as directors before third parties, but who actually control the management and administration of a company by exercising a decisive influence upon the *de jure* directors (ie, shadow directors).

In addition to the above, the Supreme Court has recently ruled that the concept of *de facto* director refers to those persons who, without having been formally appointed as directors, act as if they were formally appointed and as if all the legal or statutory requirements were met. Therefore, the main characteristic of a *de facto* director is not the material implementation of certain duties, but rather acting as a director disregarding the legal and statutory requirements to hold such position.[8]

Additionally, according to the Supreme Court, there are three characteristic features of the *de facto* director:

- the performance of management activities that are usually carried out by a company director;
- such management activities having been performed systematically and on an continuing basis (so they have both quantitative and qualitative importance); and
- the management activities being performed independently and with autonomous decision-making, but with the support of the company.

With respect to the possibility of considering a financial creditor a *de facto* director (which results in the subordination of its credit, according to Sections 92.5º and 93.2.2º of the Insolvency Act), it is worth highlighting a recent ruling from the Madrid Regional Court.[9] In this case, the debtor and the trustee

8 Among others, rulings from the Supreme Court, no. 721/2012, dated 4 December (RJ 2013, 2405), no. 421/2015, dated 22 July (RJ 2015, 3512), and no. 224/2016, dated 8 April (RJ 2016, 1232).

9 No. 200/2018, dated 23 March (JUR 2018, 152750).

claimed that one of the financial creditors should be considered a *de facto* director because, as a consequence of the provisions set out in the security documents securing the loan granted to the debtor,[10] the financial creditor was assuming complete control over the debtor, it was taking strategic decisions with respect to the debtor and its assets, and it had knowledge of, and control over, the debtor's financial statements, income and expenses.

However, based on the definition developed by the Supreme Court, the Madrid Regional Court ruled that the actions performed by the financial creditor and alleged by the debtor and the trustee could not be considered as control and management functions. Instead, the court considered that none of the three characteristic features referred to above applied and that these actions were rather aimed at supervising the actions performed by the company directors. Therefore, the financial creditor, which was exercising the supervising role conferred upon it under the financing and security documentation, could not be considered a *de facto* director.

Moreover, as further explained below, signatories of refinancing agreements pursuant to the terms of Section 71 *bis* or the Fourth Additional Provision of the Insolvency Act will not be considered *de facto* directors in respect of the obligations assumed by the debtor in relation to the business plan, unless evidence to the contrary is provided.

The liability of a *de facto* director depends on proof that he or she has systematically interfered in the management of the debtor in such a way as to distort the company's usual corporate governance.

This should not be confused with the normal influence that a majority or controlling shareholder may exercise within its legitimate rights. Such influence is usually less significant than that exercised by a *de facto* director. Joint management is commonly exercised in cases of flexible corporate governance, so that the control of a specific shareholder is diluted and the financial and managerial autonomy of the subsidiaries is respected. Therefore, the characterisation of a *de facto* director will apply solely to clear cases where the dominant or controlling shareholder regularly interferes in the company's management.

In conclusion, *de facto* directors are those who systematically give express and binding instructions (ie, not mere opinions, recommendations or general guidelines regarding the management of the whole group) to the debtor's own directors. These instructions must impede the directors' autonomous exercise of their duties of loyal and diligent management.

10 In particular, among others, the fact that the debtor needed the pledgee's authorisation to use the funds in a pledged account and certain provisions of the mortgage loan agreement, such as the regulation of a payment waterfall and an information obligation whereby the debtor had to deliver to the financial creditor its annual accounts and information about the income generated by the mortgaged asset.

13. Refinancing agreements and court-sanctioned refinancing

The Spanish legislature has recently developed a variety of pre-petition restructuring tools that include:

- individual refinancing agreements;
- collective refinancing agreements; and
- court-sanctioned refinancings (*homologación judicial*).[11]

13.1 Individual refinancing agreements

An individual refinancing agreement is a notarised agreement that satisfies the following conditions:

- There is an improvement in the ratio of assets over liabilities.
- Current assets are no less than current liabilities.
- The proportion of the resulting security interest value relative to the outstanding debt is not greater than the proportion existing prior to the refinancing.
- The value of the resulting security interest does not exceed 9/10 of the value of the outstanding debt owed to creditors.
- It does not increase the interest rate applicable to the debt prior to the refinancing.

13.2 Collective refinancing agreements

A collective refinancing agreement is a notarised agreement that satisfies the following conditions:

- It has the support of creditors (not only secured and unsecured creditors but also commercial creditors) holding at least 60% of the debtor's claims at the time the refinancing agreement is executed (as evidenced by an auditor's certificate).
- It extends the maturity or extends the credit made available to the debtor, or reduces or cancels existing financial obligations.
- It is based on a business plan that allows business activity to continue in the short to medium term.

---

11 The list of workouts implemented by the recent reforms to the Spanish insolvency regime includes the out-of-court settlement agreement of debt payment introduced under the Insolvency Act. This pre-insolvency workout, also known as 'insolvency mediation', is regulated as an out-of-court debt renegotiation mechanism which, under certain circumstances, allows for write-offs, debt-for-equity swaps, grace periods, payments in kind, and debt conversion into PPL. The procedure is led by an appointed 'insolvency mediator' who seeks consensus among the debtor and its creditors. Once the out-of-court settlement agreement is reached, it works as a pre-composition agreement whose breach (or at a prior stage, when the impossibility to reach said settlement becomes evident) will require the opening of the debtor's insolvency proceeding straight into liquidation. Although the out-of-court settlement is an alternative solution for distressed situations, it is not explained in detail in this chapter as it is designed mainly for individuals and SMEs.

13.3 Effects of the refinancing agreements

Parties to an individual or collective refinancing agreement meeting the above requirements will benefit from the following effects:

- The refinancing agreement will be shielded from claw-back actions (the protection will extend to security interests granted and perfected in connection with such agreements and, arguably, other corporate actions). However, this protection will only relate to challenges by other creditors, whereas a trustee appointed in a hypothetical future insolvency proceeding of the debtor would still be entitled to challenge the refinancing agreements if any of the statutory requirements for these refinancing agreements, described above, had been breached. This protection is absolute in the case of court-sanctioned refinancings (*homologacións judicial*) – as explained below – where not even a subsequently appointed trustee is entitled to file for claw-back. However, it should be noted that fraudulent refinancings seeking to diminish the debtor's assets can be rescinded pursuant to an *acción pauliana* brought by a dissenting creditor or any other interested party (see above).
- Signatories will not be considered *de facto* directors (and, therefore, parties related to the debtor for credit subordination purposes) with regard to the obligations assumed by the debtor in relation to the business plan, unless evidence to the contrary is provided. As a result, these creditors would not be equitably subordinated on the grounds of being *de facto* directors.
- 'Fresh money' granted as part of a refinancing agreement has priority in a potential insolvency scenario. As a result, claims derived from cash injections made available through a collective or individual refinancing agreement will be prioritised so that 50% of the pre-petition claim will be allowed as an administrative expense (with a super-priority over any other pre-petition claim); and the remaining 50% will be allowed as a general privileged claim (junior to administrative expenses and *in rem* secured claims, but senior to general ordinary unsecured creditors). This privilege granted to cash injections is dealt with in further detail below.

13.4 Court-sanctioned refinancings or *homologacións judicial*

A court-sanctioned workout or *homologación judicial* (regulated under the Fourth Additional Provision of the Insolvency Act) is a collective refinancing agreement that is supported by at least 51% of the financial claims (excluding commercial and public debts) and is additionally homologated by the insolvency court – although the *homologación judicial* is not *per se* a formal insolvency judicial proceeding. It is arguable that neither current nor imminent insolvency is a requirement to file for *homologación judicial*, although recent lower court rulings have held otherwise (ie, insolvency must be shown).

13.5 Effects of *homologación judicial*

On top of the benefits of the collective refinancing agreements detailed above, the court-sanctioned refinancing agreement will also be absolutely protected against claw-back actions by creditors or trustees. As mentioned above, despite the court sanction providing a safe harbour from claw-back actions, the *homologación judicial* will still be subject to challenge by any interested party through an *acción pauliana* where the refinancing is fraudulent and detrimental to the creditors' interest.

However, the key effect of the *homologación judicial* is the ability to cram down dissenting creditors if certain additional majorities are achieved. These majorities depend on the content of the refinancing agreement to be crammed down and whether such dissenting creditors are secured or unsecured.[12]

With respect to unsecured creditors (creditors that do not benefit from *in rem* security and the residual amount of any secured claim that exceeds the value of the collateral):[13]

- A majority of 60% of the financial claims is necessary to cram down dissidents when the content of the refinancing consists of:
  - a grace period of up to five years; and
  - the conversion of senior debt into PPLs for a term no longer than five years.
- A majority of 75% of the financial claims is necessary to cram down when refinancing consists of:
  - a grace period between 5 and 10 years;
  - any write-offs;
  - any debt-for-equity or debt-for-asset swaps;
  - the conversion of senior debt into PPLs for a term between 5 and 10 years;
  - convertible obligations or conversion into any financial instrument; and
  - payments in kind.

Regarding secured financial claims (calculated by the value of the collateral as indicated above),[14] the aforementioned majorities are extended by five percent, to 65% and 80% respectively.

---

12 A controversial issue in the case law is whether the majorities should be determined by reference to all the financial claims (*Abengoa* ruling, see n 15) or only those affected by the refinancing agreement so that the parties to the refinancing may cherry-pick which creditors and financial claims are considered for majority purposes (*FCC* and *Comsa* rulings).

13 Being the lower of:
- the value of the claim held by the creditor;
- 9/10 of the reasonable value of the collateral; or
- the maximum secured liability agreed.

14 Therefore, disputes may arise in respect of the proper value assessment of the collateral to determine exactly where the value of the security breaks, although it is still not specified how parties would address these disputes.

Table 2: Majorities required for cram-down

Court-sanctioned refinancings	**Majority**	**Affected debt**	**Cram-down of secured creditors**	**Contents**
Standard	51%	Financial debt	N/A	Claw-back protection
Reinforced (basic)	60%	Unsecured financial debt and deficiency claims	No	• Grace period < 5 years • Conversion of debt into PPL with a term < 5 years
	65%	Secured financial debt by value of security	Yes	
Reinforced (advanced)	75%	Unsecured financial debt and deficiency claims	No	• Grace period 5–10 years • Write-offs • Conversion of debt into PPL with a term of 5–10 years • Debt-for-equity/asset swap • Convertible obligations /financial instrument conversion • Payments in kind
	80%	Secured financial debt by value of security	Yes	

Credits held by specially related parties (in general terms, shareholders and directors) are excluded and do not attract the right to vote, but the effects of the workout can still be extended to them. In contrast, non-financial creditors (eg, commercial and public debt creditors) can also voluntarily adhere to the refinancing agreement but cannot be crammed down in the context of a *homologación judicial.*

When it comes to syndicated loan agreements (including bilateral agreements syndicated via intercreditor agreement) a special voting rule applies, pursuant to which all lenders within a syndicated agreement will be considered to support the refinancing workout if 75% of the syndicated debt (or such lower percentage as is agreed in the syndication agreement) have voted in favour of the refinancing agreement. In other words, in the event that a majority of 75% of the syndicated claims is achieved (or the lower majority applicable), the remaining 25% (or higher) will be crammed down and the lenders holding that debt will be deemed to have accepted the refinancing.

One issue in dispute has been whether this positive drag implies that the syndicated lenders that have not voted in favour of the refinancing:

- are considered as 'dissenting creditors' and thus subject to cram-down; or
- are deemed to have legally entered into the refinancing agreement.

The latter would imply that these syndicated lenders:

- are not entitled to challenge the approval of the refinancing agreement; and
- are subject to all the provisions of the refinancing agreement, which can go beyond the laundry list of effects that can be crammed down as indicated above.

Recent case law such as *Abengoa* (September 2017),[15] *Finarpisa* (November 2016)[16] and *Aliwin Plus* (March 2016)[17] has shed some light on this subject and is tending towards the approach that once the threshold majorities are reached, the entire syndicate is deemed to have entered into the *homologación judicial.*

It is important to note that the list of potential effects on holdout creditors is narrowly construed and limited to those identified above; it does not include the typical crammable effects of restructurings, such as change of debtor or third-party security release. Furthermore, the effects of the court-sanctioned refinancing do not have an impact on joint-obligors and guarantors, and therefore dissenting creditors affected by any grace period or write-off at the

---

15 Sevilla Commercial Court 2, 25 September 2017 (SJM SE 675/2017).
16 Sevilla Commercial Court 1, 21 November 2016 (JUR 2016, 263931).
17 Madrid Commercial Court 6, 15 March 2016 (JUR 2016, 232283).

principal obligor level will maintain their rights with regard to such joint-obligors and guarantors. In order to overcome such limitation, the vast majority of Spanish court-sanctioned refinancing agreements are becoming group schemes where not only the principal debtor files for court sanction, but also the subsidiaries and affiliates that are obligors and guarantors of such debts.

Grounds for objection to a *homologación judicial* are limited and must be brought before the same court that sanctioned the agreement. A dissenting creditor may challenge a court-sanctioned workout if the relevant required majority has not been obtained or properly calculated, or if the refinancing imposes a disproportionate sacrifice on such creditor. With respect to the 'disproportionate sacrifice' concept, the lack of a statutory definition has made it necessary for Spanish case law to develop a definition. In a nutshell, some rulings have settled two contrasting criteria for ascertaining whether the sacrifice imposed on dissenting creditors is disproportionate:

- if the dissenting creditors have suffered a worsening of their position with respect to what they reasonable expected to receive in the absence of restructuring if the debtor's business was liquidated or sold as a going concern (the 'liquidation test'); or
- if the dissenting creditors are treated less favourably than supporters of the agreement that would be junior to them under normal insolvency priority rules.

Some other rulings have found elements of disproportionate sacrifice in workouts where there is lack of proportionality between the effects of the refinancing on the creditors and on the debtor (ie, where the refinancing is not proportional to the objectives pursued), or where the business plan is not feasible.

14. 'New money' privilege

One of the measures introduced by the recent insolvency reforms in Spain in order to promote out-of-court restructurings is the privilege granted to new cash injections or 'new money' provided through the aforementioned ring-fenced refinancing agreements as a mechanism to facilitate the viability of debtors in situations of financial distress.

Thus, the Insolvency Act gives insolvency privilege to the claims of those creditors that made cash injections available to the debtor through a refinancing agreement pursuant to Section 71 *bis* or the Fourth Additional Provision of the Insolvency Act, as follows:

- 50% of the pre-petition claim will be allowed as an administrative expense, with super-priority status over any other pre-petition claims except claims secured with *in rem* collateral.
- 50% of the pre-petition claim will be allowed as a general privileged

claim (junior to administrative expenses and *in rem* secured claims, but senior to general ordinary unsecured creditors).

This privilege does not apply to cash injections made available by a specially related person (see above) through a share capital increase, credit facilities, or acts or transactions with similar purposes.

In addition, in order to further enhance access to available financing for distressed companies, the Insolvency Act recognises that claims resulting from a composition agreement will be treated as administrative expense priority claims in the context of subsequent liquidation, which promotes 'exit financings' within in-court restructuring proceedings.

Despite the above, the general view in the market is that the Spanish legislature could have taken a step further in line with the European Directive Proposal on Preventive Restructuring Frameworks, and included complete and systematic regulation and protection of interim financing or post-petition financings (like, for instance, the DIP financing regime in the US) in order to provide debtors with the ability to finance their working capital requirements during the insolvency proceedings, along with the direct and indirect costs related to such proceedings.

15. Debt-for-equity swaps

The Spanish legislature has made many efforts to enhance debt-for-equity swaps within Spanish restructurings, invoking a broad swathe of Spanish law ranging from insolvency laws, to commercial, corporate and tax regulations. The measures can be divided into five main groups:

- Debt-for-equity swaps have been included in the effects that can be crammed down on holdouts pursuant to a *homologación judicial*. However, dissenting creditors are allowed to choose between the proposed capitalisation or a write-off in an amount equivalent to the par value of the shares.
- The Insolvency Act excludes from the definition of 'specially related parties', for the purposes of equitable subordination, those creditors that have become shareholders following a debt-for-equity swap implemented in the context of a collective refinancing agreement or *homologación judicial*, or in the context of a security enforcement.
- The majorities applicable to the shareholders' meeting approving a debt-for-equity swap have been lowered to simple majorities, instead of the former 'reinforced' majorities.
- The 2007 Spanish Decree on Takeover Bids has been amended with respect to debt-for-equity transactions where the target trading company is subject to conditions of serious financial distress. As a result, the Spanish Securities Market Authority (CNMV) may exempt such

capitalisation transactions from the obligation to launch a takeover bid, provided that their objective is to restore the financial viability of the relevant company in the long term. This authorisation from the CNMV is not necessary if the capitalisation is executed pursuant to a refinancing through a *homologación judicial* and backed by the favourable opinion of an independent expert.

- Finally, and very importantly, the Insolvency Act now includes a rebuttable presumption to assess the liability of shareholders of the debtor in circumstances where they reject, unless with reasonable cause, a debt-for-equity swap, capitalisation process or the issuance of convertible obligations, which rejection frustrates a collective refinancing agreement or *homologación judicial*. As explained above, should the debtor subsequently file for insolvency, the rejecting shareholders can be subject to the culpable qualification of the insolvency proceedings and, among other things, could be held personally liable for any shortfall in creditors' recoveries.

In this regard, it is important to note that, under Spanish law and contrary to what happens in some other jurisdictions, the cram-down of the equity always requires the approval of shareholders, even when they have no economic interest. This fact has jeopardised many Spanish financing restructurings and provides shareholders with leverage in these distressed situations, notwithstanding the fact that their share value at risk is zero, or close to zero.

The above measures have sought to address this key challenge of many restructurings. However, the Spanish legislature has still not taken firm steps towards aligning shareholders' rights within a refinancing proceeding to their "real" economic rights. In fact, as the Insolvency Act has not introduced restrictions to the rights of existing shareholders in the context of the refinancing of distressed debtors, in practice, debt-for-equity swaps in the Spanish restructuring market only take place when a consensual deal (with the shareholders' approval) is put in place. Notwithstanding this, creditors can still follow other classical strategies, such as enforcement of pledges over the debtor shares, or forcing the debtor's liquidation within the insolvency proceeding, although these may be less appealing to creditors in terms of timing and cost-efficiency.

United States

John C Longmire
Willkie Farr & Gallagher LLP
Christopher S Koenig
Kirkland & Ellis LLP

1. Introduction

Chapter 11 of the United States Bankruptcy Code is designed to allow financially distressed businesses to reorganise their debts, and to preserve going concern value where possible. Rather than requiring a cessation of operations or sale of assets (although each of those outcomes is available as well), Chapter 11 is designed to facilitate capital structure changes that allow these business to continue and, hopefully, thrive.

The objectives of Chapter 11 include maximising the value of the debtor's business for distribution to its stakeholders; consolidation of all claims and actions into a single forum; establishment of a 'breathing spell' through a stay of all litigation and debt collection efforts; and equality of treatment among similarly situated stakeholders. Following a Chapter 11 filing, the debtor's business continues to operate largely as usual, except that court approval is required for any actions outside of the ordinary course of business and, generally, payment may not be made on debts that arose before the date that the Chapter 11 case was filed (the 'petition date'). Absent extreme circumstances such as fraud or gross mismanagement, the debtor's existing management remains in charge of operations during the bankruptcy case; the appointment of a third-party trustee is rare.

2. Filing for Chapter 11 protection

2.1 Who may file

Most businesses are eligible to file for Chapter 11 if they have assets located in the US. Individuals, partnerships, and corporations may file but certain types of entities, including governmental entities, insurance companies and banks, may not (some of these types of entities are subject to separate insolvency or debt-adjustment mechanisms).

A company does not need to be organised under US law or have its centre of main interests in the US to be eligible for Chapter 11. Rather, a debtor must simply have assets in the US, and courts have found that even non-core assets such as a bank account or a retainer held by an attorney in the US makes a debtor eligible to file for Chapter 11 protection.

2.2 Process of filing

A voluntary filing for Chapter 11 relief is fairly straightforward. There is a uniform petition form that must be signed by an authorised signatory of the debtor. Evidence of due authorisation (such as a board resolution) is required. Once the petition is filed with the court and a filing fee is paid, the debtor is automatically protected by the provisions of the Bankruptcy Code. There is no requirement that the debtor make a showing of insolvency, and no requirement that a court "accept" the petition.

In rare cases, creditors may also force a debtor into bankruptcy by filing an involuntary petition. Involuntary petitions may be filed by three or more unsecured creditors acting together. After an involuntary petition is filed, the debtor is not automatically placed into bankruptcy; the bankruptcy court must first determine that the debtor is generally not paying its debts as they come due.

Chapter 11 (and all other types of) bankruptcy cases are heard by dedicated bankruptcy judges who sit in each of several judicial districts that make up the United States Bankruptcy Court system. A business debtor must be organised or have assets or an affiliate in a particular district in order to file its case in that venue.

3. Debtor's powers and obligations

3.1 Operation of business

The debtor in a Chapter 11 case is known as a 'debtor in possession', and is treated for some (but not all) purposes as if it were a legal entity distinct from the pre-bankruptcy company. A debtor in possession may pay debts that arise in the ordinary course of business after the petition date (for example, for goods or services provided post-petition) without court approval. However, the debtor may not pay debts that arose prior to the petition date (for example, for goods or services provided pre-petition), or enter into transactions outside the ordinary course of its business, without the prior approval of the bankruptcy court.

In order to address some of these restrictions, debtors routinely file 'first day motions' to seek approval from the bankruptcy court to pay certain important pre-petition claims. The bankruptcy court can authorise these payments if there is a sufficient showing that they are necessary for the debtor's reorganisation efforts. For example, if (as is common) a portion of employees' pre-petition wages are unpaid at the petition date, bankruptcy courts regularly authorise the payment of these wages and other employee benefits. Debtors also routinely receive court authority to pay certain other pre-petition debts to crucial stakeholders, such as claims for payroll taxes and insurance premiums.

Debtors also routinely seek permission to pay pre-petition claims of 'critical vendors' on the basis that they are necessary to the operation of the debtor's business and would cease doing business with the debtor if their claims are not paid. These motions tend to be more controversial, as there may be disputes about which vendors should be treated as critical and thus singled out for preferential treatment.

3.2 Assumption, rejection, and assignment of executory contracts and unexpired leases

A debtor has the power to assume, reject or assign executory contracts or unexpired leases. A contract qualifies as executory if both parties have significant unperformed obligations remaining due as of the petition date. Essentially, this gives a debtor in possession the power to review all of the debtor's unperformed contracts and leases and determine which to retain and which to reject. Prior to assumption or rejection of an agreement, the counterparty cannot terminate or cease performance under the contract on account of a pre-petition breach by the debtor. However, the debtor in possession must pay for post-petition benefits it receives. If the debtor in possession chooses to reject the contract or lease, it is no longer bound by the terms of the agreement, and the counterparty can assert an unsecured claim against the debtor for damages resulting from the breach. If the debtor assumes the contract or lease, it must cure any existing breaches of the agreement and provide adequate assurance of its ability to perform future obligations under the agreement.

The debtor may also assign an executory contract or unexpired lease to a third party, even if the agreement contains restrictions or prohibitions on assignment. Similarly, a provision that allows the counterparty to terminate or modify the debtor's rights based on a bankruptcy filing is unenforceable once the debtor is in Chapter 11. In order to assign a contract to a third party, the debtor must first assume the contract (thereby triggering the obligation to cure all existing defaults), and demonstrate that the assignee will be able to perform its future obligations under the contract.

The standard that courts use to evaluate a debtor's request to assume or reject a contract is whether the decision appears to reflect a reasonable exercise of the debtor's business judgement. This is a highly deferential standard, and thus courts will rarely deny a request to assume or reject an agreement unless the decision was manifestly unreasonable or the result of bad faith.

3.3 Litigation claims

The Bankruptcy Code allows the debtor to litigate various existing claims in the bankruptcy court. The Bankruptcy Code also allows a debtor to claw back certain types of payments or other transfers made prior to the bankruptcy filing.

There are two main types of clawback actions in US bankruptcy cases. A 'preference' is a transfer made by the debtor, while insolvent, in the ninety days prior to the petition date (one year if the transferee was an insider), on account of an existing debt, that results in the recipient receiving a greater recovery than it would have received had the payment not been made, and the creditor had instead received its *pro rata* share of the debtor's assets in the subsequent bankruptcy case. No showing of fault or intent is required. The recipient of a preferential payment can still avoid clawback by establishing one of several defences, such as that the transfer was made in the ordinary course of business, was part of a contemporaneous exchange of value, or was followed by a transfer of uncompensated 'new value' to the debtor.

Debtors may also claw back transactions known as 'fraudulent transfers'. There are two types of fraudulent transfer: 'actual' and 'constructive'. In each, the lookback period is two years from the petition date (although the debtor may also utilise applicable state fraudulent transfer law, which can extend the lookback period to up to six years).

Actual fraudulent transfer claims involve the rare cases where the debtor transferred an asset, or incurred a liability, with actual intent to hinder, delay or defraud its creditors. Because evidence of such intent is rarely available, courts typically look to badges of fraud (such as transactions with insiders immediately before large payment obligations became due) as evidence from which to infer fraudulent intent.

Constructive fraudulent transfer claims are much more common. In these cases, transfers may be unwound if the debtor was insolvent at the time of the transfer and received less than reasonably equivalent value in exchange. No showing of fraudulent intent is necessary.

Pursuant to the strong-arm provisions of the Bankruptcy Code, a debtor may also avoid liens that are unperfected as of the petition date. In order to achieve this result, the Bankruptcy Code provides that the debtor in possession is deemed to have the rights and powers of a hypothetical good faith purchaser of the collateral as of the petition date. As a result, the debtor in possession can effectively treat secured claims that have not been properly perfected as though they are unsecured claims.

3.4 Fiduciary duties of directors

While a debtor is in bankruptcy, its directors continue to have traditional fiduciary duties. However, if the debtor is insolvent, the ultimate beneficiaries of those duties may be creditors rather than equity holders, and directors are required to consider the best interests of creditors when making decisions for the debtor. In addition, because any transaction outside the ordinary course of business requires judicial approval, directors of companies in Chapter 11 may be more insulated from attack over post-petition decisions than in non-bankruptcy situations.

4. Other key stakeholders

4.1 Secured creditors

Secured creditors have certain rights and protections that must be respected in Chapter 11. Among these is the principle that the debtor may not use a secured creditor's cash or other collateral, or provide DIP lenders (discussed below) with senior liens on such collateral, without providing "adequate protection" of the existing secured creditors' interests in that collateral. Adequate protection is designed to ensure that the secured lenders are in no worse position than they were prior to the use or diminution in value of their collateral. Adequate protection can take many forms, such as replacement liens on unencumbered assets or cash payments to compensate for the diminution in value of the lender's collateral. The court may also find that adequate protection is unnecessary because a secured lender is significantly oversecured. Secured creditors cannot foreclose on their collateral during the Chapter 11 case, even if there is a default, unless there is a lack of adequate protection and they are granted relief from the automatic stay (which is rare).

4.2 Unsecured creditors' committee

A committee of unsecured creditors (UCC) is usually appointed early in the case by the US Trustee (a representative of the US government serving in a watchdog capacity in Chapter 11 cases). The UCC serves as a fiduciary to represent the interests of the debtor's unsecured creditors. The UCC is generally made up of four to seven large creditors holding claims of different types (eg, landlords, bondholders, suppliers, etc) and provides the primary, non-judicial independent oversight of the debtor during the Chapter 11 case. The UCC conducts significant diligence on the debtor's business and has the right to take discovery to seek additional information. It often scrutinises the debtor's requests closely and acts as the primary creditor representative to evaluate the debtor's operations and decision-making. The fees and expenses of a UCC's professionals are paid by the debtor.

5. The automatic stay

The automatic stay arises immediately upon the filing of a Chapter 11 case, in order to create the breathing spell necessary for a debtor to reorganise, and to funnel all claims activity into the bankruptcy court. The stay prevents parties from taking any action against the debtor or its property, to litigate or collect pre-petition debts. The automatic stay also prevents parties from creating, perfecting or enforcing liens.

The automatic stay theoretically protects all property of the debtor, even if it is not located in the US; however, enforcing the automatic stay outside the US can be difficult in practice. Accordingly, debtors with significant assets abroad may seek to have their Chapter 11 cases recognised in foreign jurisdictions, if possible, to ensure that debt collection efforts are foreclosed in those locations as well.

Any action taken in violation of the automatic stay, such as an attempt to collect a pre-petition claim from the debtor, is null and void. The debtor may file a motion in the bankruptcy court for an order enforcing the automatic stay, and any party who violates the automatic stay may be subject to punitive damages if it acted with knowledge of the bankruptcy case. The automatic stay does not prevent certain government actions, including criminal actions against the debtor or the exercise of the government's "police or regulatory powers".

Although the automatic stay arises immediately upon commencement of a bankruptcy case, it can be lifted for "cause" upon the motion of a party in interest. One common cause cited is that the debtor has not provided adequate protection to a secured creditor for the use or diminution in value of its collateral (see section 4.1). The automatic stay can also be lifted to permit foreclosure if

- the debtor has no equity in the property; and
- the property is not necessary to an effective reorganisation.

The automatic stay is rarely lifted on this basis in large commercial cases, because typically the debtor will be able to demonstrate that any core asset is necessary to its reorganisation efforts.

6. DIP financing

Most Chapter 11 debtors seek new financing (usually called 'DIP financing', or 'debtor in possession financing') on or after the petition date, to finance their operations while in bankruptcy. DIP loans are commonly secured by junior liens on all of the debtor's property and/or senior, priming liens on such property. For the court to approve such liens, the debtor must show that it could not obtain credit on an unsecured basis and, in the case of priming liens, that it could not obtain credit secured by a junior lien. In either case, the debtor may have to demonstrate that the rights of existing lienholders are adequately protected (see section 4.1). To make the necessary showings about the unavailability of other sources of credit, debtors typically submit testimony from their investment bankers that various alternative lenders were asked to provide a DIP loan on an unsecured or junior lien basis, and no lender was willing to accept those terms.

Unless there is a significant equity cushion in the existing senior lenders' collateral, or significant unencumbered assets available, DIP lenders routinely demand senior, priming liens to secure their new loans. Accordingly, it can be relatively straightforward to demonstrate that no other lender would be willing to extend credit on a junior lien basis. However, it may be difficult to achieve the existing lenders' consent to have their liens primed, or to demonstrate that their rights are adequately protected if they object to a priming lien. Therefore, DIP loans are most often provided by the existing senior secured lenders. Junior secured creditors are often contractually prohibited (through intercreditor agreements with the senior lenders) from objecting to a DIP loan that the senior creditors have approved.

DIP lenders may exert significant influence over a Chapter 11 case, through such mechanisms as requiring the debtor to make expenditures only in accordance with an agreed cash flow budget, establishing deadlines by which milestone events in the bankruptcy case must occur, and providing for short-term maturities.

7. Sales of assets

The debtor may sell some, or all, of its assets outside the ordinary course of business, with the approval of the bankruptcy court. These transactions are commonly known as '363 sales', after the section of the Bankruptcy Code that authorises them. Section 363 allows a debtor to sell assets free and clear of all liens, claims, encumbrances and other interests, meaning that the buyer can be completely insulated from any liability for the seller's debts. Given that most Chapter 11 debtors are insolvent, this is a crucial provision that allows a debtor to dispose some or all of its business in exchange for cash that can be used to pay creditors.

Assets that are collateral for secured creditors can be sold free and clear of those liens, even without the secured lenders' consent, and their liens can be made to attach instead to the cash proceeds of the sale. Secured creditors may also 'credit bid' in 363 sales of their collateral, meaning that they can propose to reduce or eliminate their secured claims, rather than paying cash, in exchange for ownership of their collateral.

In order to approve a 363 sale, the bankruptcy court generally will be required to find that the proposed sale represents the highest or otherwise best available price for the assets being sold. To support such a finding, the debtor will usually retain an investment banker and conduct an in-depth marketing process. The court may also require an auction of the assets. In order to ensure that the auction process is successful, debtors will often sign an agreement, in advance of an auction, to sell the assets to a stalking horse bidder. Such an agreement is binding on the bidder, but does not bind the debtor until it is approved by the court. To compensate the stalking horse buyer for being bound to this arrangement while the debtor seeks court approval of the sale (and continues to market the assets), the court may approve various types of protections for the stalking horse buyer, such as a break-up fee (typically 2–3% of the purchase price), expense reimbursement, and requirements that competing bidders provide cash deposits, meet specified minimum bid amounts, and satisfy various other requirements. The stalking horse bid then serves as a floor against which other bids may be measured. If competing bids are received, a live auction may be held. Once a successful bidder is chosen, the debtor will seek court approval before closing the transaction.

8. Plan of reorganisation

8.1 Overview

A plan of reorganisation is usually the final milestone in a Chapter 11 case. The plan is a comprehensive document that provides for the treatment of all claims against the debtor and provides for the debtor's restructuring. A plan sorts all claims against and equity interests in the debtor into separate classes. Each class must contain only claims (or equity interests) that are substantially similar to one another, and all members of each class must receive (proportionately) identical treatment to one another. Regardless of the terms of a creditor's agreements with the debtor, if its class votes to accept the plan, the creditor will be bound to accept the treatment proposed by the plan for its class, regardless of whether that creditor voted in favour of, or otherwise accepted, the plan. Once a plan is confirmed by the bankruptcy court, it binds all creditors and other parties in interest, all claims against the debtor may be discharged, and claimants will be limited to the recoveries provided for them under the plan.

8.2 Exclusivity

The debtor has the exclusive right to propose a plan for the first 120 days of the case. This exclusivity allows the debtor to effectively control the case for a period of time by preventing creditors from proposing their own plan. The exclusivity period may be extended for cause, but not beyond 18 months after the petition date. Cause for an extension is typically demonstrated through

- the size and complexity of the case;
- the existence of good faith negotiations between the debtor and its creditors regarding the terms of a plan; and
- the amount of time that has elapsed in the case.

In large Chapter 11 cases, an initial proposed extension of the exclusivity period is almost always approved, and the court typically is willing to approve multiple extensions in complex cases if there is some evidence of good faith progress towards a plan.

Creditors may also seek to terminate exclusivity for cause, but such motions are rarely granted unless creditors can demonstrate bad faith by the debtor or evidence that the debtor does not intend to propose a confirmable plan.

8.3 Disclosure statement

When a party submits its plan to the court (and thereby makes it public), it must also submit a 'disclosure statement'. The disclosure statement is a non-binding, descriptive document (similar to a prospectus) that is designed to provide voting parties with sufficient information about the company, the plan and its impact on creditors for them to cast fully informed votes. If the debtor is reorganising (as opposed to liquidating), the disclosure statement will typically include a detailed business plan and projections of future performance.

If the plan proposes to equitise debt claims, the disclosure statement will typically include a detailed valuation of the reorganised company and its equity securities. Before the plan proponent can seek creditors' votes on the plan, the court must approve the disclosure statement. In order to do so, the court must be satisfied that the disclosure statement contains "adequate information" for voting parties to make informed decisions on the plan. Once a disclosure statement is approved, the debtor (or other plan proponent) distributes the disclosure statement, the plan and any related documents to creditors, and solicits their votes on the plan.

8.4 Classification and voting

As discussed above, a plan must classify stakeholders into classes of creditors and equity holders based on the types of debt or equity they hold. Classification is crucial, because under the plan, all members of a class will be treated the same as one another. "Substantially similar" claims or interests may be placed in the same class, but the plan proponent has significant discretion in classifying claims, except that lien priority should generally be respected.

The plan will also determine whether each class is 'impaired'. A class is impaired if the plan alters in any way the rights of its members. As one example, a class would be impaired if its members received payment in full, but the maturity date on the notes held by the class members was extended by one year.

If a class is unimpaired, the members of the class do not have the right to vote on the plan (because their rights are unaltered). If a class will receive no distribution under the plan, its members are presumed to reject the plan and do not have the right to vote. All impaired classes that receive a distribution under the plan have the right to vote.

Voting on a plan takes place by class. Each member of a voting class will receive a ballot, along with a copy of the plan and disclosure statement. After the voting deadline, an agent of the court will count the votes and determine which classes accepted the plan and which classes rejected the plan. In order for a class of creditors to have accepted the plan, affirmative votes must be received from at least

- a majority of all class members that voted on the plan; and
- two-thirds in dollar amount of all voting claims in the class.

8.5 Confirmation of a plan

After voting occurs, the court will hold a hearing on whether to confirm the plan. All parties in interest have the right to object and be heard at this hearing (even if they did not have the right to vote). There are a variety of confirmation requirements, but most notably, the 'cram-down' requirements must be met, and either all classes entitled to vote must have accepted the plan, or at least one impaired class must have voted to accept the plan. If any class votes (or is deemed) to reject the plan, a cram-down of the plan may be forced on that class (if the class is a senior class of creditors, this is sometimes referred to as 'cram-up').

To succeed with a cram-down, the plan proponent must demonstrate that the plan does not "unfairly discriminate", and is "fair and equitable", with respect to the dissenting class(es). The unfair discrimination requirement effectively means that classes of equal priority should not receive distributions of different value under the plan without reasonable justification. Two classes of unsecured creditors could receive the same value but through different means (one in cash and one in new notes, for example), but the value of such recoveries should not be different absent a rational business justification.

The "fair and equitable" requirement is also known as the 'absolute priority' rule, which provides that no class can receive less than full payment under the plan if any junior class is receiving any recovery. With respect to secured creditors, there is an additional requirement:

- the secured creditors must retain their liens and receive deferred cash payments with a present value of at least the value of their collateral; or
- the collateral must be sold and the secured creditors' liens attached to the proceeds of the sale; or
- the secured creditors must receive the "indubitable equivalent" of their claims, which courts interpret as requiring that the secured creditors will receive the same level of value as they would receive for their existing liens (eg, a replacement lien on similarly valued collateral).

An additional confirmation requirement is that the plan is "feasible" – that is, that it is not likely to result in the debtor needing to liquidate, or further reorganise, in the few years after implementation of the plan. The plan proponent typically demonstrates feasibility through financial projections, which objecting parties can challenge as unreasonable. The plan proponent need not guarantee a successful reorganisation; it need only show that it is more likely than not that the plan is feasible.

The final primary confirmation requirement is known as the 'best interests' test, which requires the plan proponent to demonstrate that the debtor's stakeholders will receive at least as much value as would be received under a hypothetical liquidation of the debtor under Chapter 7 of the Bankruptcy Code.

The best interests test is usually easy to satisfy, because a reorganisation of the debtor will typically lead to significantly higher value than a fire sale liquidation of the debtor under Chapter 7, and even a Chapter 11 liquidation will be more cost-effective than one implemented by a third party Chapter 7 trustee.

8.6 Typical types of plans

The most common type of plan of reorganisation is a debt-for-equity swap, where certain of the debtor's existing creditors exchange all or a portion of their debt for the equity of the reorganised debtor. This can remove substantial debt from the reorganised debtor's balance sheet, benefiting the debtor's new equity holders.

Some plans of reorganisation resolve substantial litigation against the debtor or related parties, either through a settlement of that litigation under the plan, or through the establishment of a litigation trust that will be beneficially owned by creditors and pursue the litigation after the confirmation of the plan.

Some Chapter 11 plans involve 'substantive consolidation', which means that the assets and liabilities of certain debtors (or in rare cases, non-debtors) are combined, as though the entities were merged, for the limited purpose of making distributions to creditors. Substantive consolidation is often approved in consensual situations as a convenience, but is a remedy that is rarely granted to creditors over a debtor's objection (the standard is similar to that applicable to piercing the corporate veil).

Some Chapter 11 plans are actually liquidation plans that provide for the cessation of operations, sale of the debtor's assets, and distribution of the proceeds to the debtor's stakeholders.

8.7 Prepackaged/pre-negotiated plans

One recent trend in Chapter 11 cases is the negotiation of plans before the debtor even files for bankruptcy. If a debtor strikes a deal with key creditors prior to bankruptcy, that agreement is usually implemented more quickly than if the debtor begins negotiations after a filing. Stakeholders may agree on either a 'prepackaged' or a 'pre-negotiated' plan. In a prepackaged plan, the debtor solicits all votes on a plan prior to filing. If votes are to be solicited pre-petition, the usual requirement that the court approve a disclosure statement before voting does not apply. Instead, the court may be asked to approve the disclosure statement after the fact, at the confirmation hearing. In a prepackaged case, immediately upon the bankruptcy filing, the plan and disclosure statement are filed with the court, and a hearing is scheduled for court approval of both documents. Prepackaged cases are extremely expedited, and a plan is often confirmed by the court within 45–60 days.

In a pre-negotiated plan, prior to filing the debtor enters into an agreement with a voting majority of creditors in one or more classes to support a plan, but the debtor does not solicit votes pre-filing (and the debtor may not even have a final version of a plan at the time of the filing). The agreement between the debtor and the supporting creditors is often called a 'plan support agreement' or a 'restructuring support agreement'. These creditors agree to vote for a plan with certain agreed-upon terms, and the debtor will often agree to give the supporting creditors certain rights and protections, including:

- an agreement not to seek a different restructuring with other parties; and
- deadlines by which certain case milestones must occur, failing which the supporting creditors may terminate the agreement.

A pre-negotiated case must have a disclosure statement approved after the filing, and before the voting on a plan, so the Chapter 11 case typically lasts at least a few months. However, the restructuring support agreement gives the debtor leverage in negotiations with other creditors and an important narrative for the debtor's other stakeholders that the debtor has already secured a path to get out of bankruptcy.

The Lehman bankruptcy

Russell Downs
PwC LLP

1. Introduction

The events around September 2008, when the world's fourth-largest investment bank went into bankruptcy, played out on our screens and newsfeeds and have come to signify the onset of the global financial crisis. For those in the financial services industry, and for many onlookers, the bank's collapse will no doubt be one of those "Where were you when ...?" moments.

Ten years have passed since this dramatic moment, providing a suitable milestone for reflection from a bankruptcy standpoint and for offering some commentary on how the relevant bankruptcy laws coped with Lehman's demise, and what were some of the key issues.

Lehman Brothers was an employer of over 20,000 people across the world, with key centres in London (for Europe), Hong Kong (for Asia) and New York (for the US). It had over 10,000 customers and a group balance sheet including custodied assets measured in the trillions of dollars. The group had been attempting to achieve a white knight takeover and indeed a number of the staff left for that fateful weekend of 13th and 14th September believing that Monday would see them in new employment – certainly not contemplating the failure of such a distinguished firm. In the event there was no such rescue and as time ticked by on the afternoon of Sunday 14th it became increasingly clear that the group would file for bankruptcy. What would happen next few, if any, could speculate on with any conviction.

The group was run on a fully integrated basis, with slick treasury management orchestrated by the US parent and the regional hubs in London and Hong Kong, and data and technology shared throughout the group. What any practitioner would take for granted now by way of resolution plan or living will, has come about since 2008, so the relevant bankruptcy officers began their contingency planning from a blank sheet of paper. The first wave of bankruptcy filings began on the morning of 15th September in Japan and Asia, before moving to Europe and concluding in the US. Not surprisingly, further appointments were made as matters developed. Within a very short interval, a group formerly controlled by a global executive with years of service on behalf of its shareholders, fragmented into a disparate group of insolvency professionals entirely unfamiliar with the business and urgently attempting to identify their respective creditor groups.

In the UK, appointments became inevitable as soon as it became clear to the directors that the companies would not be funded by their parent during the course of the Sunday, and they were made in time for the 8 a.m. market opening on the Monday morning. Lehman Brothers (International) Europe (LBIE) was the principal and regulated Lehman entity, and had a number of important branches in Europe and elsewhere.

Other notable appointments in Europe were made in Germany and Switzerland, with the latter hosting an unregulated entity used specifically for derivatives trading.

In the US, Lehman Brothers Holdings Inc (LBHI), the parent, filed on the Monday, as did its derivative trading business and a large number of other US entities. A key decision was taken to ring fence the parent's broker-dealer, Lehman Brothers Inc (LBI), to enable a rescue attempt to be made. This was achieved in the Barclays/Lehman transaction on Friday 19 September, which left a lasting legacy in terms of the conduct of the bankruptcy process.

During the course of several tumultuous days, what had been a corporate group run along divisional lines for the benefit of group stakeholders (shareholders, customers and employees) became a legal entity construct with new and independent officers, in many cases appointed by the jurisdictional courts to oversee a statutory process, with a heavy focus on managing each entity's affairs for the sole benefit of its own creditors.

In its most distilled form, the methodology for dealing with an insolvency situation is as simple as taking control of the company's assets, devising and subsequently implementing a realisation strategy for those assets, identifying and agreeing the claims of creditors, and finally orchestrating a distribution to creditors through a consensual plan or otherwise. This basic approach remained valid despite the enormous scale of the Lehman collapse.

The early days, weeks and months of the insolvency were focused around identifying the people, data systems and assets available to each entity, as well as shortlisting urgent issues requiring the most pressing attention.

2. Global protocol

It became clear that the US parent would benefit greatly from a coordinated worldwide insolvency approach that maximised the pre-bankruptcy benefits of a single amalgamation of corporate interest. This led to the development of the global protocol, which was adopted almost without exception throughout the group. The key benefits of the approach were:

- a common set of numbers as at the group's close of business on Friday 12 September;

- a vision and shared objectives about how to deal with issues between the various affiliates; and
- (crucially) access to shared data and systems.

To the bemusement of many, however, LBIE found the benefit of signing up to the global protocol underwhelming and instead preferred a series of bilateral agreements with affiliates to secure their support, where needed.

A global protocol from a purist point of view does not sit particularly well when assessed against the relevant legal framework governing the insolvent entity. There is obviously a benefit in the affiliates within a group acting in a coordinated way in order to maximise asset values, coordinate agreement of claims, and avoid unnecessary costs. The question, however, is whether the costs of signing up to such a protocol are more than outweighed by the benefits. Where the group's parent will have the most to gain from coordinated actions and improved asset returns – particularly in protecting any remaining equity value through the rest of the group – there is obviously an imperative for such a protocol. But LBIE had its own resources (people, data and systems) and, having formed the view that the benefits for its stakeholders seemed more burdensome than real, it elected to absent itself from the global protocol framework and instead opt for a series of bilateral arrangements.

In any event, as bystanders, we can agree that the global protocol put in place in the Lehman case provided one of the critical ingredients for making the bankruptcy the success that it became. It brought focus, clarity and purpose. It did require careful orchestration and investment in time to build the appropriate relationships; but discussion of claims between affiliates on the basis of a common set of books and records has taken years off the process and avoided potential challenge between those estates.

3. Bar dates

Creditors wishing to make a claim in an insolvency process must usually do so by a specified time known as the bar date. Despite the ambitions of the global protocol it did not amend the statutory bar date processes in place in different jurisdictions, and bar dates can be the biggest challenge to the success of any group insolvency situation. They are a common and routine requirement but they come with a range of timing and legal effects.

The US notably has a relatively early bar date and in the Lehman case, for many of the estates, the bar date was set at four months from the insolvency. Also, there is no accommodation for late-filed claims, which presents a very material, early hurdle on which prospective creditors must focus; the more so from an affiliate perspective where newly appointed officers are trying to get to grips with a number of complex issues.

This can be contrasted with the UK approach, where there is no set time for a bar date, and LBIE's bar date was ultimately set some nine years after its counterpart entities in the US.

One of the key characteristics of the Lehman business was inter-affiliate trading. This was not just relevant in terms of service and support by certain affiliates. The more important entities had significant trading activity across all financial products both on a proprietary basis but also for the clients and counterparties of a particular affiliate. Typically, trading was in both directions and was significant. Pre-bankruptcy, a number of formal agreements were in place to manage these arrangements. In many cases, inter-affiliate balances would be settled daily, monthly or as and when a small balance grew to be a large one. At all times, though, inter-affiliate trading was settled on a net basis. The calling for claims through the bar date process focused all of the practitioners on ensuring that they had put in the maximum possible claim in order to protect their position not only on behalf of their clients but also, no doubt, in respect of their own personal exposure – no one wanted to be criticised for having failed to put in an appropriately prudent claim. This seemed to be an invitation for creativity – many claims were put in on a gross basis (therefore ignoring set-off, which would have been part of the usual settlement basis) and other potential heads of claim were identified as being speculative. This of course put pressure on the global protocol and initially delayed plans for resolving the estates.

By way of example, LBIE filed outbound claims of over £50 billion and received inbound claims of over £40 billion. This would have a marked impact on how the estates would be taken forward and the positions taken by creditors as they assessed whether to hold on to their investment or close out any exposure.

The market has to think long and hard and search out a better solution to ensuring there is greater restraint in filing such claims, but no obvious alternative apparently exists. Once a claim has been submitted it requires considerable effort to have it removed without the claimant's consent, and it therefore provides leverage in any ensuing discussions.

4. Chapter 11 plan of reorganisation

Key events in the course of the global bankruptcy were the formulation by the Chapter 11 debtors in the US of a plan of reorganisation and its subsequent negotiation and confirmation by the bankruptcy court.

The plan was filed in March 2010 as a combined plan, including all twenty-two of the US entities that had filed for protection under Chapter 11. The timing was driven by the debtors' desire to remain in control of the development of the plan and prevent other parties from filing alternative plans. At the time it was widely recognised that there was going to be considerable further negotiation before the bankruptcy court would be asked to confirm the plan.

The debtors had to develop a plan that found an acceptable path through a number of commercial tensions, where different groups of creditors held strongly opposing views:

- *Speed v value:* The plan had to balance the competing interests of creditors who wanted a fast resolution and whose recovery, perhaps because they ranked senior to other creditors, might largely be unaffected by a fire-sale of assets, against those of creditors who wanted to maximise asset values no matter how long it might take.
- *Guarantees:* Ordinary creditors of LBHI wanted to minimise the number and value of allowed claims by guarantee claimants.
- *Consolidation:* The proposed plan was based on each entity being independent, with its own assets and liabilities, such that the rate of recovery for creditors in one estate might be significantly greater than in another. Many creditors argued that the group in fact operated as one entity and that the bankruptcy court should apply the concept of substantive consolidation such that all the combined debtors' assets and liabilities should be pooled together.

In the event, the plan was confirmed by the court and became effective in March 2012, some two years after it was originally launched.

From a UK perspective, it was vital that the claims of UK affiliates against the US debtors (and vice versa) should be properly recognised by the reorganisation plan. The administrators spent around eighteen months negotiating a settlement agreement setting out the basis of treatment of agreed claims in the plan that LBIE and the other UK entities were prepared to accept.

5. Emergence of secondary trading

The bankruptcy very quickly gave rise to unprecedented opportunities for secondary debt trading, as original creditors decided to close down their exposure at a discount for certainty, and no doubt in many cases address their own liquidity issues given the then-prevailing financial crisis. The opportunity was seized by large and smaller players across all of the Lehman entities. Given commercial confidentiality, little is known other than by way of anecdote, but the first trades began in the first few months after the bankruptcy. What is clear is that all pricing has trended up as progress has been made, and the biggest correlation is between the elimination of the protective inter-affiliate claims referenced above and the consequent improvement in underlying recovery for creditors. Many estates have made par recoveries and a good number are now in the unfamiliar territory of dealing with the allocation of post-appointment interest. Indeed, LBI and LBIE alone have made returns to creditors of almost £90 billion. Only LBIE's Waterfall judgement on currency claims, discussed below, has sparked a reduction in the pricing of its claims, although by then most claims had traded and remaining volume was very thin.

The claims purchasers' investment strategy seems to have involved coverage across all entities as a hedge against the protective claims made by affiliates who anticipated that the recoveries being reported would eventually flow out of the affiliates to claims purchasers as third party creditors. It is worth noting that estates handled this in different ways. Some gave greater disclosure than might have been expected to enable original creditors to be fully informed about the estate's outlook and of course enable analysts' models to be refreshed, whereas others disclosed less about their outlook or the progress being made in their estate.

6. The LBIE/LBI resolution

The trading relationship between the US broker-dealer LBI and the European regulated entity of LBIE was the biggest and most complex to finalise. The LBI estate was under the control of a Securities Investor Protection Act (SIPA) insolvency process rather than a Chapter 11. The issues remaining in the LBI estate were quickly distilled into the LBI/Barclays transaction and the litigation that would ensue between the two parties to determine whether the purchaser had overpaid in respect of the transaction and what assets had in fact been transferred. Additionally, LBI had not transferred a number of clients and these residual clients would need to be dealt with. It soon became clear that LBIE was the largest of its clients that had not been transferred to Barclays, and LBIE's claim covered clients as well as a proprietary house claim. The status of LBIE's claim as a 'client' or 'general' creditor under the SIPA insolvency was critical to prospective recovery. Conversely, LBI had multiple claims against LBIE and it was not clear that as an affiliate LBIE would have the same status as third party customers in respect of its claims.

A key complication was the difference in the insolvency relevant date (LBIE's being Monday 15 September 2008 and LBI's being Friday 19 September 2008) and trying to establish the impact of this four-day interim period. Whilst LBIE had ceased trading as at the date of its own insolvency, LBI had allowed a very large number of trades to settle over the following few days, such that LBIE's closing positon on its bankruptcy date looked markedly different from LBI's closing position on 19 September. In the chaos of those opening days of the insolvency it was clear that where LBI held an omnibus account for LBIE, many segregated client securities were used to settle trades of other clients in that time. This meant that there was a very significant mismatch between the securities that should have been held and those securities that were in fact held.

The SIPA insolvency process differs in a fundamental way from a Chapter 11 because it creates a customer estate for agreed customers and a general estate for other creditors. The trustee appointed determines ultimately, with the blessing of the bankruptcy court, how LBI's property should be allocated as between the customer estate and the general estate. During the course of the process it became evident that if all of LBIE's asserted customer claims were valid, there was a prospect that there would be insufficient customer property to satisfy them. Additionally, LBIE's own clients had put in protective claims to LBI pending a resolution of the LBI/LBIE position. As both sides prepared for a legal challenge to the status of LBIE's claims, the parties were able to develop a very creative settlement framework to agree their respective claims in each other's estates, and in so doing transformed the outlook for their estates, both in terms of timescale to resolve final adjudication and in terms of the economic recovery for creditors and clients alike.

7. Waterfall proceedings

'Waterfall proceedings' refers collectively to a series of three directions applications made by the administrators of, *inter alia*, LBIE, Lehman Brothers Limited (LBL) and LB Holdings Intermediate 2 Limited (LBHI2). Each application dealt with different issues but they were all aimed at providing the administrators of LBIE with clarity on how to deal with the c. £8 billion surplus it expected to have after settlement of all its ordinary provable claims.

The applications covered a number of highly complex issues, some of which arose purely because LBIE was an unlimited liability company. While the unlimited liability issues are intellectually very interesting, they are unlikely ever to be of relevance to general restructuring or insolvency, so have been omitted here.

The term 'waterfall' was first coined, in the insolvency context, by the Supreme Court in its decision in *Re Nortel GmbH*.[1] In that decision, the court set out the order in which the administrator should pay claims from the assets available (after costs), in summary, as follows:

1. Unsecured creditors
2. Statutory interest
3. Non-provable creditors
4. Equity

Waterfall I, the first application, principally dealt with three questions:

- Where did debt that was contractually subordinated rank in the above waterfall?
- Did a non-provable claim exist as a result of losses suffered by creditors because their claims were converted into and then paid in sterling rather than in their underlying currency?
- Which of the categories of claims, if any, in the above waterfall were LBIE's shareholders (LBHI2 and LBL) obligated to contribute as a result of LBIE being an unlimited liability company?

---

1 (2013) UKSC 52.

8. Ranking of subordinated debt

Subordinated debt was an important part of LBIE's regulated capital and was governed by common form Financial Services Authority subordination agreements. At the date LBIE went into administration it had a subordinated debt balance of approximately £1.25 billion.

LBHI2 held the subordinated debt in LBIE and asserted that it was only subordinate to provable non-subordinated creditors and not to statutory interest or non-provable claims. In other words, LBHI2 argued that it should rank between the first and second items in the above waterfall.

LBIE argued that it should rank just above equity or, failing that, between the second and third elements of the waterfall.

The court was asked to determine the correct construction of the subordination agreements.

After several years of litigation, this aspect was finally determined by the Supreme Court, which agreed with LBIE's arguments and put the subordinated debt firmly at the bottom of the waterfall, as quasi equity.

9. Currency conversion claims

It is easiest to demonstrate what a currency conversion claim (CCC) is by means of an illustration.

Creditor A had a claim against LBIE arising from a contract denominated in US$. The claim was for $180 million. Pursuant to Rule 2.86[2] the proof submitted by Creditor A was converted to sterling at the date of LBIE's administration, giving rise to an admitted claim of £100 million.

LBIE paid a series of distributions to Creditor A in sterling,[3] in the amounts and at the dates shown in the table below.

Because the rate of exchange was different at each payment date, after payment of the final dividend Creditor A had received its full proved claim amount of £100 million but was still $20 million short on its contractual US$ claim. This was the CCC for Creditor A.

---

2 Rule 2.86 of the Insolvency Rules 1986.

3 LBIE does not have a choice of distribution currency and is obliged by the Rules to pay dividends to creditors in sterling. Similarly, it arguably has no statutory obligation to consider the currency of underlying contracts, hold its funds in appropriate currencies or otherwise hedge against currency movements.

Table 1: Currency conversion claim – Creditor A

	£ (m)	**$ (m)**
Claim	100.00	180.00
1st distribution 30/11/12	25.20	40.32
2nd distribution 28/06/13	43.30	66.25
3rd distribution 29/11/13	23.70	38.29
4th distribution 30/04/14	7.80	15.04
	100.00	**160.00**
Currency conversion claim		**20.00**

The court was asked to decide whether such claims existed and, if they did, where they would rank in the waterfall.

Whilst both the High Court and the Court of Appeal (by majority) decided that CCCs did exist and would rank for payment after statutory interest as non-provable claims, the Supreme Court ultimately determined that such claims do not exist.

The value of CCC claims against LBIE was in the region of £1.4 billion (or about a 15% premium of US$ contractual claims) and the prospect of such claims added real uncertainty to the value of claims being held and traded in the secondary market. This was one of the main reasons why earlier settlement of creditors' entitlements to statutory interest was not achievable.

The second waterfall application, Waterfall II, was commenced after the High Court judgment was handed down in respect of the first application. It aimed to get clarification on a number of practical issues that would affect the quantum of the statutory interest and non-provable claims that could be made against the LBIE surplus.

The principal questions before the court were:

- how the LBIE administrators should calculate statutory interest payable to creditors; and
- whether the creditor claim agreement process used by LBIE had somehow waived or released a creditor's right to statutory interest or to non-provable claims (ie, currency conversion claims).

The first question had two main components: first, whether the rule for calculation of interest established in *Bower v Marris*[4] should be applied and second, in cases where the rate of interest to be applied was calculated by reference to cost of funds, what factors should be considered in determining that rate.

Stated simply, the decision in *Bower v Marris* would suggest that payments made by LBIE to its creditors in respect of their provable claims should be treated as settling statutory interest first and then principal. To put it in context, application of this rule by LBIE creditors would have resulted in additional statutory interest entitlements of at least c. £1.9 billion.

The second issue arises because the statutory obligation for an administrator to use the surplus in his hands (after payment of all proved creditor claims against a company) to pay interest to such creditors provides that the rate of interest is "whichever is the greater of the [Judgment Act rate of 8%] and the rate applicable to the debt apart from the administration".

As the Lehman group's broker-dealer in Europe, LBIE had many counterparties that traded with it under the terms of an ISDA Master Agreement (or similar German master agreement). As you might expect, these agreements included provisions to calculate a default rate of interest in the event that one of the parties defaulted – default in this case being triggered by LBIE's insolvency.

The major point at issue was therefore whether this contractual default rate of interest would be higher than the 8% Judgment Act rate.

This issue was very important for the different LBIE stakeholders because, in simple terms, the default interest rate is calculated by reference to the cost of funds of the relevant payee and, depending on the counterparty, cost of funds could represent a much higher rate than 8%.

The scheme of arrangement proposed by LBIE, which became effective on 20 June 2018, resolved these issues by agreeing to the withdrawal of the application for permission to appeal to the Supreme Court in respect of the *Bower v Marris* question, and by a settlement premium being paid to creditors with relevant ISDA (or similar) contracts. As such, no finally determinative court judgment was handed down.

Waterfall III, the third application, was only issued in 2016 and had its first hearing in the High Court in February 2017. This application dealt primarily with the remaining unanswered questions regarding the obligations of LBIE's shareholders: the rights of indemnity or counterclaim *inter se*, and rights of set-off between the contributories and LBIE. It also sought to deal with the validity of specific claims being made by LBL as a result of its being the service company within the UK Lehman group.

The third waterfall application was withdrawn after a settlement was

4 (1841) Cr & Ph 351.

reached between the parties, paving the way for the LBIE scheme of arrangement and allowing significant distributions to be made by a number of UK affiliates.

The final question, as to whether the creditor claim agreement process used by LBIE had somehow waived or released a creditor's right to statutory interest or to non-provable claims (ie, currency conversion claims), was rendered moot when the Supreme Court held that currency conversion claims do not exist in an English insolvency.

It is worth noting that there were two very large groups of creditors taking polar opposite positions in the waterfall applications. One group represented ordinary unsecured, unsubordinated creditors. The other was a specially formed partnership called Wentworth which had acquired both a high value in ordinary unsecured, unsubordinated claims, and interests in LBIE's subordinated debt and preferential equity.

Either of these creditor groups could block a settlement proposal from LBIE. It was only after the waterfall proceedings had almost run their course that the two sides could be brought close enough together to achieve the settlement compromise achieved by LBIE's scheme of arrangement.

10. LBIE pays 100%

LBIE's first distribution was in November 2012 and its final distribution was in April 2014 when it reached par (albeit its secondary pricing had reach par some years before).

Other estates have also reached a par return for creditors and will be paying out interest in addition.

This positive outcome does raise the question of whether the entities should have been placed into insolvency at the time and whether a different solution, delivering the same outcome, could have been reached sooner.

11. Conclusion

Even with the remarkable outcome achieved there is no doubt that, absent a last-minute rescue, bankruptcy for the group as a whole was the only option. For those estates that have paid creditors in full, including interest, that is perhaps harder to argue.

Bankruptcy regimes, practitioners and advisers all played their part in ensuring original creditors and secondary investors buying claims got the best possible return in the circumstances.

No two insolvencies are ever the same and it is unlikely there will be anything ever again approaching the size, scale and complexity of Lehman Brothers. But if there were, stakeholders should take considerable heart that there is a profession intent on being creative, collaborative and focused on minimising stakeholders' losses.

About the authors

Alexandra Bigot
Partner, Willkie Farr & Gallagher LLP
abigot@willkie.com

Alexandra Bigot is a partner in the Business Reorganisation and Restructuring Department at Willkie in Paris, a position she has held since 2003. Ms Bigot is regularly involved in out-of-court and cross-border restructuring matters on behalf of debtors, sponsors and hedge funds, especially with respect to troubled leveraged buyout (LBO) cases (including loan-to-own strategies) and sales of underperforming or distressed branches of international groups. She also advises investors (corporate investors, hedge funds and recovery funds) seeking investment opportunities in insolvency proceedings and out-of-court restructuring cases. Ms Bigot has significant previous experience advising private equity funds in LBO acquisitions with regard to corporate, finance and tax matters. She also gained specific experience as a former private equity investor at Lazard.

Ms Bigot is a member of the board of the Association pour le Retournement des Entreprises (ARE), of the LBO Committee of AFIC and of the International Insolvency Institute (III).

Carlo Bosco
Managing director and head of Financing Advisory and Restructuring for Europe, Greenhill
Carlo.Bosco@greenhill.com

Carlo Bosco is a managing director and head of Financing Advisory and Restructuring for Europe at Greenhill. Prior to joining Greenhill in London in 2014, Carlo spent eight years in the Restructuring Group at Lazard in New York and Milan. He has represented clients in over 25 closed transactions in EMEA and North America, in a wide range of corporate finance activities including M&A, out-of-court and in-court restructuring, rehabilitations and debt and equity financings. Corporate clients over the years include the AA, Lonmin, Avanti Communications, Airopack, Stemcor, Dynegy, Local Insight, Rural / Metro, FGIC, PMI, Limoni, Italtel and La Rinascente.

Carlo holds an MSc in finance (CLEFIN) and a BA in international economics and management (DIEM) from Bocconi University. He was selected by *Financial News* as one of the top 40 "Rising Stars" in the investment banking industry in March 2016.

Ignacio Buil Aldana
Partner and head of the London office, Cuatrecasas
ignacio.buil@cuatrecasas.com

Ignacio Buil Aldana is a partner in the finance practice at Cuatrecasas. He is head of the London office, where he has been based since September 2013. He is qualified in Spain and New York.

Ignacio has extensive experience in negotiating financing and refinancing agreements involving a wide range of capital structures, including the refinancing of LBO financings, project finance, real estate and corporate finance.

He represents borrowers and lenders, and advises financial institutions, hedge funds and private equity funds on several national and multijurisdictional financing and refinancing transactions, distressed investment strategies and acquisitions of NPL portfolios.

He worked as an associate in the New York office of a major American law firm representing several debtors and creditors in Chapter 11 reorganisations, including advising on 363 sales and DIP financings.

He has been recommended by several directories, including *Chambers Global* and *Chambers Europe 2018* ("Banking and Finance" and "Investment Funds").

Stephan Chischportich
Co-head of EMEA Restructuring, Evercore
stephan.chischportich@evercore.com

Stephan Chischportich is co-head of Evercore's EMEA Restructuring Group and is based in London. Stephan has advised companies and their stakeholders in many of the most complex debt financing and financial restructuring transactions globally. He has represented both debtors and creditors across a number of jurisdictions and has significant experience in debt financing, liability management, restructuring and distressed M&A.

He has advised on a number of high-profile transactions, including advising ZIM Integrated Shipping in connection with its financial restructuring and charter-hire renegotiations; Ocean Rig in connection with its financial restructuring and COMI shift; and senior lenders to Dubai World on an amend & extend transaction involving over $15 billion of debt obligations.

He has been recognised by *Financial News* as a "Rising Star in Investment Banking – Top 40 Under 40" and by *M&A Advisor* as an "Emerging Leader of Finance". He was a finalist in Turnaround Management Association's Young Turnaround Professional award.

Kevin Coates
Managing director, AlixPartners
kcoates@alixpartners.com

Kevin Coates is a managing director in the turnaround and restructuring practice at AlixPartners, the global financial advisory firm. He has over 20 years' experience in advising and leading management teams and stakeholders through periods of significant change and high pressure situations, gaining a broad range of financial management, turnaround, advisory and restructuring experience across various sectors from the mid-market to large corporates.

Kevin has developed and led numerous distressed M&A transactions, carve-outs, pre-packaged insolvency sales and distressed refinancings. Prior to joining Alixpartners, he spent 10 years each with the restructuring teams of EY and Zolfo Cooper, including 12 months working for the restructuring team of a major UK clearing bank. He has a degree in civil engineering and is a Fellow of the Institute of Chartered Accountants in England and Wales, the Association of Business Recovery Professionals and the Insolvency Practitioners Association (where he holds an insolvency practitioner's licence).

Russell Downs
Partner, PwC LLP
Russell.Downs@pwc.com

Russell Downs is a partner in PwC's business recovery services practice, focusing on large-scale corporate insolvency. He has worked on the Lehman Brothers engagement for eight years during which he has addressed some of the company's most challenging issues. Russell led the resolution of the US broker-dealer relationship, leading to $10bn of recoveries and the development of the consensual proposal with relevant clients to enable distributions of $8bn. In addition, he conducted the Waterfall proceedings, a complex set of UK court directions. Most recently, he has led the negotiation, proposal and approval of the surplus scheme, leading to distributions of £6bn.

Away from Lehman Brothers, Russell has acted as special manager of certain Carillion Plc subsidiaries and as administrator of Beaufort Securities.

Mark Firmin
Managing director and head of UK Insolvency & Regional Restructuring, Alvarez & Marsal
mfirmin@alvarezandmarsal.com

Mark Firmin has over 25 years of experience providing restructuring advice and support to under-performing businesses and their stakeholders. He specializes in helping boards to implement strategic, operational and financial restructurings and also helps businesses to develop contingency plans. His work often includes helping to quickly stabilise the business, improve stakeholder communication, generate additional cash headroom, implement an accelerated sale, and develop contingency plans.

He has led a large number of insolvencies and has been particularly successful in keeping businesses intact throughout the insolvency process, thereby maximising value for stakeholders and preserving jobs.

Prior to joining Alvarez & Marsal, Mark was UK head of restructuring at KPMG.

Richard Fleming
Managing director and head of European Restructuring, Alvarez & Marsal
rfleming@alvarezandmarsal.com

Richard Fleming has over 30 years of restructuring experience across a wide range of industries and has played a key role in a number of high-profile stressed, distressed and insolvency cases in the public and private arena.

Richard acted as the administrator of MF Global and Leeds United FC and led the company-side restructuring of Southern Cross Plc, the largest nursing home operator in the UK at the time with 41,000 employees. He led the restructuring of JJB Sports Plc and Blacks Leisure Plc, breaking new ground by taking these privately listed companies through company voluntary arrangements without any share suspension, paving the way for subsequent equity raises.

He has acted as administrator to more than 20 retailers including Threshers, Peacocks and La Senza, and has led or advised lenders on numerous CVAs including Homebase, Travelodge, Fitness First, Suits You, Toys "R" Us, Prezzo and Carpetright.

Sandra Gómez San Esteban
Associate, Cuatrecasas
sandracristina.gomez@cuatrecasas.com

Sandra Gómez is an associate in the finance team of the Cuatrecasas London office and a member of the Madrid Bar Association. She graduated in law and business administration from the University of Navarra and she holds a master's degree in corporate law from the University of Navarra.

Her practice focuses on the secondary loan trading markets, where she advises financial institutions and investment funds, mainly based in the UK, in the acquisition of distressed debt and insolvency claims. She also advises on debt restructuring and refinancing deals, corporate finance and direct lending transactions.

Martin Gudgeon
Partner, PJT Partners
Gudgeon@pjtpartners.com

Martin Gudgeon is a partner and head of the European Restructuring and Special Situations Group at PJT Partners, based in London.

Prior to joining PJT Partners, Martin worked at Blackstone for eight years, serving as a senior managing director. Before that he was the chief executive and head of restructuring at Close Brothers; and before that he was at Hill Samuel, where he spent two years on secondment to Macquarie Bank in Sydney.

Martin's clients have included debtors, creditor groups and governments in all major jurisdictions in EMEA. He is a chartered accountant and a member of the Chartered Institute of Electrical Engineers. He undertook his accountancy training at Price Waterhouse and received his BSc (Hons) in engineering from Durham University.

Luke Hartley
Director, Lincoln Pensions
L.Hartley@lincolnpensions.com

Luke Hartley is a director at Lincoln Pensions, having joined in January 2017 from the pensions advisory practice at AlixPartners (formerly Zolfo Cooper). He has over twelve years' experience in employer covenant assessment and his work includes triennial reviews, annual monitoring, corporate restructuring and M&A activity, from both trustee and sponsor perspectives. Luke has particular experience in litigation, distress and regulatory involvement and has worked on a number of landmark cases. He is an active participant in the Employer Covenant Working Group and co-wrote the working group's guidance on the best practice assessment of employer covenant.

Luke is a fellow of the Association of Chartered Certified Accountants and has a BSc (First Class) in economics from the University of Warwick.

Alex Hutton-Mills
Managing director, Lincoln Pensions
A.Hutton-Mills@lincolnpensions.com

Alex Hutton-Mills is a managing director of Lincoln Pensions and co-founded the business with Darren Redmayne. He qualified as a solicitor in Norton Rose's corporate finance department.

Alex has extensive experience in UK pensions matters and their impact on corporate finance transactions, in particular, M&A, capital markets and restructurings. He has advised on multiple M&A and restructuring transactions across a range of industries including UK and cross-border public and private M&A, debt and equity capital raisings, joint venture arrangements and restructurings.

Alex co-founded the pensions advisory business of Lincoln International (now Lincoln Pensions) in 2008 having previously worked at Citigroup where he was part of the Global Special Situations and Insurance and Pensions Structured Solutions groups. At Citigroup, he was a member of the team that successfully completed the innovative, non-insured buy-out of the Thomson Regional Newspapers pension scheme.

Shirish Joshi
Managing director, Restructuring and Special Situations Group, PJT Partners
Joshi@pjtpartners.com

Shirish Joshi is a managing director in the Restructuring and Special Situations Group of PJT Partners, based in London. Before joining PJT Partners' predecessor firm, Blackstone, in 2007, Shirish worked in the European Special Situations Group of Houlihan Lokey. He began his career in the Mergers & Acquisitions Group at Morgan Stanley & Co in New York. He studied finance at the Brigham Young University and undertook graduate work in law & accounting at the London School of Economics.

Christopher S Koenig
Associate, Restructuring, Kirkland & Ellis LLP
chris.koenig@kirkland.com

Christopher Koenig, formerly of Willkie Farr & Gallagher LLP, is an associate at Kirkland & Ellis LLP. Chris graduated from Johns Hopkins University (BA, 2010) and the University of Illinois College of Law (JD, 2013). His practice focuses on the representation of both debtors and creditors in connection with Chapter 11 restructurings, out-of-court restructurings and cross-border matters in Chapter 15 cases.

Chris represented Westmoreland Coal Company and its affiliated debtors in their Chapter 11 cases, the COFINA Agent in the Commonwealth of Puerto Rico bankruptcy cases, the independent directors of the debtors in the FirstEnergy Solutions Chapter 11 cases, and the independent directors of Clear Channel Outdoor Holdings, Inc in the Chapter 11 cases of iHeartMedia, Inc. Chris also represented Momentive Performance Materials, Inc in its Chapter 11 cases, and the largest senior secured creditor in the Chapter 11 cases of LightSquared, Inc and its affiliated debtors.

Olena Koltko
Financial sector specialist,
The World Bank Group
okoltko@worldbank.org

Olena Koltko is a financial sector specialist with the financial inclusion, infrastructure & access team in the Finance, Competitiveness and Innovation Global Practice at the World Bank Group. Olena is part of the Credit Infrastructure Program, where she works on insolvency and secured transactions projects in Eastern Europe and Central Asia, the Middle East and North Africa and Sub-Saharan Africa. Olena joined the World Bank Group in 2012 as part of the Development Economics Vice Presidency. Prior to that, she practised law in the United States and in Ukraine.

Graham Lane
Partner, Willkie Farr & Gallagher LLP
glane@willkie.com

Graham Lane is a partner in the Business Reorganisation & Restructuring Department of Willkie Farr in London. He advises par and distressed debt investors, private equity sponsors and other stakeholders in all types of restructuring and insolvency matters, with a particular focus on complex cross-border projects.

Graham has over 15 years' experience gained from roles in significant market-leading restructurings, including Premier Oil, Agrokor, Danaos, MF Global, Eitzen, European Directories, Sea Containers and Japan Airlines. He is also known for his broad experience in the French market having been involved in Vivarte, CGG, Latécoère, Eurotunnel, and many other significant French restructurings.

Amongst other accolades, Graham is cited in *Chambers UK* 2019 and the *IFLR 1000 UK 2019*. In the *IFLR 1000*, he is described as "Highly Regarded" in the area of restructuring/ insolvency and is described by his clients in *Chambers* as having "well-honed commercial and legal acumen".

Graham is a member of the Insolvency Lawyers' Association and the International Insolvency Institute. He is a guest lecturer at the Centre of Commercial Law Studies at Queen Mary, University of London, and is a frequent speaker at international restructuring conferences.

John C Longmire
Partner, Business Reorganisation & Restructuring Department, Willkie Farr & Gallagher LLP
jlongmire@willkie.com

John Longmire graduated from New York University (BS, 1987) and St John's University School of Law (JD, 1995). John is based in Willkie's New York office. He has received numerous awards and recognitions for his work in complex restructuring matters. For example, *Chambers USA* has ranked John among New York's leading attorneys on several occasions; he has been included in *Best Lawyers in America* each of the last six years; *Expert Guides* lists him as one of the leading restructuring attorneys in the world; *Turnarounds and Workouts* included him as one of its 12 Outstanding Restructuring Lawyers (2015); *Best Attorneys in America* has named him among the top 100 lawyers in the US; and *Global M&A Network* has included him in a list of the top 100 restructuring professionals. John was also recently shortlisted for *The Deal's* Lawyer of the Year in the energy and power sector. Recent engagements include the restructurings of Westinghouse Electric Corp, CGG, SA, Relativity Media and Danaos Corp.

Matthew Mawhinney
Assistant director, Deloitte
mmawhinney@deloitte.co.uk

Matthew Mawhinney is an assistant director in restructuring services in Deloitte, London and has spent the last eight years predominantly focusing on contingency planning and implementation projects of complex multi-jurisdictional corporate structures.

During his career, Matt has gained experience of complex restructuring and contingency planning engagements plus options development and implementation for varying stakeholders. Work has focussed on detailed day 1 insolvency plans, continuity of service and value preservation across a range of sectors including the public sector, financial services, real estate and oil and gas.

Recent projects have included the liquidation of Abraaj Investment Management Limited, the CVA of New Look Retailers Limited and contingency planning on behalf of the Cabinet Office in respect of the restructuring of a critical government supplier. In addition, Matt has led the administration of Paragon Offshore through the successful implementation of the wider Chapter 11 restructuring.

Matt is a chartered accountant and qualified insolvency practitioner.

Ronen Nehmad
Consultant, The World Bank Group
rnehmad@ifc.org

Ronen Nehmad is a consultant with the Credit Infrastructure Program Finance, Competitiveness, and Innovation Global Practice at the World Bank Group. He is currently completing a JD/MBA degree from Osgoode Hall Law School and the Schulich School of Business in Toronto, Canada.

Craig Rachel
Senior vice-president, AlixPartners
crachel@alixpartners.com

Craig Rachel is a senior vice-president in the transactions team at AlixPartners, the leading advisory firm.

Craig has worked in professional services for over ten years, the past six being spent executing complex M&A, valuation and refinancing transactions at AlixPartners. He has a particular focus on the consumer space (covering retail, pubs, bars and restaurants) but has advised on situations across a broad range of sectors. After qualifying as an accountant with PwC, he joined the equity research team at investment bank GCA Altium, before joining the Zolfo Cooper corporate finance team in 2012. Zolfo Cooper Europe was acquired by AlixPartners in 2015.

Vanessa Rudder
Director, Alvarez & Marsal
vrudder@alvarezandmarsal.com

Vanessa Rudder has over 19 years of experience in complex cross-border restructuring and insolvency cases across a broad range of jurisdictions including the UK, Australia and across Europe and Asia.

Both her UK and cross-border engagements have covered a variety of industries including the retail, healthcare, telecommunications, construction, PFI and steel and commodity sectors.

Vanessa's recent engagements include large UK and cross-border contingency and insolvency planning, options analysis, cash flow reviews, pre-pack planning, estimated outcome analysis and scheme of arrangement transactions.

Prior to joining Alvarez & Marsal, Vanessa spent eight years with PwC in London and 10 years with Ernst & Young in Australia. Vanessa also did a 12-month secondment to RBS's Global Restructuring Group. She is a chartered accountant and qualified insolvency practitioner.

Javier Segura Valero
Associate, Cuatrecasas
javier.segura@cuatrecasas.com

Javier Segura is an associate in the finance team of Cuatrecasas and he is a member of the Madrid Bar Association. He is based in the London office. As part of the Pro-International Advocacy Program (PPAI), he has also worked in the São Paulo and Madrid offices, among others, where he gained experience in corporate law, tax law and litigation matters.

He currently advises international clients on refinancing and restructuring transactions, and direct lending transactions. He also provides assistance to UK-based financial institutions and investment funds in the acquisition of distressed debt and insolvency claims on the secondary loan trading markets as well as the acquisition of non-performing loans.

Mark Shaw
Head of London Restructuring, BDO LLP
mark.shaw@bdo.co.uk

Mark Shaw's practice covers a range of restructuring, insolvency and expert witness assignments. He has led some of the highest-profile matters of recent years. Most of his cases are cross-border with significant value or issues at stake.

Representative matters include: Abengoa (energy, telecoms, transport etc, €6bn); ARM Asset Backed Securities (finance, $250m); Britannia Bulk (shipping, $1bn+); *Carlyle Capital Corporation v Conway & others* (finance, claim of c. $2bn, $20 bn+ structure); various CDOs (aggregate $2bn+); Dawnay Day (property/finance, £1bn+); Dewey & LeBoeuf (legal, $225m); *LIA v Goldman Sachs* (finance, $1.2bn); *LIA v SocGen & others* (finance, $2.1bn); further LIA matters (finance, $800m+); Northern Rock (finance, £100bn+ structure); Northsea Base Investments (shipping, $180m); Tata Steel (industrial, £7bn+); and *Torre Asset Funding v RBS* (property/finance, £660m structure).

Mark holds a first-class degree in accountancy and is a chartered accountant and authorised insolvency practitioner.

Graeme Smith
Managing director, AlixPartners
gsmith@alixpartners.com

Graeme Smith is a managing director specialising in corporate finance and restructuring advice at AlixPartners, the leading advisory firm. He uses his experience and network to help companies and investors achieve their goals through M&A transactions, restructurings, and access to both equity and debt financing. He has two decades of UK and cross-border experience in advising clients on buy- and sell-side M&A, raising or refinancing equity and debt, valuation matters, special-situations M&A, and financial restructurings. His experience was achieved across a broad range of industries but with a particular focus on consumer-based sectors, including hospitality & leisure and retail. Recent mandates include the restructuring of Prezzo, the UK casual dining group, advising the lenders to the Toys "R" Us propco vehicle, and the valuations of the Formula 1 group and the Iceland Food Group. Graeme is a chartered accountant and a mediator accredited by the Centre for Effective Dispute Resolution.

David Soden
Partner, Deloitte
dsoden@deloitte.co.uk

David Soden is a partner in the restructuring services team in Deloitte in London, responsible for financial institutions. A licensed insolvency practitioner in the UK and Dubai, David has over 15 years' experience in international insolvency assignments. He has worked on formal insolvency assignments and performed complex security/option reviews and asset-based insolvency valuations for lenders and other stakeholders.

David is a member of the Financial Services Regulatory Steering Group and has developed significant experience in the implementation of the Banking Resolution and Recovery Directive.

He has also led the liquidations of Abraaj Investment Management Limited and the Dubai private bank in the Espirito Santo Financial Group, both of which have involved managing a complex group of stakeholders, and resolving disputes across a number of jurisdictions.

David is a Fellow of the Institute of Chartered Accountants in England and Wales and a Member of the Association of Business Recovery Professionals.

Lionel Spizzichino
Partner, Willkie Farr & Gallagher LLP
lspizzichino@willkie.com

Lionel Spizzichino is a partner in the Business Reorganisation and Restructuring Department at Willkie in Paris. He has extensive experience in complex cross-border restructurings, and French pre-insolvency and insolvency matters including out-of-court restructuring, insolvency proceedings, restructuring litigation and distressed mergers and acquisitions, and frequently advises corporate entities on presenting open bids on assets of distressed companies. His clients include corporate debtors, creditors and investors in a wide range of sectors such as retail, media, chemical, financial services and the automotive industry. He regularly advises investment funds, recovery funds and hedge funds.

Lionel is a member of the Association pour le Retournement des Entreprises (ARE), the Institut Français des Praticiens des Procédures Collectives (IFPPC – French Insolvency Practitioners' Association), the Association Française en Faveur de l'Institution Consulaire (AFFIC) and the Turnaround Management Association (TMA).

Mahesh Uttamchandani
Practice manager, The World Bank Group
muttamchandani@worldbank.org

Mahesh Uttamchandani is the practice manager for SME Access to Finance and Financial Inclusion, Infrastructure & Access in the Finance, Competitiveness and Innovation Global Practice at the World Bank Group (WBG). He manages Payment & Market Infrastructures, Responsible Financial Access, Credit Infrastructure, the global Financial Inclusion Support Framework programme and the global Financial Consumer Protection programme. He also jointly leads (with an IFC co-head) the Universal Financial Access 2020 initiative. He was previously practice manager for SME Access to Finance and Credit Infrastructure.

Mahesh also served as a global lead for Credit Infrastructure Global Solutions Group, where he led the WBG's work in the areas of secured transactions, credit reporting and insolvency, including the insolvency and creditor/debtor rights initiative.

Mahesh joined the World Bank's Legal Vice Presidency in 2006 and has since held various positions at both the World Bank and IFC.

Prior to joining the WBG, Mahesh worked at the EBRD and as a commercial litigator at a leading Canadian law firm.

Mahesh is a member of the executive committee of CGAP, a board member of the legal journal, *International Corporate Rescue* and a board member of INSOL International. He has published and taught at university level and lectured extensively in North America, Europe and Asia.

Matthew Whiting
Co-head of EMEA restructuring, Evercore
Matthew.Whiting@Evercore.com

Matthew Whiting is co-head of Evercore's EMEA Restructuring Group and is based in London. Matthew has over 15 years of experience in the financial services industry and specialises in in-court and out-of-court financial restructurings and deleveraging transactions for debtors and creditors. Prior to joining Evercore, he spent the majority of his career in the restructuring groups at Lazard and Rothschild in both London and New York. During his time at Lazard and Rothschild, he was responsible for sourcing and executing balance sheet restructurings and capital raises.

Matthew has represented clients in a wide range of industries and geographies. He has completed transactions in shipping, real estate, industrials, financials, media, automotive and gaming in the United States, Europe, Mexico, Africa and the Middle East.

Index

Page references to figures and tables are in *italics*. References to notes will be followed by the letter 'n' and note number.

About Globe Law and Business

Globe Law and Business was established in 2005, and from the very beginning, we set out to create law books which are sufficiently high level to be of real use to the experienced professional, yet still accessible and easy to navigate. Most of our authors are drawn from Magic Circle and other top commercial firms, both in the UK and internationally.

Our titles are carefully produced, with the utmost attention paid to editorial, design and production processes. We hope this results in high-quality books which are easy to read, and a pleasure to own. All our new books are also available as ebooks, which are compatible with most desktop, laptop and tablet devices.

We have recently expanded our portfolio to include a new range of journals, available both digitally and in hard copy format, and produced to the same high standards as our books.

We'd very much like to hear from you with your thoughts and ideas for improving what we offer. Please do feel free to email me on sian@globelawandbusiness.com with your views.

Sian O'Neill
Managing director
Globe Law and Business

www.globelawandbusiness.com

Related titles in restructuring

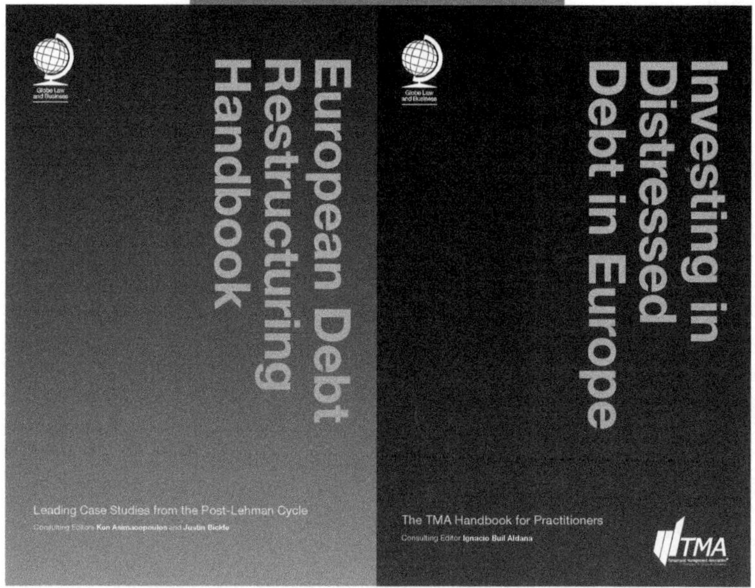

Go to **www.globelawandbusiness.com**
for full details including free sample chapters

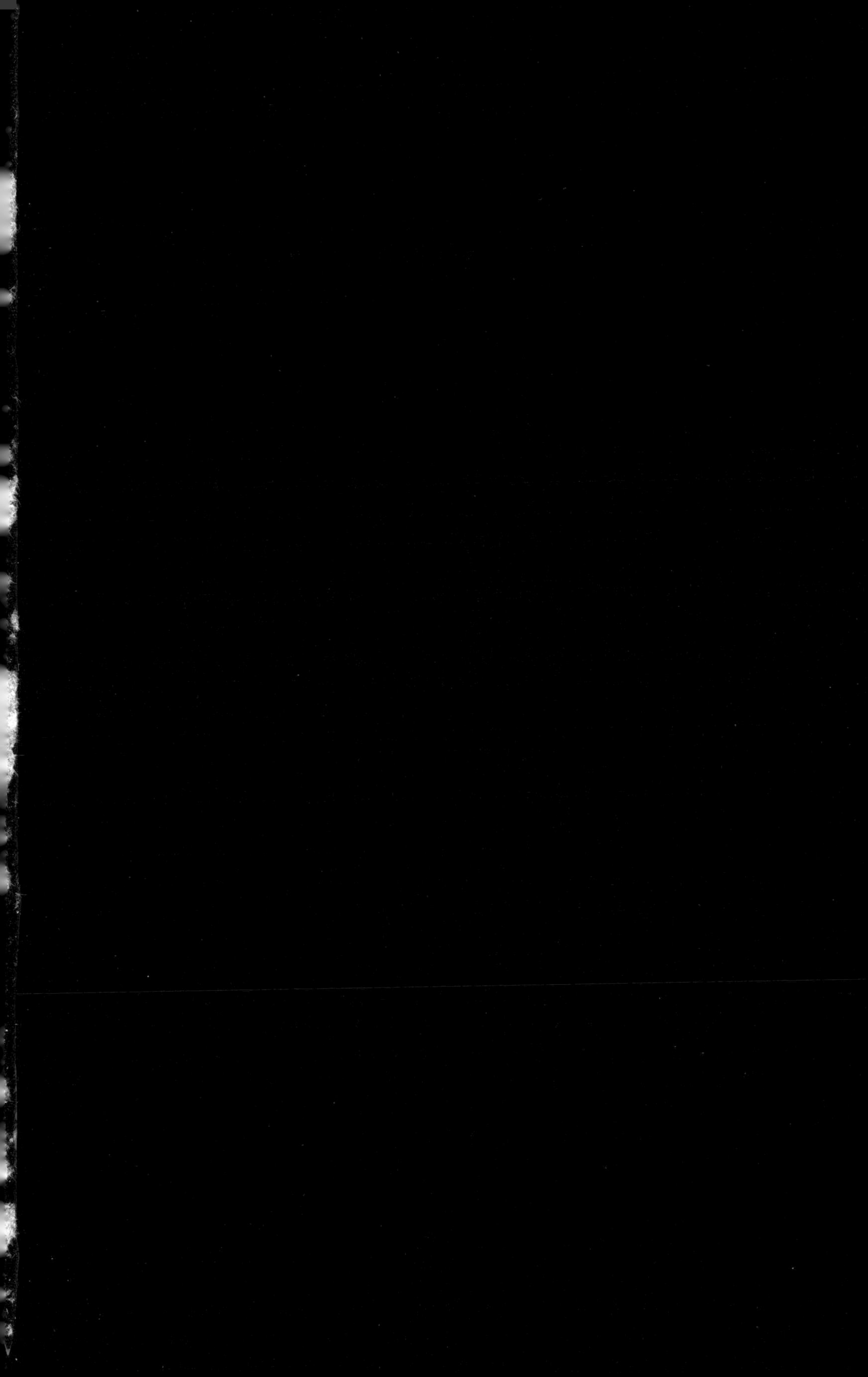